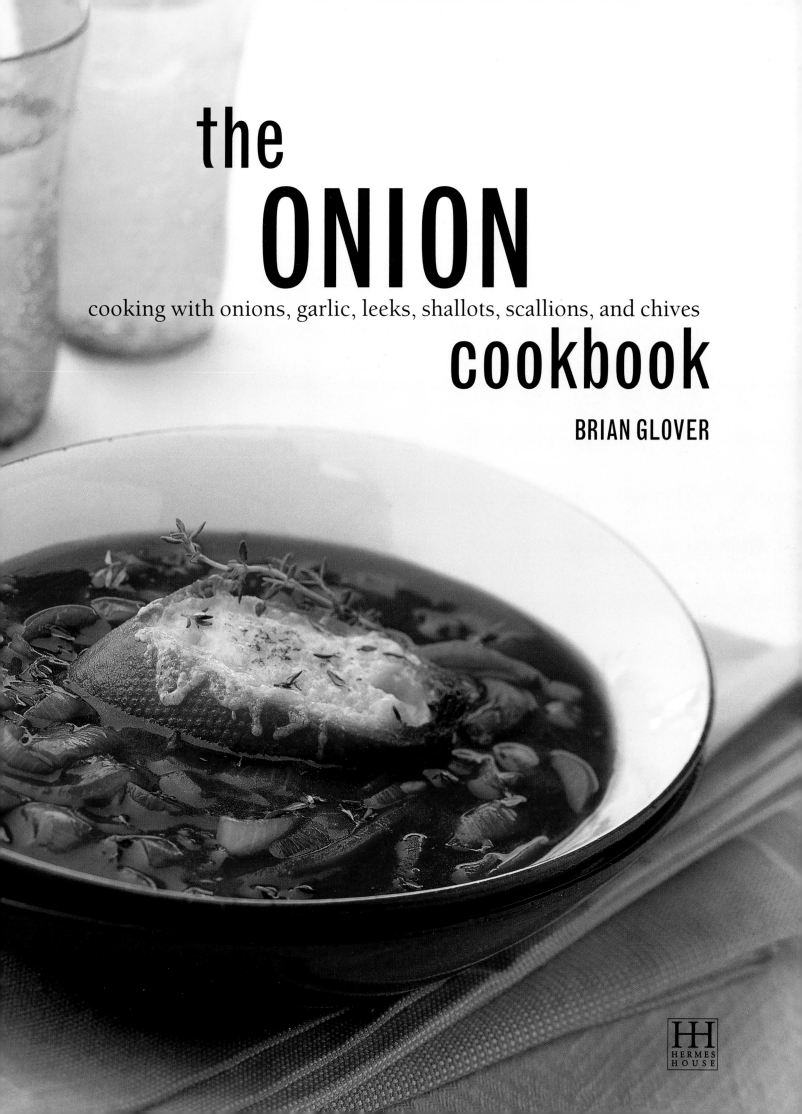

the ONION

cooking with onions, garlic, leeks, shallots, scallions, and chives

cookbook

BRIAN GLOVER

HERMES HOUSE

This edition is published by Hermes House

Hermes House is an imprint of Anness Publishing Ltd
Published in the USA by Hermes House, Anness Publishing Inc.
27 West 20th Street, New York, NY 10011; fax 212 807 6813
info@anness.com

A CIP catalogue record for this book is available from the British Library

Publisher: Joanna Lorenz
Executive Editor: Linda Fraser
Editor: Susannah Blake
Copy Editors: Bridget Jones (recipes) and Gwen Rigby (reference)
Indexer: Hilary Bird
Designer: Isobel Gillan
Photographer: William Lingwood
Food for Photography: Sunil Vijayakar (recipes) and Tonia Hedley (reference)
Stylist: Helen Trent

Front cover shows Frittata with Leek, Red Bell Pepper and Spinach.
For recipe see page 183

Previously published as *Onion*

1 3 5 7 9 10 8 6 4 2

NOTES

Standard spoon and cup measures are level.

Large eggs are used unless otherwise stated.

CONTENTS

INTRODUCTION

Members of the onion family have been cultivated ever since people started to form communities and grow their own food. Wild onions were gathered and eaten even before that. With a few exceptions, onions are now used in the cooking of almost every culture across the world. There is no country where this indispensable vegetable, in one form or another, is not now grown.

The evolution of the first, wild onions into the cultivated plants that we know today is not entirely clear. Many varieties, such as the common or garden onion, only seem to exist in their cultivated form and are not known to grow wild at all. There is a "missing link" in the development between the wild species of the plant and today's cultivated onions.

The mystery surrounding this transition suggests that the cultivation of onions occurred a very long time ago. People would seem to have perceived onions as good things to eat very early on in history, and onions are among the first plants to have been grown to add flavor to the human diet.

Onions belong to the allium family, which contains more than 300 species. Many of these different varieties are grown in gardens, some as ornamentals in flower borders, others as herbs and edible plants in vegetable patches. For a long time, botanists disagreed about whether the alliums belonged to the larger plant group of lilies (*Liliaceae*) or amaryllis (*Amaryllidaceae*), but now most place them in an order all of their own—the *Alliaceae*.

From the grower's point of view, alliums are very easy to identify. They form bulbs, or fleshy leaf bottoms; they have long, narrow, flat or tubular leaves, usually blue-green in color; they have round, globular heads of flowers made up of many individual flowers; and all, to one degree or another, have the same unmistakably characteristic onion smell, especially when the bulb or leaves are damaged or broken.

pejorative associations have been made. They are forbidden to certain social groups, and are sometimes considered taboo or to have evil powers. The effect of their odor on the breath and sweat has led them to be labeled as vulgar, and unacceptable in polite society.

The relationship of the onion family to people throughout history is marked by these contradictory attitudes. While onions and other alliums are revered and praised and popular in dishes around the world, they are also frowned upon and rejected by many cultures and social groups.

Left: Alliums are an important crop in France as its traditional cooking has always made very good use of these vegetables, especially onions and garlic.

The pungent onion smell is caused by the presence of allicins—chemicals that include volatile sulphur compounds —which are released by the action of enzymes when any part of the plant is cut or bruised. It is these compounds that make the eyes water when an allium is chopped and which give onions that are used in cooking their characteristic flavor and bite.

The alliums' inescapable chemical signature has brought them to people's attention from the earliest times. Their smell and taste have made them into plants with an ancient and special place in the evolution of human culture.

From the earliest records, it appears that onions have always been regarded as important foodstuffs, and imbued with symbolic and religious meaning: they were grown in the best fields and can be found in important tombs and paintings. However, along with this reverence and value, a number of

Opposite: Onions have been cultivated for thousands of years. Their distinctive blue-green leaves and round flower heads make them easy to recognize.

Right: Delicately flavored bunching onions and scallions are popular in Vietnamese cooking, and can always be found at their food markets.

Onions and Other Alliums Throughout History

Whether praised or criticized, the onion family has attracted attention from the very earliest times. In different societies and at different periods in history, these vegetables have been bestowed with symbolic and spiritual meanings and have been considered vital in herbalistic and shamanistic medicine. The onion figures prominently in folklore, literature and even painting: few other vegetable families have such a value-laden history.

The actual origins of the onion are not known. However, they do seem to have been among the first families of plants to have been cultivated and selected. The recorded evidence suggests that onions were first cultivated over 5,000 years ago, around 3000 B.C., in Asia Minor—the area of central Asia that now includes modern-day countries such as Iran, Pakistan and Afghanistan. These onions would have been close relatives of the cultivated varieties that we are familiar with today.

Garlic probably began in this area too, and was then taken to Greece and on to Egypt. A type of garlic (*Allium sativum*) still grows wild in some parts of the Mediterranean, particularly on the island of Sicily. Shallots are also likely to have originated in central Asia and, according to food historian Alan Davidson, were known and used in India before they traveled to the Middle East.

Onions were also being cultivated in parts of China around 3000 B.C. These would have been bunching onions (varieties of *Allium fistulosum*), rather than bulb onions. The Chinese also grew leeks, although these were a different variety from European leeks and derived from *Allium ramosum*.

At some point in the Han dynasty, dating 206 B.C.–A.D. 221, bulb onions (*Allium cepa*) and true garlic (*Allium sativa*) were introduced into China, probably from India. The bulb onion is still known as *hu-t'sung* or "foreign onion" in Chinese.

The cultivation of onions and garlic is mentioned in some of the early Vedic writings of ancient India. They are also noted in scribal records from Sumer (*c.*2400 B.C.), which record that the city governor's onions and cucumbers were grown in "the gods' best fields." The mentioning of the various alliums in these early texts shows that they were considered to be a most important crop.

Below: Onions and garlic have been an essential cooking ingredient in many countries, such as Brazil, for centuries.

ALLIUMS IN ANCIENT EGYPT

By the time of the ancient Egyptians, there is evidence that onions, garlic and leeks were being grown and consumed in huge amounts. Onions figure prominently in the decoration and hieroglyphics of one of the Egyptians' best-known legacies—the pyramids. They appear on the walls of the pyramids of Unas (*c*.2423 B.C.) and Pepi II (*c*.2200 B.C.) and onions were found in the eye sockets of the mummy of Rameses IV, who died in 1160 B.C.

The Greek historian Herodotus, in 450 B.C., reporting on his travels in Egypt, writes of inscriptions on the walls of the pyramids that show a breakdown of the cost of building these great monuments. Among the items listed is an entry showing how much was spent on "black radish, red onions and garlic" for the laborers on the pyramid at Giza.

Centuries later, the 17th-century diarist John Evelyn remarks in his *Acetaria* (1699) on "How this noble bulb was deified in Egypt ... and that whilst they were building the pyramids, there was spent on this root ninety tun of gold among the workmen." When the laborers' onion and garlic ration was cut, they are believed to have gone on strike.

Below: Egyptian laborers working on the pyramids received rations of onions, garlic, leeks and beer. It was believed that all the alliums provided physical strength and prevented disease.

Right: Onions have been found in eye sockets, armpits and body cavities of ancient Egyptian mummies, which were stored in decorative cases. This may have been because onions acted as antiseptics or because they were believed to have supernatural powers.

Above and above right: Onions are commonly depicted in the wall paintings in Egyptian tombs. It is thought they acted both as symbols of eternal life and as food and medicine for the journey into the afterlife.

The significance of alliums to the ancient Egyptians seems to have been very complex. Onions were placed in tombs as food for the journey into the next life and as symbols of eternity because of the circle-within-a-circle structure of the bulb. Many paintings show onions as part of religious symbolism. They were also known as powerful antibiotics and antiseptics. Laborers were fed on onions, leeks and garlic as these vegetables were believed to keep them fit and well for their manual work.

There is evidence also that the lingering smell of the onion in the body had great significance for the ancient Egyptians. The passage of the onion smell through the body was considered a sign of good health and fertility in women, though it was taboo for certain priests to eat or smell of onions.

The onion family was also popular with the Egyptians' neighbors, the Hebrews. In the Bible in Numbers XI:5, the Israelites led out into the desert by Moses complain about how hungry they are, and remember "the cucumbers, and the melons, and the leeks, and the onions and the garlic," which they used to enjoy in their captivity in Egypt.

The association of alliums with this part of the eastern Mediterranean remained strong for many centuries. For instance, in many European countries, the name for shallots (*Allium cepa*, Aggregatum Group) is derived from the ancient Palestinian port of Ascalon. This was reflected in their old Latin name (*Allium ascalonicum*) given by the Romans. No doubt Ascalon was the place from which shallots were first imported to Rome, and the name stuck.

Centuries later, the tree onion (*Allium cepa*, Proliferum Group), and the shallot-related potato onion, were still both called Egyptian onions by the English and French.

Below: Onions and other alliums are mentioned several times in the Bible. The most famous occasion is when the Israelites recall the pleasures of eating onions, leeks and garlic before their flight from Egypt (Numbers XI:5).

ALLIUMS IN GREEK AND ROMAN TIMES

The classical Greeks used alliums too. Hippocrates (*c.*400 B.C.), who is credited with founding modern medicine, notes that onions, garlic and leeks were grown in kitchen gardens or harvested from the wild. The food historian Alan Davidson points out that a section of market in Athens was called simply *ta skoroda*, meaning "the garlic," suggesting that the trade in alliums was an important feature of everyday Athenian life. The alliums even merit mention in Homer's great epic poem, the *Odyssey*.

Like the Egyptian pyramid builders, the Greeks believed in the onion's ability to promote health, virility and potency. Onions were used to prepare athletes for games, and competitors not only ate onions but also rubbed onion juice on their bodies. Greek soldiers were fed on onions to develop a martial vigor, and it was said that the enemy always knew when the Greek army was advancing by the powerful smell of onions that preceded the arrival of the troops.

In Rome, bread and onions were the standard diet of the poor. Archaeologists excavating Pompeii have found onion-shaped cavities where onions were growing in gardens, just as the writer Pliny the Elder (A.D. 23–79) described in his *Historia Naturalis*.

Because onions played such a vital role in the diet of the poor in Rome, they were held in some contempt by sections of the wealthy élite. The priestesses of Cybele, for instance, refused entrance to their temple in Rome to anyone who smelt of garlic. The poet Horace considered the smell of garlic a mark of real vulgarity and called it "more poisonous than hemlock," and Juvenal mockingly writes of onions as "kitchen gods."

Leeks seem to have been universally popular at all levels of Roman society, which may well have been because they were milder and tainted the breath less. There are many leek recipes in Apicius' 1st-century *De Re Coquinaria*, a cook book intended for the literate middle classes. Apicius was a shadowy figure, and there may have been more than one person known as Apicius involved in the book over a considerable period of time. The recipes show a great love of leeks, and to a lesser extent onions, in a range of sophisticated dishes that include Beets with Leeks in Raisin Sauce,

Below: As with the Greeks, the Roman army was fed on onions and garlic, and took them on their invasions. They are credited with introducing garlic, onions and leeks to Britain, Germany and Gaul.

Above: The Roman emperor Nero was nicknamed porrophagus or "leek eater" because he ate so many of them in his belief that they helped his singing voice and oratory.

Peppercorn Leek Sauce and Quinces Stewed with Leeks. *De Re Coquinaria* contains few recipes for garlic, however, which suggests garlic was less popular with middle-class Romans.

The Romans not only cultivated and cooked with alliums, but are thought to have been instrumental in taking these vegetables into all parts of Europe.

While Romans enjoyed eating onions and other alliums, they did not imbue them with the same significance as the ancient Egyptians and the Roman satirist Juvenal (*c.*A.D. 60–140) mocks the Egyptians' contradictory beliefs:

*How Egypt has grown mad
    with superstition
She makes gods of demons as
    is well known
It is a deadly sin to eat an onion
But every clove of garlic has a
    holy power.
A pious country, and with fine
    houses
But every garden is overrun
    with gods.*

ALLIUMS IN THE MIDDLE AGES

After the Romans' introduction of edible alliums to other parts of Europe, these vegetables soon became established as an important part of the European diet. They were popular in the Middle Ages, especially among the poor. Even before the introduction of cultivated varieties, it is certain that wild alliums, such as rocambole (*Allium scordoprasum*) and ramsons (*Allium ursinum*), would have been gathered and eaten. The English words leek and garlic come from the Anglo-Saxon word *leac,* meaning plant, and *garleac,* meaning spear-shaped plant. In Anglo-Saxon, the leek was known as *porleac* and the onion *ynioleac.* Onions get their name from the Latin *unio* via the French *oignon* and Anglo-Norman *union.*

Alliums became an important crop in medieval Britain, particularly leeks, which were one of the few vegetables to withstand a normal winter unprotected. In the *Forme of Cury* (*c.*1390), a cook book written for Richard II, a *salat* was made from *persel, sawge, grene garlec, chibolles* [Welsh onions], *oynouns and leek* all dressed with oil and vinegar. And *porray* (from *porrum,* the Latin for leek) was a white soup made from leeks, almonds and rice.

The trade in alliums was important in medieval Europe. Onions from Brittany and garlic from Picardy are recorded as having been sold in London food markets as early as the 13th century.

By Chaucer's time, in the late 14th century, it is obvious that leeks were considered commonplace, everyday fare. He often uses the phrase "Not worth a leke" to suggest something that is entirely worthless.

Because they were so hardy, leeks could be grown in the coldest places and are associated particularly with Scotland and Wales, becoming, in Wales, a symbol for Celtic hardiness and survival. Legend has it that the Welsh wore leeks, like feathers, in their caps, as a badge of identification during their victory over the Saxons in A.D. 640. It is probable that these would have been wild alliums—ramsons or rocamboles maybe—rather than the familiar modern-day leeks. But by Shakespeare's time, the Welsh wearing of leeks on their national day—St. David's Day, March 1—had clearly become well established. In the play *Henry V*, Pistol taunts Fluellen about his Welshness by promising to knock "his leek about his pate upon Saint Davy's day."

To this day, leeks still figure as a part of Welsh identity. They are an essential ingredient in cawl, a comforting soup or stew of lamb and leeks, which may be considered traditional Welsh soul food. Championship leek growing is still a major competitive hobby in many areas

Left: In medieval herbals and medicinal manuscripts, many members of the onion family were recognized to have curative and therapeutic properties.

Left: In Chaucer's Canterbury Tales *the Summoner's vulgar character is shown by his love of garlic, onions and leeks.*

The ribald and lewd associations of onions and leeks started early in Britain. This Anglo-Saxon riddle dates from before the Norman conquest of 1066:

I stand erect and tall, well-rooted
I stand proud in bed
I am hairy below. Sometimes the
*   fair peasant's daughter ...*
... grips my body and holds me
*   hard ...*
I will bring tears to her eyes.

Above: An illustration of garlic from Pierre Jean Francois Turpin's Flore Médicale *showing the bulb structure.*

of south Wales. Most people, however, have taken to wearing the less odorous daffodil on St. David's Day.

Although onions were important in dietary and medicinal terms in medieval Europe, the Roman inhibitions and prejudices about how onions smell and the effect they have on an individual's moral character also prevailed.

Throughout the Middle Ages, alliums were associated with vulgarity. For the Egyptians and Greeks, the alliums were thought to promote strength, fertility and vigor, and it was only a short step until onions became associated, in ribald terms, with licentiousness and sexual prowess. In the 14th century, Chaucer's lecherous Summoner in *The Canterbury Tales* is described thus:

Wel loved he garleek, onions, and
*   eek lekes,*
And for to drinken strong wyun, reed
*   as blood.*

Similarly, in William Langland's *Piers Plowman*, an allegorical poem dating from the 14th century, Gluttony is offered "a pound of garleek" as an inducement to step into the ale-house rather than go to church.

In France, the various members of the onion family were also associated with sexual potency. King Henry IV, for instance, was commonly reputed to have been baptized with garlic water, so prodigious was his sexual potency and so strong his breath.

Within late-medieval philosophy, edible bulbs such as garlic and onions were considered among the least noble of food plants. Existence was structured into a Great Chain of Being, a hierarchy which placed God at the top and inanimate objects, such as plants, at the bottom. All creation was ascribed a level in this hierarchical way of seeing the world and bulbs were placed at the very bottom.

THE ALLIUMS' FALL FROM GRACE

Despite their associations with the poor, vulgar and lecherous, onions, garlic and leeks continued to be popular in British cooking until the 17th century. Eating them uncooked, however, began to be frowned upon and was seen as a distinct social taboo, particularly for women and those who held social pretensions or aspirations.

Towards the end of the 17th century, there was a noticeable rise in the social prohibition against garlic, the most odorous of the alliums. The diarist John Evelyn, a great grower and eater of vegetables, wrote a treatise on salads as a preface to his *Acetaria* in 1699. Regarding "garlick" he writes: "We absolutely forbid it entrance into our saleting, by reason of its intolerable rankness, and that made it so detested of old … to be sure it is not for ladies' palates, nor those who court them."

Below: In some sections of society onions were considered as only fit for poor people as in this scene of humble living called "Preparations for Lunch" by Bernard Lepicie.

Above: Toward the end of the 17th century, alliums became unpopular in genteel society and tended to be associated with the poor and vulgar. Although onions were still used in cooking, they were rarely used as a main ingredient in their own right.

Throughout the following centuries, garlic features little in British cookery books, and although onions continue to appear in countless dishes, they rarely figure as a main ingredient in their own right. In Hannah Glasse's *The Art of Cookery Made Plain & Easy* (1747) onions are pickled, stewed, "ragoo'd with cucumbers" and made into a pie. Garlic, however, is not included. Leeks are not mentioned at all by Glasse. As with onions and garlic, they had become associated purely with peasant food and thought unsuitable for the middle classes (at which audience most 18th- and 19th-century cookbooks were aimed). Isabella Beeton, the great bastion of the 19th-century middle-class kitchen, sums up the doubtful regard in which leeks were held when she advocates boiling them really well or else "they will taint the breath."

Throughout Anglo-Saxon Europe and much of the United States, the social taboo surrounding the effect of onions and garlic on human breath and sweat lasted for almost three hundred years. Undoubtedly, onions, leeks and, to a lesser extent, garlic were still eaten, but to smell of them was considered socially impolite and a mark of low breeding. In countries outside Europe and the United States, similar social taboos were attached to the eating of onions and other alliums. For example, in Japan, to smell of onions or garlic has traditionally been perceived as being discourteous and has a great social stigma attached to it. Japan is still the one country in Asia that makes very little use of garlic in its cooking.

From the time of the earliest records, onions, and in particular garlic, have been accused of exciting sexual and libidinous desires: Egyptian priests were denied garlic precisely because they had to remain celibate. To this day Kashmiri Brahmans and Jains are forbidden from eating strong-tasting foods, in particular onions and garlic, because they are thought to heat the blood and have the ability to inflame carnal desire. Some Chinese Buddhists avoid the prohibited "five strong-smelling vegetables" for the same reasons.

The Hindu sacred texts place great emphasis on the idea that a man is what he eats and rules are given for the right foods. The three upper castes, Brahmans, Kshatryas and Vaisyas, should avoid onions and garlic in their diet. The Sanskrit poem, *Mahabharata,* suggests that onions and garlic should not be eaten by "honourable people."

Left: Garlic became very unpopular in countries such as Britain toward the end of the 17th century, but garlic and bay sellers such as this one were still able to eke out a living in France where garlic was not frowned upon to such a great extent.

THE REHABILITATION OF ALLIUMS

Some countries in northern Europe maintained their antipathy toward onions and garlic, but much depended on the general food culture of a society. In the 1580s, when the German ambassador of the Holy Roman Emperor visited the court of the Byzantine emperor Nicephoros II, his entourage was appalled by the food and the smell of garlic on the emperor's breath. For the northern Europeans, the great consumption of large amounts of vegetables, including onions and garlic, was little short of scandalous. In large parts of northern Europe, especially in comparatively rich countries such as Britain, Germany and the Netherlands, good food was synonymous with meat.

However, many cultures, typically those around the Mediterranean, never fell out of love with the onion family. It was for this reason that the vegetable-loving cultures of the Mediterranean region were for centuries looked down upon as gastronomically uncivilized.

In France, in particular, onions, garlic, leeks and shallots—in fact the whole allium tribe—remained extremely popular at almost every level of society. Brittany, a region well known in the 20th century for its bicycling onion sellers, and the west of France, were particularly linked with cooking with onions and garlic.

The French trade in onions and garlic began early; onions from Brittany were imported to London as early as the 13th century. The trade continued until well into the 20th century, with onion sellers cycling around southern English towns selling their familiar strings of onions and garlic from their bicycles. Food writer Lindsay Bareham notes that the last of these onion sellers was still working in the mid-1990s.

Onions and garlic were, and still are, an intrinsic part of much French provincial and peasant cooking. Garlic festivals, such as the garlic and basil fair at Tours on St. Anne's Day, July 26th, occur throughout France, usually when the new season crop has been harvested. Even when the alliums were at their most unpopular in Britain, in the 18th–19th centuries, onions were still celebrated in France. As food historian John Ayto points out, the classic sauce, *sauce soubise*, was named after an 18th-century French general and courtier Charles de Rohan, Prince de Soubise, showing that aristocracy did not see any shame in being associated with onions.

In sophisticated Paris, onions had their ups and downs but by the early 19th century they were actually thought quite *de rigeur* in polite society. The poet Shelley, writing of a trip to Paris, seems quite delightedly shocked at the

Above: In the early 19th century, Parisian society considered onions and garlic positively fashionable.

thought of the onions' fashionable status: "What do you think? Young women of rank eat—you will never guess what—garlick!"

In Spain, too, onions were consumed with gusto despite the fact that certain elements of society frowned upon the practice. An old Andalusian saying states that "*Olla sin cebolla, es baile sin tamborin* [a stew without onion is like a dance without music]." In Cataluña they celebrate the new crop of their local, large green scallions—*calçots*—with a

Onions in the United States

Columbus, and then the first pilgrims, took onions and garlic to North America, while the Spanish introduced them to Central and South America. But many varieties of wild onion, leek and garlic grew indigenously in North America and were used by native Americans in cooking and, especially, in medicine. Chicago was named after the Illinois Indian name for "the place which smells of onions." *Chicagoua*—the plant that gave Chicago its name—was probably a form of wild garlic or ramps (*Allium tricoccum*). This species and other wild onions, such as *Allium cernuum* and *Allium canadense,* still grow profusely throughout North America. Père Marquette, the French Jesuit explorer and missionary, who camped on the shores of Lake Michigan in 1670, wrote of being saved from starvation by eating the various kinds of wild onion and garlic that grew there. Later generations of Americans took these plants to their heart, and much onion breeding took place in the first decades of the 20th century. The emphasis was on producing sweet, early-summer-cropping onions, which have a high water and sugar content. There was also a move toward producing low-sulphur and hence less smelly onions.

special feast called *la calçotada. La calçotada* consists of masses of scallions, grilled over charcoal and then served with salsa romesco, made from chilies, nuts and garlic.

Despite the popularity of alliums in such countries, these odorous vegetables were slow to return to favor in England. Onions, shallots, even leeks, but most especially garlic, remained fairly unpopular and became associated with "foreign food." Writing in 1861, in her hugely influential *Book of Household Management*, Isabella Beeton observes rather sniffily of garlic: "It was in greater repute with our ancestors than it is with ourselves ... on the Continent, especially in Italy, it is much used, and the French consider it is an essential in many made dishes". Mrs Beeton gives only one dish that includes garlic—a Bengali recipe for hot mango chutney—highlighting the influence of Indian cooking on the English kitchen.

Why did the alliums stay so popular in some cultures but attract such great opprobrium in others? One answer may lie in the nature of cooking in different cultures. In northern Europe, especially England, and in North America, regional, peasant and rural cooking lost ground

Above: During World War II when onions were in short supply in Britain, leeks became even more important.

in the face of a growing move toward industrialization as people moved to big cities in search of work. Alliums have always been associated with regional, peasant cooking. These traditions remained strong in all the Mediterranean countries and had a great influence on the middle-class cooking of the day. In Britain, cooking was effectively cut off from its rural and peasant roots and a "genteel" style of middle-class cooking —ironically influenced by notions of French *haute cuisine*—was adopted in its place.

By the late 20th century, the health benefits of the vegetable-based Mediterranean diet, including lots of onions and other alliums, was vaunted in the United States and Britain as a much healthier way of eating. This had always been the case in poorer areas of Europe, where onions have always remained a vital and much celebrated way of injecting flavor into the diet.

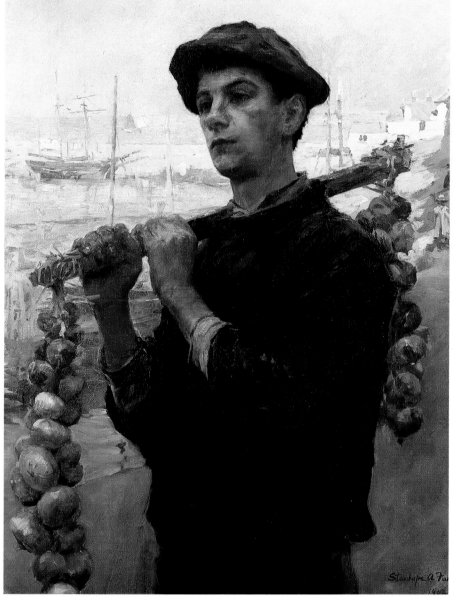

Left: French onion sellers, like this one depicted by Stanhope Alexander Forbes, were once a common sight in many English towns.

ALLIUMS OVER THE LAST HUNDRED YEARS

Apart from long-standing religious and social taboos, the history of the onion family over the last century or so has been one of gradual rehabilitation. In the United States and Australia, the massive influx of immigrants from garlic-loving cultures (Greek, Italian, Hispanic), has had an effect. In Britain, the growing love affair with Indian "curries," especially after World War II, was important, too.

Italian and Greek food, both heavily garlic- and onion-reliant, came into great vogue in the 1960s. Food writer Elizabeth David, whose books on Mediterranean and French cooking were published in the 1950s and '60s, had a huge impact on breaking down the social taboos against garlic.

There had been a few earlier voices. *The Gentle Art of Cookery* (1925), written by Miss Olga Hartley and Mrs C. F. Leyel, included a whole section on onions, including soups, stuffed onions and a recipe for an Alsatian *gâteau aux oignons*. Mrs Leyel was the founder of Culpepper's herbalist stores, head of the Society of Herbalists, and was obviously an adventurous cook and traveler. She includes garlic as one of the essential ingredients in her "Alchemist's Storecupboard." In 1933, the food writer Ambrose Heath wrote his *Book of the Onion*: a whole book (albeit small) devoted to recipes containing onions as a major ingredient. But these were lonely voices.

As the century progressed, the old middle-class sanction against using (and hence smelling of) onions and garlic started to falter. By the 1960s

Below: Onions and bicycles have long been associated with each other because of the traditional French onion and garlic sellers who, even today, can be seen selling their produce.

onion-smelling breath or body odor became less of a problem than it may have been in previous centuries.

Nowadays, onions, garlic and leeks are celebrated as never before. Garlic and onion festivals are held in places as distant as the Isle of Wight in England, and Gilroy, California. New varieties of onion are constantly being developed and bred, providing a year-round supply. Some restaurants devote themselves to wholly garlic-based menus, introducing such unusual dishes as garlic ice cream. Thousands of websites on all members of the onion family have been launched.

Exciting discoveries are being made about the medicinal qualities of the alliums. Today, the onion family is perhaps more popular and considered more indispensable than at any other time in its long and complex history.

Above: Specialty growers selling many different kinds of garlic, shallots and onions are a familiar feature of French and Italian markets.

Right: These enormously long strings of garlic for sale at Korla market in the Kinjiang Province in China demonstrate the popularity and importance of this allium in Chinese cooking.

and '70s, using garlic in food became a mark of culinary sophistication and trendiness. The famous "garlic dinner," cooked by American chef Alice Waters in 1976 in her Berkeley restaurant Chez Panisse, launched a huge garlic revival in mainstream American food culture and was extremely influential in establishing the important Californian garlic-growing industry.

Whereas the taboo started in the 18th century as a middle-class attempt to mark themselves out from the lower classes, it was to be the middle classes themselves in the 20th century who started using garlic as a mark of their sophistication and extensive travel. No doubt, as the food writer Jane Grigson noted, standards of hygiene improved in the 20th century, and diets and digestion with them, so the issue of

MYTHS, FOLKLORE AND MEDICINE

Throughout their long history, all manner of special powers have been attributed to the onion family, especially to garlic, and many myths and taboos have built up around them. To some extent these have grown out of the alliums' potent medicinal properties.

ALLIUMS IN MYTH AND FOLKLORE

Priests, shamans and healers have used alliums throughout the ages, and it is inevitable that the onion family has been attributed mystical powers. The ancient Egyptians considered that the layered structure of the onion made it a symbol of eternity, and they were certainly aware of the onion's curative powers. For the Egyptians, the onion not only cured disease and gave vitality, it also replicated the cycle of life itself. As such, it was also a fertility symbol: used in tombs to grant souls a fertile afterlife; used to ascertain female fertility; and denied to priests who might be incited to lustful acts of procreation if they ate onions.

For the Greeks, too, alliums were bestowed with sacred significance and linked to the afterlife. Theophrastus records that garlic should be placed on the side of the road at crossroads as a gift to placate Hecate, goddess of the Underworld, and this practice was continued well into the 11th century A.D. when the Christian Church put a stop to it. In Homer's *Odyssey*, the power of an onion (probably *Allium moly*) allows Odysseus to enter the lair of Circe. A well-known creation myth of Turkish Muslims records that, when the devil was expelled from Paradise and fell to earth, garlic sprung up where his left foot landed and onions from where his right foot came to rest. An Indian legend concerning the origins of garlic tells that when King Rahu, lord of the demons, stole the elixir of life and was punished by the god Vishnu by being decapitated, garlic sprang from where his blood fell. To this day, the followers of Vishnu refuse to eat any alliums.

From ancient times, onions have always had something of a diabolic, other-worldly connection, but they also suggest the triumph of life over death.

Above: The many different members of the onion family, including garlic, leeks, shallots and chives, all contain allicins—compounds which are believed to have natural antibacterial and antifungal properties.

The devil in onions, present in their fiery bite and effect on the palate, was also thought to incite men to lust and carnal desires. Again and again during the Middle Ages, a connection is made between eating onions, drinking alcohol and sexual incontinence. Or, as Thomas Nashe put it in his book *The Unfortunate Traveller* (1594) "Garlic ... makes a man winke, drinke and stinke." This attitude toward the alliums persisted beyond the Middle Ages in cultures as disparate as Imperial China, caste-structured India and 19th-century Britain.

All these beliefs come into play in one of the best-known myths that surround the allium family—that of the vampire. This myth began in the 16th century in central and eastern Europe but culminates in Bram Stoker's late 19th-century classic, *Dracula*.

Above: In country districts, strings of garlic, such as these sold by a French garlic seller, were often hung on thresholds or on children's cradles to ward off evil spirits.

In the vampire myths, garlic wards off evil and protects potential victims against the undead. Traditionally, in Romania, garlic was used in amulets to protect against the evil eye. In Stoker's *Dracula*, the threshold, windows and hearth are all rubbed and strewn with garlic flowers to prevent Dracula from entering his victim's bed chamber. The hero is also offered garlic as a protective talisman by the peasants on his way to visit Dracula's castle.

In the 19th and 20th centuries, the story becomes a sexual allegory: virgins may protect themselves against male desire by using garlic—men do not like the objects of their desire to smell of garlic. Garlic's part in the Dracula myths brings together all the various qualities ascribed to the "stinking rose" through history. In this story we find garlic's other-worldly, dark associations; garlic's connection with sexuality and desire; garlic's quality as a life force in the face of death; and even its ability to fight off infection as a natural antibiotic.

THE ALLIUMS IN MEDICINE

Alliins, the chemical compounds that create allicins, which give all onions their characteristic smell, are also the source of their remarkable medicinal and curative qualities. Alliins are the thioallyl or sulphur compounds present in all alliums. These compounds are volatile, which means that they break down when any part of the plant is cut or bruised. When the cell walls are damaged and exposed to the air, the compounds are converted by enzyme action to diallydisulphides or allicins—which work as effective antibacterial and antifungal agents. Of the everyday culinary alliums, garlic, with its naturally low water content, has the highest concentration of alliins (1–2 percent) and hence the greatest medicinal value.

Throughout history the health-giving properties of all the alliums, especially garlic, have been recognized by many writers and many cultures, especially in folk-medicine and herbalism. Garlic was thought of so highly as a medicinal herb that Galen, the Greek medical codifier of the 2nd century A.D., labeled it the

Above: The ancient Egyptian Eber Codex, The Book of the Dead, *suggests garlic as a remedy for a wide variety of medical problems.*

poor man's theriac, or cure-all. This passed into medieval English as the "poor man's treacle" (or treat-all), and for many centuries garlic was used to treat a great variety of complaints. As John Trevisa, the 13th-century writer, says, "it [garlic] is cleped tryacle of cherles among auctours in olde tyme."

Early medicinal uses

The earliest texts to mention the use of onions as medicine are the 5,000-year-old Ayurvedic texts from India. Garlic is mentioned as a useful treatment for digestive disorders, throat and bronchial complaints and even for typhoid. The Egyptian *Eber Codex, The Book of the Dead,* is a medical work of therapies and cures from around 1550 B.C. Garlic is again mentioned here as useful for treating many complaints, as diverse as headaches and the pains of childbirth. Throughout the classical and medieval period, writers again and again extol the curative properties of the alliums. The most common complaints mentioned include chest and bronchial problems

(Nero was not alone in thinking alliums improved the voice), worms, intestinal problems, bladder problems and lack of libido. They were also used to treat open wounds, to guard against infection from animal bites and to treat colds, headaches, hemorrhoids, sunburn and even leprosy.

The Greek Hippocrates (*c.*400 B.C.), the father of modern medicine, thought garlic good for wounds and toothache. Dioscorides, the Greek doctor who traveled with the Roman army (which was largely fed on onions, leeks and garlic) in the 1st century A.D., notes its use against tapeworms and snake bites. He was also convinced that garlic could help clear the arteries and cure coughs. Pliny the Elder (A.D. 23–79) in his *Historia Naturalis* gives over 60 garlic remedies, including cures for bites by wild animals and low libido. This latter is a common theme in the use of garlic, and links in with the idea that all the onions excite the carnal appetites.

Right: An early illustration of garlic (Allium sativum) *showing the flowers and the mature bulb.*

Below: Hippocrates, the father of modern medicine, praised the healing powers of garlic and posited it as a cure for a great number of diverse ailments.

Allium sativum L.

Medieval medicine and beyond

These notions held by the Greeks survived well into the Middle Ages. The 14th-century French herbal *The Four Seasons of the House of Cerruti* claims that white onions help to bring forth milk in nursing mothers and promote virile semen in men, and the herbal also considers garlic to be an undoubted aphrodisiac. Food historian John Ayto quotes an observation from *Andrew Boorde's Dietary of Helthe* (1542), which claims that "onions do promote a man to veneryous [sexual] actes," much as the Roman writer Pliny had done centuries earlier.

Medical thought and practice was governed throughout the Middle Ages by the doctrine of the humors, which explained how humans interacted with the natural world. The humors were the four bodily fluids: blood, choler, melancholy and phlegm, which were thought to determine character and physical health. The four elements of fire, water, air and earth also had characteristic qualities: hot, moist, cold and dry respectively. All living things—plants, animals, human beings—were governed by one or more elements and displayed one, or a combination of, these qualities.

Onions were considered hot and moist and were thought to govern the blood, the humor of the sanguine personality. Garlic was considered hotter and drier and thought to be good for treating the cold and wet phlegmatic personality. In John Trevisa's 13th-century translation of *De Proprietatibus Rerum*, he says of garlic "if colerik men ete to moche therof it maketh the body to hoot ... and is cause of madnesse and of frenesye," but later he admits its use: "and garlek abateth the ache of guttes aboute the reynes [period pains] also." John Evelyn, in his *Acetaria* (1699), observed that garlic was "dry toward excess ... and more proper for our northern rustics, especially [those] living in uliginous and moist places. Whereas leeks are hot, and of vertue

prolifick ... the Welch, who eat them much, are observ'd to be very fruitful." In the doctrine of humors, a plant's fecundity is thought to reflect its good effect on human fertility.

Other cultures also developed systems of categorizing the natural world and hence food. In China, the alliums are yang in the yin-yang balance of properties. Yang foods are male, dry and hot so, during the T'ang Dynasty (A.D. 618–907), garlic was endorsed as good for heating the blood and as a tonic. The Iranian "Araqi" classification ranks garlic as one of the hottest foods.

The alliums, especially garlic, have repeatedly been mentioned for use as treatments for open wounds, bites by venomous snakes and wild animals and cleansing the blood. Trevisa writes in

Above: Nicholas Culpepper, the 17th-century apothecary, extolled the curative virtues of onions and other alliums in his popular herbal, The English Physician.

the 13th century that garlic has "many maner vertu yfounde ... to putte out venym and all venemous thinges." Thomas Tusser, the 16th-century writer of agricultural doggerel, says that "now leeks are in season, for pottage full good and spareth the milch-cow, and purgeth the blood." Nicholas Culpepper in his well-known 17th-century herbal remarks that onions "Provoke urine and women's courses, helps the biting of mad dogs and other venonmous creatures ... [it] kills the worms."

There is also evidence that, in pre-Colonial America, native Americans used roasted wild onions and honey to neutralize snakebites and to help heal open wounds. Even as late as World War I (1914–18) garlic was used by the British as an antiseptic on a large scale, as noted by Mrs Grieve in her *Modern Herbal* (1931). The garlic was pounded to express the juice, which was then applied on swabs to open wounds to help staunch bleeding and prevent the wound from becoming infected.

Left: This medieval illustration shows the harvesting and bunching of garlic, which was believed to be good for treating a phlegmatic personality.

Alliums as preventives

In general, onions and garlic have been considered to be preventives and act as a general tonic against both infection and infestation. They are mentioned as preventives in outbreaks of the plague, for instance, both in France and England. The alliums' prophylactic properties were often linked with their use as talismans to ward off disease, rather than as remedies to be imbibed or rubbed on the body.

The Egyptian *Eber Codex* advocates wearing garlic around the neck as a way of driving out tapeworms. Greek and Macedonian mothers hung garlic around their babies' necks or cradles to ward off disease. In ancient China, onions, garlic and bunching onions were considered part of the "five strong-smelling foods" (*wu han*) and were hung on red cords at the threshold to protect the household against disease. John Evelyn (1699) considered garlic "a charm against all infection and poyson," even though he despised it in salads. Pre-colonial native Americans considered that wild onions worn around the neck protected the wearer from colds and bronchitis. Most famously, of course, a garland of garlic was supposed to guard the wearer from being attacked by vampires. Even in garlic-phobic Japan, in the northern town of Tsukuba-Khinoya, there is an annual festival, which dates from the Heian period of more than 1,000 years ago, when garlic is hung at the entrance to the house to prevent disease from crossing the threshold during the coming year.

Alliums in the modern diet

Many contemporary writers consider that the onion family, particularly garlic, should be an essential part of our diet. Alliums aid good digestion, maintain a balanced blood pressure and work as a general tonic to help stave off infection. Recent research seems to confirm most of the herbalist lore that has built up through the ages.

Left: With the growing interest in the healing potential of food, organically grown food, such as these leeks, is becoming more popular.

Below: Of all the members of the onion family, garlic in particular is renowned for its healing properties.

Above: Links have been made between garlic and cancer prevention, and experts agree that even a small amount every day will help strengthen the immune system.

There is evidence that garlic reduces blood pressure, helps lower LDL (low-density lipo-protein) cholesterol and may prevent the build-up of cholesterol within the arteries. Raw garlic has always been considered an effective antibiotic. There is evidence that although garlic is not as strong as modern antibiotics, the way in which it works is so different that it can kill strains of bacteria that have become antibiotic-resistant. Garlic and onions generally have great antifungal and antiviral properties, and they play their part in maintaining a healthy intestinal flora and fauna.

Research is also progressing to examine the link between garlic and cancer. Garlic certainly has antioxidant properties and contains selenium, which is known to strengthen the body's ability to resist cancer. Clinical tests have also shown that garlic reduces the size of certain tumors in animals or prevents them from growing. Most experts agree that even a small amount of garlic every day—say one clove—will help maintain good health and strengthen the immune system. Garlic can also help thin the blood and prevent blood from clotting.

Lore, remedies and old wives' tales

• As a remedy for corns, bandage a cut slice of garlic over the corn and replace it every day until the corn drops off.

• A syrup made from garlic steeped in vinegar and honey is good for asthma, coughs and general bronchial problems.

• To soothe a dry and painful cough, take a spoonful of honey mixed with a little crushed raw onion or garlic.

• It was once recommended that a roasted onion be applied to the affected ear as a cure for earache; it was also said to be good for boils.

• All onions are good for getting rid of moles in the garden. Drop peeled garlic or cut onions into their holes.

• Chopped garlic, bandaged to the soles of the feet and renewed daily, was thought a remedy for smallpox and even leprosy.

• Cut garlic rubbed over the lips will prevent them from being burned by the sun.

• Mixed with lard and applied to the chest or back as a poultice, garlic is thought good for whooping cough and other chest conditions.

• A cut onion will rid a room of other strong smells, such as paint.

• An Irish folk-belief is that garlic planted on a Good Friday will protect people from fever during the whole year.

• A cut onion is said to attract all infection from the air into it and will kill airborne infection.

• To cure baldness, rub the sap of a cut onion mixed with honey on the bald patch until the skin reddens—then wait.

• According to Brewer's *Dictionary of Phrase & Fable*, the phrase "to know your onions" is probably derived from Cockney rhyming slang, as in "onion rings"—"things." However, some have suggested that it refers to the man who edited the *Oxford English Dictionary*—C. T. Onions.

THE WORLD OF ONIONS

While we tend to think of onions as being more or less the same, there are many different varieties, colors and sizes. Some are better suited to roasting, others to frying; some are delicious cooked whole, others are better for chopping, slicing and eating raw. The same is true of the other members of the onion family—especially shallots, garlic and leeks. This fully illustrated reference section will help you to identify all the main varieties of edible alliums and give guidance on how best to use them in the kitchen.

THE ALLIUM FAMILY

There are more than 300 distinct species in the allium family, many of which have been used as food plants. For culinary purposes the best-known species are the onion (*Allium cepa*), the shallot (*Allium cepa*, Aggregatum Group), the leek (*Allium ampeloprasum* var. *porrum*), bunching onions (*Allium fistulosum* and *Allium cepa*, Proliferum Group), garlic (*Allium sativum*) and, finally, the various chives (*Allium schoenoprasum* and *Allium tuberosum*).

Onions, shallots, leeks and garlic are commonly known only in their cultivated forms. Although we do not know the wild forms of many of these plants, we can make informed guesses as to their origins. Many wild forms of edible alliums still exist around the world, as well as many varieties of allium that are purely ornamental.

The one thing that connects all the members of the allium family is their characteristic smell. Alliums contain chemical compounds known as alliins. When a plant is bruised or damaged, the alliins immediately begin to break down into the sulphur compounds known as allicins, which produce the instantly recognizable smell and flavor. The release of these volatile compounds can make us cry when we chop onions. If you wander through a woodland carpeted with wild garlic (*Allium ursinum*) in the late spring, the acrid, pungent smell is almost overpowering. Place a bunch of unwrapped garlic chives in the refrigerator, and you will find that within a few hours the eggs, milk and butter will be tainted with their strong smell. Onions are some of the most potent flavoring ingredients available for use in the kitchen, so it is no wonder they have been used by cooks for countless generations.

WILD ALLIUMS

Ramsons (*Allium ursinum*) are one of the most common wild alliums in Britain and they grow in damp, shady areas throughout Europe. They form broad, fresh green leaves and have lacy heads of white flowers in late spring. The whole plant is very odorous and will affect the milk of any goats or cattle that graze on it. Ramsons used to be fed to chickens before they started laying, as a spring tonic and to "kick-start" them into productivity. The leaves are good wrapped around fish before grilling over charcoal. The flowers may be added to salads, and young leaves may be shredded into omelets or rice dishes; they were commonly used instead of scarce onions during World War II. Ramsons have left their mark in a number of English place names, such as Ramsbottom in Lancashire and Ramsey on the Isle of Man.

Rocambole *Allium scorodoprasum* and *Allium sativum* var. *ophioscorodon* have both been called rocambole. The first is commonly called the sand leek, for it likes to grow in sandy soils; the second is a form of garlic. Both have coiled or twisted stems and grow widely across Europe. They have a good, mild flavor and were once exceedingly popular in salads and for flavoring cheese. John Evelyn, the 17th-century diarist and gardener who was quite against garlic, thought rocambole far more socially acceptable: "a clove or two of roccombo, of a yet milder and delicate nature, which by rubbing the [salad] dish only, imparts its vertue agreeably enough" (*Acetaria*, 1699).

Above: The pink-flowered wild sand leek has a mild, garlicky flavor, which has been popular with cooks for centuries.

Babbington leek or kurrat (*Allium ampeloprasum* var. *babbingtonii* or *Allium ampeloprasum* var. *kurrat*) is probably related to the elephant garlic (*Allium ampeloprasum*). It is grown in the Near East for its narrow leaves. The sectioned bulb may be used as a mild version of garlic.

Other wild onions that have been used in the kitchen are crow garlic (*Allium vineale*) in Europe; *A. canadense*, *A. tricconum* and *A. cernum* in America.

Left: The flowers of ramsons can be found in European woodlands in spring.

ONIONS

These are all varieties of *Allium cepa*. Onions are grown for the bulb, formed by layers of fleshy, swollen leaf bottoms; the actual stem of an onion is the small layer of hard tissue at the top of the roots. The onion probably originated in western and central Asia, in an area stretching from modern-day Israel to India, and has been cultivated since the earliest times. It is likely that various kinds of onion were first cultivated around the Middle and Near East.

The uses of onions in the kitchen are myriad. They are used in the savory cooking of almost every country and culture. They are fried, boiled, roasted, baked, stuffed and grilled.

There are many different kinds of onion and they are classified for kitchen use according to size, shape and color.

Yellow onions

These are the most common type of onion and are characterized by a light brown skin and greenish white to pale yellow flesh. There are different varieties within this basic type, but they are commonly known as Spanish onions, regardless of their place of origin; Bermuda is the similar generic title for this kind of large, mild onion in the United States. For culinary purposes, Spanish onions are usually large, round and mild. Other types of yellow onions include brown onions, which have thick brown skins, and French onions, which

Left: Spanish, or yellow, onions are usually large and have a mild flavor.

have a stronger flavor. Generally, the younger and greener the onion, the more pungent the flesh. Several varieties of yellow onion have been favored for the mild sweetness of their flesh, such as the Vidalia from the northwestern United States and the Maui from Hawaii. The Walla Walla, named after the town in Washington State where it was first grown, was brought to the United States by Corsican immigrants in the early 20th century. Most onions in the northern hemisphere are autumn-cropping from a spring sowing, but some varieties have been bred to overwinter from an autumn sowing and crop in summer. Of these, the Japanese varieties are best known in Europe. The Vidalia is a summer-cropping onion in America.

Below: Brown onions have a thick, brown skin.

Above: French onions tend to have a stronger, more pungent flavour than Spanish onions.

Uses in the kitchen Yellow onions are suitable for most kitchen purposes. Choose large round onions for baking, stuffing or cutting into rings. Longer or squatter onions are better for slicing or roasting whole. Some people consider them too strong to eat raw, although a mild yellow onion is good in potato salad or in marinated fish dishes, such as ceviche and herrings.

Uses in the kitchen
Red onions usually have a much milder, sweeter flavor than yellow onions and they are popular in salads; this is, no doubt, also because of their attractive pink-tinged flesh. They are frequently used raw in salsas, relishes, antipasti and marinated dishes. Red onions are also good roasted, either whole or cut into wedges, which concentrates the sweetness of their flesh. They are less useful for basic frying, when they have less flavor than other varieties and their lovely pink color tends to turn to a murky mauve or dull brown.

White onions

Above: Red onions have beautiful purple-red skins and pink-tinged, mild flavored flesh that is excellent in salads and salsas.

Red onions

As with yellow onions, there is a great variety of size and shape among red onions, but all are characterized by shiny, papery skins of a glorious purple-red. The flesh is basically white, stained red at the edges of each layer. The color is released by contact with acids, such as vinegar or citrus juice, and red onion slices tossed in vinegar will soon turn a beautiful, uniform deep pink.

These are usually medium to large onions with a papery, white outer skin and white flesh. They tend not to vary as much in size, shape and flavor as yellow and red onions. They are usually fairly strong in taste.

Uses in the kitchen White onions may be used for all general cooking purposes, although many people consider them too strong for eating raw. Their even size and shape make them good for baking whole or stuffing.

Cipolla or borettane onions

These are quite small, flattish or squat onions with a pale golden skin and pale yellow flesh, while some varieties are tinged with pink. Cipolla or borettane onions are popular in Italy and some varieties are grown in France, too. They have an excellent, sweet flavor combined with an agreeable strength of taste.

Left: Evenly shaped white onions have a stronger flavor than red onions and are good for stuffing.

Right: A string of mixed onions makes an attractive sight hanging in a cool spot, and will cover all your onion needs in the kitchen.

Left: Cipolla onions are common in Italian markets and are excellent for braising, pickling and in salads.

Uses in the kitchen

Because they are generally small and have such a characteristic shape it would be a shame to use these onions for slicing or chopping so, generally, they are peeled and cooked whole. They are excellent caramelized or cooked *à la grecque* in a mixture of olive oil, wine and spices. They are also excellent for roasting whole, bottling and pickling.

Below: Tiny silverskin onions have a strong flavor and crisp texture.

Pickling onions

This is a general term for many different varieties of small onion. Some varieties may simply be immature yellow or red onions; others have been specially bred to produce small onions.

White silverskin pickling onions These strong-flavored tiny "pearl" onions are almost always used for pickling. When a small, pickled silverskin onion is added to a martini, the drink is called a Gibson.

Yellow and red pickling onions These are usually larger and milder than the silverskin varieties. They also keep much better than silverskins. Store them as you would normal onions.

Uses in the kitchen These onions are excellent for pickling whole in spiced vinegar and for roasting whole, or for caramelizing. Small onions are good added whole to casseroles and stews. Typically, the bourguignonne garnish, characteristic of the cooking of Burgundy in France, uses fried onions and button mushrooms to finish stews.

Grelots

This is the French term for small, flattish onions with a green skin and very white flesh. They are very like a bulbous scallion. Various types of this kind of fresh onion (they must be eaten fresh as they will not store well) are often labeled salad onions in supermarkets and food stores. They have a generally mild-flavored flesh with a crisp bite.

Above: Small yellow pickling onions are good for adding whole to stews and casseroles.

Uses in the kitchen Grelots are used extensively sliced raw in salads, but are good in many quick-cooked dishes, such as omelets and frittatas, or sliced into stir-fries. They are less useful for general frying or long-cooked recipes, when they tend to disintegrate.

Below: Pickling onions are favorites for traditional English pickled onions.

SHALLOTS

These are a distinct sub-species of *Allium cepa*, and are grouped botanically under the umbrella term Aggregatum Group, from the Latin meaning "a whole formed from several units." This is what distinguishes shallots from onions: they form clusters of several bulbs at the leaf bottoms. Their name comes from the ancient Palestinian port of Ascalon (now the port of Ashkelon in southern Israel), where it is thought they were first grown, but it is more likely to have been the port from where they were first exported to Rome. There is quite a variety of different shallots, but most are smaller than onions, composed of finer layers and they contain less water. As a result, they have a more concentrated flavor than onions, which makes them useful in the kitchen.

Banana shallots are the largest variety and get their name from their elongated shape. They have a smooth tan skin and a slightly milder flavor than other shallots.

Pink shallots and *échalote grise* are perhaps the most strongly flavored shallots and are the most popular varieties in France. Pink shallots have a reddish

Left: Banana shallots (or frog's leg shallots) are large and mild, and may be used in the same way as small onions in most recipes.

skin and pink-tinged flesh; *échalote grise* are paler but still have a pinkish cast to the flesh. They have a crisp texture and pungent, but not harsh, flavor, which is good raw and cooked.

Brown, English or Dutch shallots are probably the most common shallots found in food stores. These small, tan-skinned shallots often separate into subsidiary bulbs when they are peeled. They are good general-purpose shallots with good-flavored but reasonably mild flesh.

Asian or Thai red shallots are small, round red bulbs, which are used extensively in the cooking of many Southeast Asian countries. They vary from the strong to exceptionally strong in taste and are used most commonly in spice pastes, when they are pounded with other ingredients. Because of their low water content they are also excellent for slicing and frying to make crisp-fried shallots, which are common as a garnish on Thai salads and curries.

Chinese "shallots" are actually a different species (*Allium chinense*) and not a shallot at all. It is a wild species that is cultivated in China (*jiao tou* in Cantonese or *rakkyo* in Japanese).

Below: French shallots generally have a good, strong flavor and separate into several small sections when peeled. They are excellent in raw and cooked sauces and in salad dressings.

Left: Pink Thai shallots are used extensively in Thai curry pastes and are also used as salad garnishes. They are exceptionally pretty pickled in rice vinegar with herbs and spices.

Uses in the kitchen Shallots are excellent roasted whole, caramelized or pickled. Raw, they are essential in salad dressings and a wide range of French dishes. Chopped raw shallot is often sprinkled on a seared, rare steak *à la bordelaise*. Cooked, shallots are an essential ingredient in many sauces that need the flavor of onion but not its bulk. Shallots have a low water content, which means that they can burn and toughen easily, so care should be taken when frying. Potato onions may be used like ordinary onions.

They are grown mainly for pickling, and that is the form in which they are usually seen in the West.

Potato onions are related to shallots and belong to the Aggregatum Group of *Allium cepa*. The species is peculiar among the onions in that it develops entirely underground, in the same way as garlic. Because of this, it is a little hardier than other onions and shallots and, in the past, it was often planted in autumn. It forms clumps of small, yellow-skinned onions that store well. As many as eight small onions may form per clump.

Potato onions were once far more popular than they are now, especially in the mild west of England and Ireland; from where they were taken to the United States. They filled a gap between the end of the stored autumn-cropping onions and the new crop of shallots in late summer. Today, the potato onion is regarded as a bit of an oddity, mainly restricted to the herb patch, but the bulbs are of good flavor and are just as useful as ordinary onions in the kitchen. It is an interesting rarity that avid gardener-cooks might like to consider growing.

Right: English or Dutch shallots are generally brown skinned and have a mild flavor.

LEEKS

As a cultivated vegetable, the leek has even more ancient origins than the onion. It is probably derived from the wild *Allium ampeloprasum*, although some botanists call it a species in its own right (*Allium porrum*). The wild leek is a native of the Mediterranean and islands such as the Azores, Madeira and the Canaries. This wild leek has been traced back as far as Jericho 7,000 years ago. "Leeks" of a different species—*Allium ramosum*—have also been cultivated in China for thousands of years. Although there are many hundreds of varieties of cultivated leek, in fact, they vary only in size and winter hardiness. Some leeks have been bred to grow to vast dimensions and others to withstand quite severe winter frosts.

In the kitchen, the cook is mainly concerned with size. Traditionally in the northern hemisphere, leeks have been seen as a winter vegetable. These large leeks are one of the few vegetables to survive outdoors without protection. In recent years, baby leeks have increased in popularity, and while these may simply be immature, miniature versions of ordinary leeks, there are now special

Below: Baby leeks are good for serving whole. Steam, then brown in a hot griddle pan to bring out their flavor.

varieties that are grown to mature quickly and provide slender, tender leeks throughout the summer.

In leeks, the "bulb" or layers of leaf bottom are elongated to form what is commonly regarded as a stem, although botanically the stem is strictly the sometimes slightly bulbous bottom of the leek just above the roots. The leek divides into the white, fleshy basal portion and the green leaves or "flags." All the fleshy part of the leek may be used, but the green part is tougher and requires more cooking. Leeks have an almost universally popular flavor that is both milder and more rounded than that of onions. It lacks the pungency of onions but makes up for it in the gentle depth of its flavor.

Uses in the kitchen Young, fresh leeks may be used raw, shredded in salads (a favorite with the Romans), but their chief use in the kitchen is when they are cooked. They are superlative in soups. Leeks cook more quickly than onions, so they should be added to stews toward the end of cooking. Whole, they are good braised or blanched, then grilled. Baby leeks are almost always cooked whole. They are excellent if briefly boiled or steamed, then dressed in oil and vinegar.

Below: Large leeks, with their sweet, mild flavor, are among the most popular of alliums in the modern kitchen. They are excellent in soups and cooked salads.

SCALLIONS

Most of what are sold as scallions in the United States are simply early-maturing varieties of onion (*Allium cepa*). However, the need for a year-round supply and recent breeding, especially by the Japanese, means that some scallion varieties now have genes from Welsh onions (*Allium fistulosum*) in their makeup. If the cross-section of the leaf is circular, then the onion is a variety based on *Allium fistulosum*; if the cross-section of the leaf is crescent-shaped, then it is derived from *Allium cepa*.

As the English name suggests, these onions probably started out as the spring thinnings from ordinary onions. In culinary terms, the distinction between the different types of scallion is purely one of size—they vary from the really tiny (thinner than a pencil) to those that are as large as, if not larger than, a baby leek. Some varieties of scallion have a markedly bulbous bottom, and show a relation to the type of salad onions the French call *grelotes*; others are more leek-like, with no particular basal swelling.

Scallions have a mild, sweet flavor with a fresh green snap, which makes them good in salads. Use thinner scallions for salads and thicker ones for cooking. Red scallions have been developed: these look pretty in salads, but do not differ significantly in flavor from white scallions.

Left: Bulb scallions are the best ones to use for grilling whole or for cooking in dishes such as Chinese stir-fries, or deep-frying whole in batter.

Uses in the kitchen In Britain, scallions have traditionally been served whole (trimmed) in salads. They are good as crudités with a black olive tapenade and are excellent chopped or sliced into mixed or composite salads; they are widely used like this throughout the Middle East. They make a good addition to Mexican salsas. Scallions are also excellent cooked, and are an essential ingredient in many Asian stir-fries, because they cook quickly. They grill well, taking only a few minutes to cook. In Cataluña, in northeast Spain, they are widely used in this way: known as *calçots*, they are grilled over hot coals and served with all sorts of grilled meats and with a nut/chili sauce called *salsa romesco*. The tops of young scallions may be used as a garnish in the same way as chives, and scallion curls and brushes are popular garnishes in Chinese food.

Below: Thin scallions are excellent in salads, whether left whole or chopped small.

BUNCHING, WELSH AND TREE ONIONS

Bunching or Welsh onions (*Allium fistulosum*) are very popular in China and Japan. They are called Welsh as a corruption of the Germanic *welsche*, meaning foreign. This label was probably given when they were first introduced into Europe from Asia. In Wales itself they used to be known as "holtzers," and they were once a popular flavoring because they grew in early spring when few other vegetables were available. They are also known as *chiboules* or *cibols*. In Chinese cooking, bunching onions are used in stir-fries instead of scallions. The onion grows in clusters of bulbs, so individual onions may be removed, leaving the plant growing. The flavor is mild.

Right: Tree onions, or Egyptian onions, are vigorous, clumping onions that grow well in the herb patch.

Below: Bunching onions are the most popular type of onion in China and Japan, and are used like scallions.

Tree onions (*Allium cepa*, Proliferum Group) are true perennials for the herb patch. As with bunching onions, individual onions may be removed from the plant for use in the kitchen. Tree onions also form little bulblets at the tips of the stem, which may also be used in the kitchen or may be planted to form new plants. A particularly vigorous and tall form of the tree onion,

known as the Catawissa onion, was a popular pot herb in America during the 19th and early 20th centuries.

Uses in the kitchen Both the basal stem and the green flags may be used in sauces, stir-fries and salads, but because tree onions are slightly tougher than scallions, they do not grill well. The bulblets are good chopped in sauces and salad dressings.

Above: Chive flowers have a surprisingly oniony flavor and make a pretty addition to salads in early summer.

CHIVES

European chive (*Allium schoenoprasum*) is a common wild plant, occurring from northern Russia to the Mediterranean and as far east as the Himalayas. Various larger-growing varieties have been selected for domestication. Chives are one of the first herbs to start into growth in the early spring, and the first shoots are remarkably strong and pungent; later on, as the plants develop, they become milder. The flowers also have a mild oniony taste and are good in salads and as a garnish. Chives are usually eaten raw or very lightly cooked.

Chinese chives (*Allium tuberosum*) are also known as *kuchai* (*gow choy* in Cantonese) or, garlic chives. They have a much more pungent smell and taste than European chives and because of their strong flavor are usually cooked. They come in two forms: the leaf form has flat, slightly twisted leaves with a pronounced garlic smell; the flowering stem with a round, hollow stem is normally sold with flower buds intact. A third kind, Chinese yellow chives (*gow wong*), are simply a version of Chinese chives that have been blanched by excluding all natural light. They are highly regarded by the Chinese as a vegetable in their own right for stir-frying. Garlic shoots are also used in Chinese cooking and are sometimes known as garlic chives.

Uses in the kitchen European chives are widely used as a garnish, but they have a surprising amount of flavor, especially when picked young from the garden. They are excellent in egg and cheese dishes, but care should be taken that they are not left in contact with eggs or dairy products as they will taint them. Chives are useful for adding a mild oniony taste to salad dressings, soups and sauces, and are particularly good in potato dishes. Chinese chives are more robust and need brief cooking. They are excellent in stir-fries, in rice dishes and stirred into soups and stews.

Right: Chinese chives are often sold in tight bud and may be chopped and used in stir-fries.

Below: Chives (Allium schoenoprasum) are popular throughout Europe and North America, and give a mild, oniony flavor that is particularly good in cheese and egg dishes.

GARLIC

At various times, garlic (*Allium sativum*) has been the most lauded and the most despised of all the onion tribe because it is the fieriest and most pungent. It is one of the few culinary alliums that forms its bulb underground rather than on the surface of the soil.

Typically, a garlic bulb, or head, is formed of several separate cloves, each wrapped in its own papery skin, and the whole head is enclosed in another papery skin. Garlic is widely cultivated, but needs a long growing season and a period of cold weather to initiate proper bulb development.

Most cultures consider it a herb or flavoring rather than a vegetable in its own right, but many dishes exist that include several whole heads of garlic rather than the odd clove that more timid cooks employ. A whole head of garlic, gently roasted until it becomes sweet, mellow and purée-soft, may easily be consumed by one person at a sitting. There are French recipes for chicken or lamb with forty cloves of garlic, which achieved an almost mythical status in garlic-phobic Britain of the 1950s. Some Asian dishes contain huge amounts of garlic by Western standards, such as southern Indian dishes of whole garlic cloves cooked with spices and coconut milk.

Left: Young, new-season or wet garlic that has not been dried has a particularly sweet and mild flavor.

There are many different varieties of garlic, most of them geographically specific and therefore adapted to local climate and conditions. Garlic stores well when it is dried, but has a different taste from when it is used green and freshly pulled. There are some garlics with very white skin, while others are stained or mottled deep pink. Some garlic varieties separate naturally into tiny cloves, while others are characterized by large, fat cloves. Generally, the larger and less dried the clove, the milder and less pungent it is, but this is not an unbroken rule.

Above: Solo garlic is a mild form of garlic in which each small bulb comprises a single clove.

Below: Garlic is often sold in strings and will keep for several months if hung in a cool, dry place.

Middle East and in all Mediterranean countries. Crisp, fried garlic is a popular garnish to Burmese food, and in both Thailand and Korea pickled garlic is an accompaniment to many meals.

Garlic alters in flavor according to how it is prepared and for how long it is cooked. Crushed garlic, either raw or briefly cooked, is the most pungent and strongly flavored; a whole head of garlic, slowly roasted, will have a mellow, nutty, toasty flavor. Garlic may be fried, baked, roasted or braised. It is a ubiquitous ingredient in most spice pastes, Spanish salsas, Italian pestos and Mexican moles. It is also widely used in all types of cuisine in dressings, marinades, soups and stews.

Left: Smoked garlic is infused over wood smoke. It is good in garlic mayonnaise, marinades and salad dressings.

Below: There are many different kinds of garlic, which are often geographically specific: white garlic is popular in California. California Late and Silverskin are well-known varieties.

Elephant garlic (*Allium ampeloprasm*) There is some confusion in food stores between this variety and large-growing varieties of true garlic. Elephant garlic is actually more closely related to the leek than to garlic proper. It has a mild, creamy, garlic flavor, and the cloves are very large in comparison with ordinary garlic. Another variety of allium (*Allium gigantum*) has also been known as elephant garlic, but most gardeners grow this as an ornamental, for its very large, purple drumstick flowers, rather than as a food plant.

Solo is a variety of garlic that has been specially bred to develop just one, large clove, making it easy to peel and prepare. It is useful for dishes using a lot of garlic, but expensive to use in any quantity. The flavor is fairly mild.

Wet or new season garlic may simply be labeled "fresh" or "green" garlic. Typically, in the northern hemisphere, this is ready in late spring to early summer, when the papery skin has not fully developed and dried out. Usually the head is used whole: it is creamy white, streaked and flushed with green and pink, and has a delicious mild flavor that is ideal for European garlic soups and to roast whole.

Smoked garlic usually consists of large, whole heads of garlic that have been hot-smoked so that they are partly cooked and infused with wood smoke. They have a light, tan-brown exterior skin that should be peeled before the cloves are used for crushing into mayonnaise, for making garlic butter, or for tossing with pasta.

Garlic shoots—the first shoots of early spring—are considered a great delicacy in many areas of southern Europe (Italy, France and Spain) and are used in much the same way as chives or scallions. They are also much used in Chinese stir-fries. Soup made from garlic shoots is a great favorite and is considered a splendid health tonic—a sort of "spring clean" for the blood and circulation. The shoots are also pickled for use later in the season in relishes, salads and sauces.

Uses in the kitchen Garlic is an almost universal favorite for flavoring in cuisines all around the world. It is widely used, both raw and cooked, to flavor all kinds of dishes. It is used raw in dressings, salsas, butters and salads. Cooked, it is used in huge amounts in most Asian countries (apart from Japan), Mexico and South America, the

ALLIUM FLAVORINGS AND INGREDIENTS

There are a large number of allium flavorings and ingredients available. Some are made from onions, while others are not even related to the alliums but impart an oniony flavor.

Asafoetida

This is a pungent spice obtained from a resin from the root of a giant fennel (*Ferula asafoetida*). It is not related to the alliums but does give a distinct garlicky taste to the dishes in which it is used. It was favored in Roman cooking and was used by the Roman epicurean Apicius in the 1st century A.D. Today, asafoetida is used in Afghanistan, India and Pakistan. It is usually bought ground and should be kept well sealed, because the smell of the uncooked spice is disagreeable. It is used in Indian Brahman cooking instead of the forbidden onions and garlic.

Onion seed or kalonji

The name onion seed is a complete misnomer, because the Indian spice kalonji is not a relation of the alliums, but is related to the familiar, blue-flowered annual "love-in-the-mist" (*Nigella sativa*) of our flower borders. It is much used in India, especially in Bengali cooking. It is good stir-fried with green vegetables, and sprinkled on the top of Indian breads and pancakes.

Dried onion flakes

These are simply dehydrated thin slices of onion, but as onions are available all year round, they are rarely used today. They should be rehydrated in warm water for 15–20 minutes before using, or they may be gently fried, to form crisp fried onions, which are much used as a garnish for Thai salads and curries. Dried shallot flakes are also available.

Crisp fried onion flakes

These are ready-fried crisp scraps of onion, which are useful as a garnish in salads, soups and rice dishes, or may be added to egg dishes. Once the package is opened, the flakes should be used quickly or they will get rancid.

Left: Pungent asafoetida is much used in Indian vegetarian cooking.

Above right: Dry-roasting kalonji seeds will bring out their nutty flavor.

Right: Fried onion flakes are good sprinkled on salads and rice dishes.

Below: Dried shallot flakes may be added directly to slow-cooked stews.

Garlic salt

This is a mix of dried garlic and salt. It can be used to add instant garlic flavor to dishes such as garlic bread, but the drying process alters garlic's flavor, and many cooks prefer to use fresh garlic.

Garlic pastes

Ready-prepared garlic pastes are widely available. However, as with dried garlic, some of the preservatives used in the preparation of commercial garlic pastes alter the flavor and can give a slightly metallic tang to the finished dish. It is better to make your own roasted garlic paste, which will keep for 1–2 weeks covered with olive oil in a screw-top jar in the refrigerator.

Above left: Garlic salt is used in Cajun cooking for their blackened dishes.

Above: Fried garlic and garlic granules

Below: Small onions, garlic and shallots are popular in pickles.

Right: Minced garlic

Bottled or pickled alliums

In many countries, onions, garlic and shallots are pickled or bottled in vinegar or oil. These preserved alliums make a delicious addition to mixed salads, egg and rice dishes. Bottled green shoots of sprouting garlic are a popular spring flavoring in Spain, Italy and China. They are occasionally available fresh at Asian food stores.

CULTIVATION

The fact that the onion family has been cultivated since the earliest times and that it has spread far and wide across the globe suggests that onions are easy to grow. This is largely true: for the most part, onions are easily grown, hardy plants that are adaptable to a wide range of climates and soils. Certain varieties have been bred that are more suited to specific climatic conditions, and these different types vary in flavor and strength. Generally, the quicker an onion grows, the milder its flavor will be. Ideal quick-growing conditions, such as those found in large parts of Spain, the western United States and Hawaii, foster sweet, mild onions, such as the Vidalia from Washington State and the Maui from the Hawaiian island of the same name. Onions that grow more slowly, say in northern Europe, tend to be stronger and more pungent. Home-grown onions, which have had to survive the vicissitudes of the garden,

Below: Seedlings of the onion Vera Prima, ready for planting out.

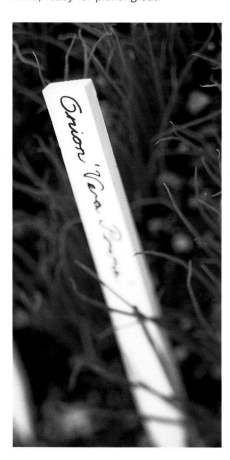

possibly with periods of drought and neglect, tend to be stronger in flavor and odor than commercially grown onions, which have led a pampered and well-watered life.

Onions can be grown in almost any type of soil but most members of the onion family like a friable, open, slightly sandy soil. The best way is to plant in ground that has been manured in autumn before planting. All members of the onion family prefer an open, sunny position: they do not grow well under the shade of trees or buildings, nor do they like the competition of roots from trees or large shrubs. Onions like to be well fed, but not with a fertilizer with a high nitrogen content, as this will make them grow large leaves rather than foster the formation of the bulb or stem.They also need to be well watered, as this helps the bulb to swell, but they can stand short periods of drought.

Onions (*Allium cepa* vars.) are biennial plants, which means that they form a bulb or storage organ one year, in order to flower and set seed the next. If the climate is mild enough, onions left in the ground during winter will shoot, flower and set seed in late spring.

The gardener grows the onion for the bulb it produces in its first year of growth. If it is properly dried off and stored, this bulb will survive throughout the winter dormant period and will not attempt to grow again until the following spring. Onions that are kept in a place that is too warm or damp may well shoot while they are in storage. An onion that does this is still edible, but the winter dormancy has been broken and it will not keep.

Onions are grown by two methods: either from seed, or from small, infant onions called sets. Shallots and garlic are, effectively, grown only from sets, while leeks and scallions are grown exclusively from seed. The bunching onions and chives are perennial plants (they live for several years and do not die upon flowering) and may be grown either from seed, division (when the plants are separated to make several new plants) or, sometimes, from little bulblets produced by the adult plant.

GROWING ONIONS FROM SEED

Onions are fairly hardy plants, and small seedlings, growing outdoors, will survive a mild frost. Therefore, seed may be sown outdoors in mid- to late spring, or, with some varieties in mild climates (zones 7–8), in the early autumn.

Sowing onions outside

1 Prepare the ground by removing all weeds, then fork it over and rake it to form a fine tilth and a level surface.

2 Make a drill about ¼ inch deep with a thin stick or the corner of the rake head.

3 If the soil is dry, water the bottom of the drill before sowing.

4 Sow the seeds thinly along the bottom. Cover with the soil and firm it lightly with a rake. If sowing on a heavy, clay soil, a thin layer of sharp sand trickled along the bottom of the seed drill will prevent the seed from rotting before it starts to shoot.

5 The seedlings should germinate in 10–15 days. When they are 2–3 inches high, thin them to 3–4 inches apart. Water if conditions are very dry and keep free from weeds.

6 When the seedlings are growing strongly and the leaves are beginning to meet, thin them again to 5–6 inches apart. The thinnings at this stage of growth may be used as salad or scallions. Unless you are intending to grow very large onions, you will not need to thin the onions again.

7 If you prefer small onions, space them closer together or let them grow as clumps of seedlings—you will then get clumps of small bulbs that you can pull as they are needed. Autumn-sown onions are often left to grow as clumps of seedlings, as these often overwinter better than the single seedlings.

Sowing onions indoors

In colder climates or on cold, heavy soils, sow onion seeds indoors under glass and then plant them outside in the garden in late spring. The seeds may be sown in early to mid-spring.

1 Fill a seed tray with sterilized seed compost, level the surface and firm it slightly by pressing down gently with your finger.

2 Sprinkle the seed thinly on the surface of the compost.

3 Cover with either a thin layer of sifted seed compost or sprinkle with a thin layer of fine vermiculite to a depth of about ¼ inch.

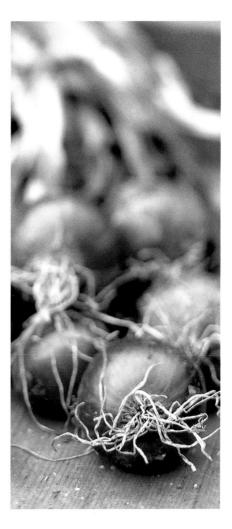

Above: North Holland Blood and Red Mate are both good growing varieties of onions.

4 Using a watering can with a fine rose on the spout, lightly water the seeds, label and cover with a propagator lid or a plastic bag. Gentle heat under the tray will aid germination, but is not essential. As soon as the seedlings begin to emerge, move the tray into full light, but protect the delicate leaves from scorching in strong sunlight.

5 When the seedlings are 2–2½ inches high, prick them out into trays of compost, spacing them 2–2½ inches apart.

6 Alternatively, sow the seeds in divided trays or seed modules, 3–4 seeds per module. When the seedlings are growing strongly, thin to one seedling.

Planting onion seedlings outside

Seedlings grown inside will need to be planted outside in late spring. Harden off the seedlings before planting out by standing the trays outside for about 12 days. Cover and protect from heavy rain or frosty weather in a cold frame or greenhouse. When the seedlings have been hardened off, plant out 6–7 inches apart, in rows 10 inches apart. The tiny bulb should be no deeper than it was in the seed tray. Water well and protect from birds.

Some varieties of onion have been specially bred (mainly in Japan) to overwinter in a mild, temperate climate. These should be sown in late summer/ early autumn. The seedlings or young plants overwinter, then grow in the spring. These onions are ready for harvesting in the early summer of the year following sowing, and usefully fill the gap between the end of the stored onions and the new season's crop of spring-sown onions. The most famous of these onions are the Vidalia onions, grown in the town of the same name in Washington state. The Vidalia onion is famous for being particularly sweet and mild.

GROWING ONIONS FROM SETS

Onions can also be grown from sets, which are small, immature bulbs. Sets have been grown and treated so that, once planted, they will continue to grow to form a full-size onion. Because onions are biennial there is a danger that the set will bolt, that is run to flower, rather than grow to make a fair-size bulb. However, some sets have been heat-treated to kill the flower and prevent bolting. Onion sets are planted in early to mid-spring and will stand a little light frost. They are best planted in open, well-dug soil which has been manured the autumn before planting.

If the soil is heavy, put a little sharp sand beneath each set. Push into the soil in rows, allowing 4 inches between sets and 10 inches between rows. The top of the set should be just visible. Apart from watering in extremely dry weather and weeding, they should need no more care.

Sometimes birds will work their way down a row pulling out the sets before they have time to root. If this happens, simply push them back into the soil, making sure that they are firm. If birds are proving to be a particular problem, try laying twigs over the soil, or covering the sets with netting. This may well be the best solution to the problem.

Good varieties of onion

Spring sowing: Buffalo, Giant Fen Globe, Ailsa Craig, Sturon, North Holland Blood, Long Red Florence, Red Baron, Southport Red Globe, Red Mate. Autumn sowing: Express Yellow, Imai Early Yellow, Vidalia, Senshyu Yellow. Pickling onions: Paris Silver Skin, Shakespeare.

Championship onions and leeks

Around the world, specialty and competitive growers prepare deep beds of special soil in which to grow mammoth onions and leeks. There is great competition between growers. Show leeks are blanched by growing them through drainpipes or wrapping them in thick, corrugated cardboard, and they are fed with "secret" compounds of liquid fertilizer to encourage growth. Some onions can grow to over 6 pounds, while leeks can grow up to 1 yard long, with a stem as thick as a person's arm. Good varieties for championship onions are Mammoth and Beacon.

GROWING LEEKS

Leeks are grown from seed in exactly the same way as onions. Sow outside in mid- to late spring or inside under glass in early spring. Sowing seeds indoors provides a longer growing season and produces bigger leeks. Leeks sown outside should be thinned to about 1 inch apart. Inside, prick out the seedlings into trays or modules about 1 inch apart. In early summer, plant the leeks outside. Indoor-sown leeks should be hardened off first.

1 If you want long, blanched leeks, dig a trench of prepared soil. The trench should be about 12 inches across and about 10 inches deep. Fork over the bottom of the trench thoroughly and dig in some well-rotted manure or fertilizer. Heap the removed soil alongside the trench for infilling later.

2 Half-fill the trench with removed soil, then make holes with a stick or dibber 8–10 inches apart. They should be about 1–1½ inches across and 5–6 inches deep.

3 Drop the seedlings into the holes so that the leaves poke out of the top.

4 Water the leeks well, by pouring water into the hole to wash soil over the roots.

5 As the leeks grow, gradually return the remaining soil to the trench. This blanches the stem, and forces the leeks to grow a longer, white stem.

6 For leeks for general cooking, holes may be made in well-prepared soil, rather than a trench. Drop in the leek seedlings and water in as above. Some gardeners on heavy clay soil find they get better results if they grow leeks in raised beds of deeply prepared soil.

Below: De Saint Victor leeks have distinctive blue-purple leaves; they are winter-hardy and have excellent flavor.

This aids drainage, whereas a trench may fill with water on badly draining land. Support the sides of the beds with planks of wood, bricks or old railway sleepers. The beds should be about 4 feet wide so that they can be cultivated without stepping on the soil.

Good varieties of leek

Bleu de Solaise: a handsome leek with blue-purple foliage; Autumn Giant: an early maturing leek that will last to late winter in the ground; Musselborough Improved: a good winter-hardy variety; King Richard: a quick-growing variety, good for harvesting as baby leeks; Jolant; De Saint Victor: winter-hardy.

Fertilizing onions and leeks

In ordinary conditions, onions need little or no feeding during the growing period, although they may be fed with a potash fertilizer when the bulb is well formed. This helps the bulb ripen and prevents it developing "thick neck." Leeks need no extra feeding during the growing season, as long as the ground was manured to start with.

GROWING SHALLOTS

Shallots are generally grown from sets rather than from seed. They grow as clumps of bulbs, each one of which may be grown on as a set. They are grown in exactly the same way as onion sets, but they grow much more quickly.

1 In late winter to early spring, plant shallot sets in open, well-dug soil that has been well manured the autumn before planting.

2 If the soil is very heavy, place a little sharp sand under every shallot to aid drainage and prevent the bulb from rotting in the wet earth.

3 If any of the sets are pulled up by birds, press them back into the soil. Alternatively, protect the sets with a layer of netting or by laying a few twigs over the soil.

4 The shallots will be ready to harvest by midsummer.

Good varieties of shallot

Atlantic: golden-skinned shallots with a high yield; Pikant: a pink-fleshed shallot of fine flavor; Giant Iona; Topper.

Pests and diseases

The potent chemicals that alliums produce generally give them an in-built defense against pests and diseases. Garlic, in particular, seems resistant to most garden pests.

Rabbits, rodents and deer give all alliums a wide berth because they find the smell and taste offensive. Moles, too, avoid making their runs near an onion or garlic bed. Despite this, mice or rats are known to eat onions in storage, so, when storing alliums, they should be protected from these vermin.

In very wet summers, and on heavy, poorly drained land, onions can be susceptible to downy mildew, which can cause rotting. Affected onions should be pulled up and discarded, but not on the compost heap. Onions should not be grown on the same patch of ground for about 3 years.

The major pest of onions is onion fly. They lay their eggs in the bulb, which is then eaten by the maggots that hatch from the eggs. There are no chemical treatments that protect onions against this harmful pest, but companion planting is said to be effective in deterring them. Plant tagetes (French marigolds) and parsley in rows among the onions if the pest is known to be prevalent.

Leeks sometimes get a rust disease, which causes rust-colored spots on the foliage. However, it does not affect the leek stem, so there is no need to spray or discard the leek plants, but do not put affected leaves on the compost heap.

Above: Once harvested, shallots are best strung for storage and kept in a dry, frost-free place. They should keep throughout the winter if stored in this way.

GROWING GARLIC

Garlic is grown from individual cloves in a similar way to onion and shallot sets. There are many different varieties of garlic that have been specially bred to suit specific climates. It is better to order an appropriate variety from a seed firm, rather than using a head of garlic from the supermarket, as it may have been imported. These will, however, often grow. Garlic needs a long growing season and also a period of 1–2 months of cold weather (32–50°F) to make a good-size head.

Garlic is different from other alliums (apart from the seldom-grown potato onion) in that the head, or bulb, grows underground rather than on the surface of the soil. Because of this, garlic is best planted in the autumn, to be harvested in mid- to late summer the following year. It will tolerate some frost. Little or no growth will be visible above ground until the following spring.

1 Plant individual cloves 4–6 inches apart in rows 10 inches apart just below the surface in well-dug soil. Place a little sand beneath each clove if gardening on heavy, clay soil to help drainage and prevent rotting.

Growing garlic shoots

Garlic shoots can easily be grown by planting cloves of garlic in pots of good, free-draining compost from early spring onward. Keep well watered in a sunny, open position. Harvest the young shoots when they are about 6–8 inches high. More shoots will soon grow to replace them.

Good varieties of garlic

Moraluz: large white heads; Cristo; Mediterranean.

GROWING SCALLIONS

Scallions are grown from seed. Sow as for bulb onions in rows about 8 inches apart. Scallions mature quickly, so sow short rows in succession every 3–4 weeks during spring and early summer. If you sow the seed thinly, there is no need to thin out scallions, simply pull the onions as you need them.

Good varieties of scallion

Santa Claus: a Japanese variety with deep-red stems; White Lisbon: a traditional, white, quick-growing scallion.

GROWING BUNCHING ONIONS

Asian varieties of bunching onions are grown in a similar way to scallions, but you can keep on harvesting them over a longer period, so thin the plants to about 4 inches apart.

Good varieties of bunching onion

Summer Isle; White Evergreen; Ishikura, Kujo Green.

GROWING WELSH ONIONS AND TREE ONIONS

These perennial onions are best bought as small plants at an herb nursery, although it is possible to grow them from seed sown indoors in early spring. If growing from seed, prick out clumps of little seedlings in 3-inch pots. Harden off the seedlings and plant them out in early summer. If you have a mature plant, you can create more by simply digging the plant up and dividing it into smaller plants. Replant small sections from the healthy, outer edge

Above: Freshly harvested garlic ready for cleaning and stringing for storage.

of the clumps, rather than from the congested center. Bulblets from the top of the stem of tree onions will also grow into new plants if pushed into a pot of good compost.

GROWING CHIVES

Chives are propagated by division. They prefer a good, moist soil, but will grow more or less anywhere. Divide the plant when it is actively growing in early or mid-spring and set the divisions about 10 inches apart. Chives should be harvested as you need them. During the growing season, they can be cut down to ground level 2–3 times and they will sprout again, with fresh, full-flavored leaves. Water well after cutting back. In the autumn, pot up chive plants, cut them back and keep them in a cool, frost-free place indoors where there is plenty of good light. This is a good way to have fresh chives available for use throughout the winter.

HARVESTING AND STORAGE

The harvesting of alliums depends on the length of time that they can be stored. Onions, shallots and garlic, which, if stored correctly, can keep throughout the winter, should be harvested when they are fully grown. Leeks, scallions and chives, which have a shorter shelf life, are better left in the ground until they are needed.

ONIONS, SHALLOTS AND GARLIC

It is obvious when onions, shallots and garlic are ready to be harvested. With onions and shallots, the leaf stem keels over at the top (neck) of the bulb. With garlic, the leaves start to die back, wither and keel over. When this happens, it is fairly certain that the bulb has finished its growth for the season and is as big as it is going to get.

Sometimes onions develop a "fat" or "thick" neck. This is not a disease, but a physiological condition. Some varieties are more susceptible than others; wet weather is an additional factor. The neck of the onion becomes thick and remains green, and the leaves do not keel over but stay upright and healthy. The onion still continues to grow, rather than to ripen and dry off. If left in the soil, the onion would eventually bolt, or run to flower. Such onions are perfectly good to eat, but they will not keep for a great length of time, so use them as quickly as possible.

When the onion leaves keel over, it is best to leave them in the soil for a week or so, especially if the weather is dry and sunny. After that, gently pull the onions up to expose the roots to the air and leave them on the ground to finish drying and for the root to wither. If the weather is cold and wet, remove the bulbs to a dry but well-ventilated place: lying on the greenhouse staging is ideal, or on a frame made of netting. Do not remove stems at this time. When the onions have thoroughly dried, the stems may be twisted off and the onions placed in trays with ventilation holes.

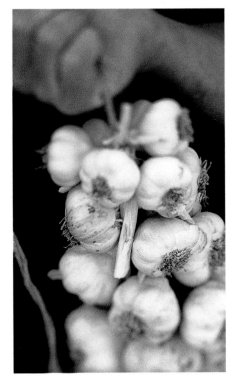

Above: Stringing garlic is an excellent way of ensuring that it stays dry and well ventilated.

Left: Lift onions with a fork, then let the bulbs dry off either on the ground, if dry, or on a rack under cover.

Stringing onions, shallots and garlic

If the stems are left intact, the onions may be strung together to form ropes or skeins, either by braiding the stems together or tying them together with string or raffia. Shallots and garlic should be treated in the same way. An alternative method of "stringing" garlic is simply to thread a stiff wire through the dry necks of the bulbs.

Strung onions, shallots and garlic may then be hung up for storage, which is an excellent way of keeping them well aired. All three should keep through to the following spring if stored in a dry, well-ventilated room or shed that is cool and just frost-free. Check your store of onions throughout winter and discard any that feel soft. Toward the end of winter, some onions may begin to sprout. Use these immediately. Do not try to store garlic ropes in the kitchen, however decorative, or they will sprout.

How to string onions, shallots and garlic

Onions, shallots and garlic can all be strung together in the same way. Either tie them into a skein with string or raffia, or braid together the dried stems.

1 Take the first bulb and tie a loop of string around the neck. Pull the string tight to allow for shrinkage later.

2 Add more bulbs, each one just above the last, forming a loop of string around the neck of each. Bind any surplus stem into the skein.

3 When you have reached the end of the skein—usually about 12–15 onions —tie all the stems together firmly, folding over any surplus.

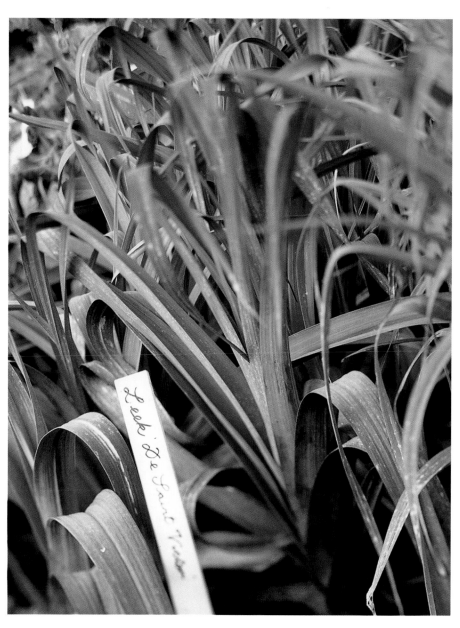

Above: Young leeks, like these 4 month old De Saint Victors, may be harvested as soon as they begin to thicken.

LEEKS

These are best left in the ground rather than lifting them as they mature. Simply harvest as and when you need them in the kitchen. They will withstand quite hard frosts and can be left in the ground throughout the autumn. When dug, the leeks will keep for about a week in a dry, well-ventilated room. Washed and prepared, leeks should be stored in a plastic bag in the vegetable drawer of the refrigerator.

SCALLIONS AND CHIVES

If the scallions have been sown thinly enough then, as they mature, you can simply pull them from the ground as and when you need them. Once pulled, they should be stored in the refrigerator, wrapped in a plastic bag.

CHIVES

These should not be pulled, but can be snipped near to the soil with a pair of kitchen scissors. Harvest chives as they are required in the kitchen. They will keep for a few days in the refrigerator, well-wrapped in a plastic bag or tub.

PREPARING ONIONS AND OTHER ALLIUMS

This section looks at most of the basic techniques for preparing and cooking onions, leeks and other alliums. It is worthwhile spending a little of your time studying and mastering these techniques, since they ultimately help to save time and tears.

CHOOSING ONIONS AND OTHER ALLIUMS

When buying onions, choose firm, undamaged specimens with light skins. Reject any that feel soft when gently squeezed, show signs of dampness or with green shoots at the top. These rules apply to shallots and garlic too, except new season's garlic which should have moist, fresh skins.

Examine the leaves of scallions and leeks—they should be fresh and not brown or slimy. Be careful when buying leeks in late spring and early summer, since they may well have a hard, central core. This core is the developing flower stem and it will not soften on cooking.

When preparing onions, discard any that have brown patches or are brown or slimy at the center. The onion will be tainted, and even if the bad portion is cut off and discarded, the onion will still taste nasty.

Green shoots at the center of a garlic clove, and dried-out, old or withered garlic cloves should be discarded—they will give a bitter or musty taste to the finished dish.

PEELING ONIONS

1 The easiest way to peel an onion is first to cut off the top and bottom.

2 Slit the skin with a sharp knife and peel it off.

Peeling whole onions

Onions or shallots used for braising or for adding to a *boeuf bourguignonne*, for example, must be left whole. Some cooks even find it easier to slice onions, which can be quite slippery and tough, if the root end is temporarily left intact.

1 To peel an onion or shallot, when it is important that the onion stays whole, trim any root from the bottom, making sure you leave the bottom intact.

2 Then, working from the neck down, make a shallow slit in the skin from top to bottom with a small, sharp knife.

3 Pull the skin off the onion, working from the neck down.

Peeling small onions and shallots

If you are peeling a lot of small onions or shallots, it is easier if you first blanch them in boiling water. This is particularly helpful when peeling varieties that have tenaciously clinging, tight skins. This also works with garlic cloves.

1 Cut off the neck of the onions or shallots and cut a thin slice off the bottom, but leave the root bottom intact, or the onions may fall apart in cooking.

2 Place in a bowl and add enough boiling water to cover.

3 Leave for about 3 minutes, drain, then slip the onions or shallots out of their skins.

TRIMMING AND CLEANING LEEKS

Particles of soil can easily become trapped in between the leaf layers of a leek. The tighter the layers, the less likelihood there is that soil will have managed to penetrate.

Baby leeks and tight, ready-trimmed leeks from the supermarket are unlikely to be very gritty, but it is still worth checking before cooking, since nothing ruins a leek dish more than the mere trace of grittiness from hidden soil. Leeks fresh from the garden are always the worst culprits and therefore need to be washed thoroughly.

Trimming and cleaning large leeks

1 When preparing large leeks, trim off most of the loose green leaves, or flags, cutting at the point where the layers begin to get tighter.

2 Discard any loose green leaves but, unless the recipe specifies the white part of the leek only, do not discard the green part of the bulb.

3 Trim off excess root. Discard one or two outer layers of the leek, which are tough, fibrous and quite likely to have been damaged.

4 Make a slit starting about 1 inch from the bottom of the leek to the top, cutting through to the center.

5 Carefully wash the leek under cold running water, fanning out the layers with your fingers to make sure you wash away all the dirt. Hold the leek so that the water runs from the bottom to the top, so dirt will not be washed back into the layers of leaves.

Trimming and cleaning baby leeks

1 Cut off as little of the green leaf as possible, as it is tender enough to eat.

2 Baby leeks are usually clean enough to cook whole, but check one by cutting a slit through to the center.

3 Peel off the outer layer of the leek if it looks tough or damaged.

4 Wash the leeks by shaking them well in a bowl of cold water.

5 If leeks appear dirty only at the top end and you want to cook the leek whole, cut a short slit in the leek. Then either wash the leeks under the cold tap or soak them in a bowl of cold, well-salted water for 30 minutes to draw out the dirt. Soaking also leaches out vitamins, so this should be a last resort.

Preparing in advance

It is unwise to prepare any of the onion family too far in advance. Raw alliums can develop "off-flavors" as a result of the sulphur compounds that are released when their cell walls are broken. Though safe to eat, they can taint delicate dishes of eggs, cream and butter. If you want to prepare alliums ahead of time, fry them briefly in a little fat from the recipe (or blanch them in boiling water for a few minutes).

SLICING AND CHOPPING ONIONS, SHALLOTS AND LEEKS

1 The easiest way to slice an onion is to cut it in half with a sharp knife, from neck to root.

2 Place the halves, cut sides down, on the cutting board.

3 Hold down one half firmly, but tuck your fingertips in, away from the blade of the knife, then, using the knuckles to guide the knife blade, cut down to make slices. Repeat with the other half.

Cutting crescent-shaped slices

Crescent-shaped slices of onion are good in salads and stir-fries. Thicker wedges are excellent for roasting.

1 Leave the root end of the onion intact and cut the bulb in half vertically, from neck to root.

2 Lay the onion, cut-side down, on a board and, using a sharp knife, cut thin slices following the curve of the onion.

3 Leave these thin slices attached at the bottom for frying or separate them into layers for salad garnishes.

Cutting onion rings

1 Choose evenly shaped round onions. Look at the neck of the bulb and check that there is only one shoot, or neck— this means that there is more chance of getting perfectly round onion rings.

2 Cut a thin slice from one side so that it will not slip on the cutting board.

3 Cut down to form thin or thick slices. Push out to separate into rings.

Chopping onions

1 Slice the onion in half from top to bottom and lay it cut-side down.

2 Slice across the onion, leaving a small section uncut at the root end.

3 Slice down through the onion at right angles to these cuts from neck to root. Leave the root end uncut to prevent the onion from falling apart.

4 Finally, slice across the onion at right angles to the second set of cuts and the onion will fall into dice on the cutting board as you cut.

Slicing leeks

1 Cut across the width of the leek in the thickness you need.

COOK'S TIP

The green part of the leek often takes a little longer to cook than the tender white part, so put it into the pan a few minutes earlier.

2 When stir-frying, cut across the leek obliquely in a series of diagonal cuts. This exposes a larger surface area of the central portion of the leek to the heat, ensuring that it cooks quickly.

Chopping leeks

1 Using a sharp knife, carefully cut the leek in half vertically, from top to root. Lay the leek, cut-side down, on the cutting board.

2 Make a series of cuts along the length of the leek from bottom to top, leaving the root end intact to prevent the leek from falling apart.

3 Cut across the leek and it will fall into dice on the cutting board.

PREPARING SCALLIONS AND BUNCHING ONIONS

Scallions and bunching onions are easily prepared. Cut off only any tough or damaged green leaves. Peel the thin, outer layer from the onion and trim the root end. Wash thoroughly in a bowl of cold water or under a cold tap. For stir-frying, simply slice at an oblique angle, holding the knife blade at about 40 degrees to the length of the onion.

Scallion brushes

These are traditionally served with Peking duck. The fringed end of the onion may be used to dip into the hoisin or plum sauce for brushing it on the pancakes.

1 Cut the scallion into 2½–3-inch lengths.

2 Make a series of lengthwise cuts at one end of the scallion, using a sharp knife or kitchen scissors to produce a tassel effect. Leave at least half the onion uncut to form a handle.

3 Place the scallions in a bowl of ice water and chill in the refrigerator for 30–45 minutes to allow them to curl.

Making scallion curls

1 Cut the scallion into 2½–3-inch lengths.

2 Cut each piece in half lengthwise, then cut these pieces lengthwise into long, thin shreds.

3 Place in a bowl of ice water and chill in the refrigerator for 30 minutes to allow the shreds to curl.

Making scallion tassels

1 Make a series of short, lengthwise cuts at each end of the onions using a sharp knife or kitchen scissors to produce a tassel effect. Make sure you leave at least 1 inch of onion uncut at the center.

2 Chill the scallions in ice water for 30–45 minutes, until the ends curl.

CUTTING CHIVES

1 Hold a bunch of chives in your hand, snip the bunch level at one end with kitchen scissors, then snip off the amount you need.

2 Cut straight across to form little rings, or obliquely to form slanting chives.

PREPARING GARLIC

The taste of garlic differs depending on how it is prepared. This is because varying amounts of the natural sulphur compounds, which are contained in garlic, are released depending on how you cut it. The finer you chop or crush garlic, the stronger the flavor will be.

Peeling garlic

The easiest way to peel garlic is to place it on a cutting board and use the blade of a wide-bladed knife flat to crush the clove.

1 Lay the blade of a knife flat on the clove and press down firmly on the blade with your fist or the heel of your hand, breaking the skin of the garlic.

2 The skin will then peel off easily. This also bruises the garlic, which allows the flavor to come out.

COOK'S TIP

To remove the smell of garlic from your hands, sprinkle them with salt, then rinse in cold water before washing them with hot water and soap. Alternatively, rub them all over with the cut-side of a lemon before washing in hot water.

Blanching garlic

If peeling a lot of garlic, you can blanch the cloves to make them easier to peel.

1 Cut off the top and bottom of each garlic clove and place in a bowl of boiling water for 2–3 minutes. Drain, then slip the cloves out of their skins.

Chopping garlic

1 When chopping or crushing garlic, first remove any green shoot at the center of the cloves. The shoot is most apparent in late winter/spring and can taste bitter. Cut out the shoot with the tip of a knife or pinch it out.

2 For a mild flavor, cut garlic into thin slices, across the clove, or chop roughly.

3 For a stronger flavor, finely chop the garlic by first cutting the clove in half from top to bottom, then cutting along and then across the clove.

Crushing garlic

To attain a much stronger flavor, crush the garlic rather than chopping it.

1 Crush the garlic in a mortar with a pestle or, alternatively, crush it on a cutting board with the flat blade of a knife to make a paste. Adding a few flakes of sea salt to the garlic will make crushing much easier.

2 Easier still, press the peeled clove through a specially designed garlic press or crusher.

GARLIC GADGETS

The only tools you really need to prepare garlic are a good, small, sharp knife, a cutting board and, of course, your hands. However, there are plenty of pieces of equipment on the market that are designed to help with the preparation of garlic. Most of this equipment has just one aim in mind—to minimize handling the garlic and therefore preventing the hands from smelling of it.

Garlic peeler

Garlic peelers are made of a simple rubber tube with a textured inside surface. The garlic clove is placed inside the tube, which is then pressed down on and rolled back and forth on the work surface to loosen the skin for easier peeling.

Garlic press (pump action)

A pump action garlic press is the most familiar type of garlic crusher. Some presses have a very useful reverse action that helps to extract the garlic that can become trapped in the holes. Garlic presses can also be used for preparing onion and ginger juice.

Garlic press (screw action)

A different type of press to the pump action but the result is basically the same. As you screw down the handle, the garlic is pressed out of the head. It is easy to use, but not so easy to clean.

Mortar and pestle

These are very useful pieces of general kitchen equipment and are excellent for crushing large amounts of garlic or making garlicky pastes, such as aioli.

Below: A mortar and pestle are the traditional devices for crushing garlic.

Garlic crush

A garlic crush is similar to a pestle but has a larger domed bottom. It is most effective when used with a bowl-shaped board. It produces a similar result to garlic crushed with the flat blade of a large knife.

Garlic slicer

A garlic slicer acts like a miniature mandolin. The garlic clove is placed in the holder, then slid back and forth over the sharp blade. This gadget is particularly useful if you are slicing large amounts of garlic or ginger.

COOKING ONIONS AND OTHER ALLIUMS

There are many ways of cooking onions, all of which will produce very different results both in the flavor of the onion and in the dish in which it is used.

FRYING ONIONS

Onions can be fried in a number of different ways and each gives its own unique result. Onions that are quickly fried until they are brown will retain all the pungency of the raw onion and may taste quite bitter if allowed to get too brown. Quick-fried onions are generally used in dishes where they will receive further cooking, such as stews and casseroles—dishes that also benefit from the dark color the browned onions impart to the sauce.

Slow-fried onions, cooked over low heat in a covered saucepan and not allowed to brown at all, will develop a wonderful, mellow, sweet taste that can add a great depth of flavor to the finished dish. This process is called sweating, and is an essential first step in preparing many soups and sauces. It works well with leeks, too.

Caramelizing onions is a combination of these two methods. First the onions are cooked slowly until soft but not browned, then the heat is turned up and the onions are cooked uncovered until they brown. In some recipes, a little sugar is added to speed up the caramelizing process. When the onions are cooked slowly to a mahogany brown, they are used as the base of many rich, brown soups and many classic sauces. They are also good to eat just as they are as an accompaniment to meat, poultry or cheese.

Different kinds of onion, or onions at different stages of growth, react in different ways to these basic cooking techniques. Green, unripened onions will not fry to a dry crispness. Red onions tend to be "wetter" than yellow Spanish onions and so they tend not to brown and caramelize so easily. Shallots, on the other hand, are quite dry-fleshed and will soon dry out and turn bitter and hard if they are fried and browned too quickly. To keep onions soft and prevent them browning when frying, add a pinch of salt to draw out their moisture.

Quick frying

1 Heat whatever fat the recipe calls for in a large, heavy frying pan over medium heat until hot. Add the thinly sliced or chopped onions and cook for about 5 minutes, stirring frequently, to prevent them from sticking to the pan, until the onions begin to turn brown at the edges. Do not allow to burn, as this will spoil the flavor.

Slow frying

1 Cook the onions over very low heat for 10–15 minutes, until they collapse and turn a deep golden yellow color. Stir the onions occasionally while they cook to prevent them from sticking to the pan and browning, as this will spoil their mellow flavor.

Sweating

This cooking process can be used for onions or leeks and is often the first step in soup making, as it concentrates and mellows the flavor, producing a rounder taste. Sweating or slow-frying requires very low heat that cooks, but does not brown the onions or leeks as this destroys the mellow, sweet flavor.

1 Cook the onions as for shallow frying, but cover the saucepan with a lid to produce much softer, sweeter results.

2 Some cooks like to press a piece of waxed or nonstick baking paper on top of the onions before covering them with the lid. This sweats the onions even more intensely.

Remedies for onion odors
• Try rubbing the soles of your feet with pure peppermint oil. Within 30 minutes the smell on your breath should be of mint.
• Chewing fresh parsley is the best-known antidote to onions and garlic on the breath. The chlorophyll in the parsley neutralizes the sulphur chemicals released by the alliums, which cause odors.
• Cover over the onion smells by chewing cardamom or fennel seeds—these seeds are traditionally offered after Indian meals as breath fresheners and an aid to digestion.
• Drink an herbal infusion of mint, fennel and/or sage.

Thai crisp-fried shallots

These are excellent for garnishing salads, rice and soups.

1 Peel the shallots and slice to a medium thickness.

2 Cook the shallots gently in oil for about 8 minutes, until they soften.

3 Raise the heat and fry the shallots briskly until they brown and crisp. Remove with a slotted spoon and drain well on paper towels.

COOK'S TIP
Dried shallot or onion slices can be fried from dry to form a crisp-fried garnish. Take care not to burn them.

CARAMELIZING

To caramelize onions or shallots, they need to be cooked slowly until their natural sugars turn an appetizing brown color. Caramelized onions or shallots add a depth of flavor to soups, sauces and stews. They are also good served with liver, steak or sausages.

The speed with which onions will caramelize depends on the heat of the pan. Onions or shallots caramelized over very low heat for 45 minutes will slowly turn a deep mahogany brown. The cooking time will depend on the onions' sugar content. Caramelized onions are used most famously in *soupe à l'oignon*. For a quicker result, raise the heat and add just a little sugar to aid caramelization, but stir frequently to prevent the onions from sticking to the pan.

Caramelizing onions in a saucepan

1 Cook onions slowly, covered, in butter or oil until they soften and turn golden.

2 Continue cooking, uncovered, until they begin to brown at the edges, stirring them frequently.

3 Add ½–1 teaspoon sugar to help the onions caramelize more quickly.

Caramelizing onions in the oven

This technique can be quite useful if you are busy, because the onions do not need to be stirred quite as often as onions caramelized in a saucepan.

1 Place thickly sliced onions in a roasting pan or on a baking tray, season with salt and pepper to taste, add herbs, such as thyme or rosemary, and sprinkle with a little olive oil.

2 Cover the onions with aluminum foil and cook at 375°F for 30 minutes.

3 Uncover the tin, stir in 1 teaspoon sugar and sprinkle a little wine or balsamic vinegar on the onions.

4 Return the baking sheet to the oven, uncovered this time, and cook for another 25–35 minutes, stirring once or twice, by which time the onions should be very soft and browned.

COOK'S TIP
A thick layer of onions will caramelize better than a thin layer, which will brown too quickly. Keep an eye on them in the oven. If they brown too quickly, lower the heat and be sure to stir once or twice.

Caramelizing shallots or baby onions

Shallots and baby onions are usually caramelized whole, but they can also be cooked in thick slices.

1 Brown the shallots or baby onions lightly on all sides in a little butter or oil. Raise the heat slightly, sprinkle in a little sugar, then let the shallots cook until the sugar begins to caramelize.

2 Add seasoning, herbs, if using, and a fairly shallow layer of a liquid to suit the recipe, such as wine, stock or vinegar. Cook gently, covered, until the shallots or onions are tender but still whole.

3 Then cook, uncovered, at a higher heat until all the liquid has evaporated.

FRYING GARLIC

Because of garlic's relatively low moisture content, it fries and browns more quickly than onions. It will burn easily and develops a bitter, acrid taste. Therefore, when a recipe calls for onions and garlic to be fried together, add the garlic to the pan when the onions are almost cooked.

In Asian cooking, garlic is often fried in oil at the beginning of cooking. Sometimes it is removed and discarded afterward because only the flavored oil is wanted in the dish; at other times, the garlic is an integral part of the dish. Again, care needs to be taken that the garlic cooks to an even, light brown, when it has a delicious toasty flavor.

Frying garlic slices

1 Heat a wok or deep frying pan until hot, add some cooking oil and allow it to become hot.

2 Add finely sliced garlic to the wok or pan and immediately stir it through the oil. It will begin to color immediately.

3 Remove the garlic with a slotted spoon as soon as it is a light brown.

Frying whole garlic cloves

Fried cloves of garlic make a delicious addition to green salads, especially those with goat cheese.

1 Choose large, plump garlic cloves and peel them. Bring a large saucepan of water to a boil and throw in the garlic; cook for 3–4 minutes, then drain.

2 Repeat the blanching process, then drain and dry thoroughly.

3 Heat a shallow layer of oil in a wok or frying pan, then fry the garlic gently until it turns an even, medium brown.

4 Remove with a slotted spoon and drain well on paper towels.

GRILLING

Cooking onions, leeks and scallions in this way gives a delicious result. They are perfect for serving as a vegetable side dish. Grilling—either over hot coals or on a grill—gives onions, leeks and scallions a sweet, mellow flavor.

Grilling onions

Onions, particularly mild, sweet onions such as Spanish onions, grill very successfully and are especially good when cooked over hot coals.

1 Peel the onions and slice them horizontally into thick slices, discarding the thin slices from the top and bottom of the onion. Carefully spear the slices on an oiled metal skewer, passing the skewer through the slice so that all the layers are kept flat.

2 Brush the skewered onion slices with oil, season, then grill for 5–6 minutes on each side or until the onions are soft and slightly charred.

3 Alternatively, place the onion slices in an oiled grill basket, brush with oil and season, then grill each side.

Grilling scallions

Scallions are delicious grilled and are very good as an accompaniment to grilled fish, poultry and meat dishes or served with cheese. They are very popular in Mexico and Cataluña where they are known as *calçots* and eaten with a spicy chili sauce.

1 Choose big, fat scallions with large bulbs for grilling.

2 Trim off any damaged leaves and the outer skin; trim off the root, too, but leave the end intact.

3 Brush with a little oil and grill, either over charcoal or on a cast-iron, ridged grill pan, for about 2 minutes on each side, or until softened and browned but not too charred. In Cataluña the outer skin is often peeled off before eating.

COOK'S TIP

Whole grilled cipolla onions make unusual and delicious canapés. After cooking, marinate the grilled cipolla onions in vinaigrette and serve on rounds of toasted bread or simply with thick slices of fresh crusty bread.

Grilling leeks

Baby leeks, when very small, may be grilled in a similar way to scallions. However, leeks are usually blanched for a few minutes in boiling water before grilling, since they have tougher skins than scallions.

1 Bring a large pan of lightly salted water to a boil and throw in the trimmed leeks. Cook baby leeks for 2–3 minutes and cook larger leeks for 4–5 minutes, then drain.

2 Cool a little, then gently squeeze the excess water out of the leeks. Leave baby leeks whole. Cut large leeks in half lengthwise or into short logs. Dry on a clean dish towel or paper towels.

3 Brush the leeks with oil, season with salt and pepper to taste, then grill baby leeks as for scallions, allowing 3–4 minutes on each side. Grill large leeks for about 4–5 minutes on each side.

COOK'S TIP

Grilled leeks may be served hot, warm or cold. They are particularly delicious with a simple dressing of oil, tarragon vinegar and a little mustard.

ROASTING ONIONS

Onions are delicious roasted. They can be roasted in their skins, which will produce a soft, juicy, sweet center, or they can be peeled, which produces a more caramelized taste and a much crisper texture.

Roasting onions in their skins

1 Remove any damaged skin and cut off excess root, leaving the bottom intact.

2 Brush with oil, if desired, then roast at 375°F until they feel soft when gently squeezed (1–1½ hours).

3 To serve, cut a cross in the top and add butter or cheese. A flavored butter with herbs or chile is especially good.

Roasting peeled onions

1 Small, peeled onions may be roasted whole. Larger onions may be cut into wedges (leaving them attached at the root bottom, so they don't fall apart on cooking) or, alternatively, they can be cut into halves or quarters.

2 Alternatively, make 2–3 cross-cuts from the top down to ½ inch from the root bottom. As they roast, the layers of the onion will open out.

3 Whole onions will roast more quickly if first blanched in boiling water for 3–4 minutes. Toss in oil, season, and cook, uncovered at 375–400°F. Whole onions take about 40 minutes, wedges about 30 minutes.

STUFFING ONIONS

Onions make natural containers for stuffings, and these may be prepared in two ways.

Preparing raw onion cups for stuffing

1 Choose round, even-shaped onions, not flat or pointed onions. Large Spanish onions are best.

2 Peel, and cut a thin slice off each end so that the cups will stay upright.

3 Using a sharp knife, cut the onion in half horizontally.

4 Using a sharp, pointed knife, cut around the second or third layer of onion, counting in from the outer layer.

5 Gradually loosen the center of the onion from the outer layers, leaving a cup of 2–3 layers.

6 If any of the cups has a hole in the bottom, cover it with a small piece of the removed onion. Fill with stuffing and cook according to the recipe.

To prepare whole onions for stuffing

Whole onions need to be blanched first so that they will cook evenly. The flesh can then be scooped out and mixed with the stuffing. Allow one large onion per person.

1 Choose round, even-shaped onions, peel, but leave the top and especially the root bottom intact.

2 Cover in boiling lightly salted water and cook for 15 minutes, then drain thoroughly and set aside until cool enough to handle.

3 Cut off and remove a cap from the top of the onion.

4 Using a small, sharp knife and a pointed or serrated teaspoon, remove the center of the onion to leave a shell 2–3 layers thick.

Making stuffing

The most popular stuffings for onions are either meat, or bread crumbs with herbs, spices and cheese. The stuffing usually incorporates the chopped onion that has been removed.

Raw onion cups are best suited to meaty fillings as they need cooking for 1–1½ hours at 350–375°F. They cook best on a bed of sauce or a mixture of olive oil and lemon juice, so that the onions may be basted while they cook. This helps to stop them from drying out and keeps them moist. Blanched, partially cooked whole onions should be brushed with a little oil or melted butter and baked for 45–60 minutes.

Watering eyes

Peeling and chopping onions makes you cry because these actions release the volatile chemicals that give onions their strength and bite. They travel to the eyes and nasal cavities through the water vapor in juicy onions. The stronger and juicier the onion, the more it will make you cry. Shallots and garlic, though often containing more of the offending allicins, contain less water, so produce less vapor and hence fewer tears. Leeks are very mild and hardly ever cause tears during preparation.

Most cures for onion tears have to be taken with a pinch of salt, but here are a few that people claim help.

• Chilling an onion in the refrigerator for several hours (or the freezer for a few minutes) is said to "lock-in" the water vapor and prevent it from reaching your eyes.

• Peeling onions under water will prevent the water vapor from reaching your nose and eyes, but no one's suggesting you try chopping onions underwater!

• The chemicals mostly reach your tear ducts through your nose, so try breathing through your mouth rather than your nose.

• If you are preparing a lot of small onions, try peeling them by the blanching method—this reduces the chemical spray that's released when onions are peeled.

• When preparing onions, try leaving the bottom (root) end intact, or cut it last of all. This basal portion of the onion contains the highest concentration of tear-causing allicins.

• An old wives' tale suggests that if you bite on a crust of bread while preparing onions, then you won't cry. Maybe the crust forms a barrier to prevent the onion's water vapor from reaching your nose and eyes.

PICKLING AND PRESERVING

Once, pickling was an important way of storing vegetables through the lean winter months, but nowadays onions are pickled because people like the taste. Although onions, shallots and garlic keep well in their natural state, pickling has always been a popular way of keeping them because their naturally strong flavor survives the pickling process so well and stands up to the strong tastes of vinegar and spices.

Pickling onions

Choose small, firm even-shaped onions for pickling, and peel them by the blanching method. Onions to be pickled are usually salted to remove water and to ensure they keep well.

For crisp pickled onions, cover with cold vinegar. For a softer pickle, the onions may be cooked in the hot vinegar for up to 10 minutes.

1 The onions can be layered with sea salt in a nonreactive (i.e. nonmetallic) bowl.

2 Alternatively, put the onions in a bowl and cover with a strong brine solution. Set aside to soak. .

3 Weight the onions to ensure that they are covered by the brine.

4 After 1–2 days in the brine (this depends on the size of the onions), the onions should be rinsed and patted dry, then packed into clean, sterilized jars.

5 Pour spiced vinegar onto the onions.

6 Extra spices can be added to the jar if desired, then tightly seal the jars for storage.

COOK'S TIP

Spices, which can be added for extra flavoring, may include mustard seeds, peppercorns, coriander seeds, allspice, chiles and cloves.

Simple spiced vinegar

Heat together 5 cups of vinegar (light or dark malt has the best keeping qualities) with 2 pieces of dried ginger root, 2 blades of mace, 2–3 dried red chiles and 1 tablespoon each mustard seeds, coriander seeds and black peppercorns. Add a few bay leaves, a piece of cinnamon stick or 2 or 3 star anise to taste. The longer you heat the flavorings with the vinegar, the stronger the taste will become. For a sweeter vinegar, dissolve 3 tablespoons of brown sugar in the vinegar.

To sterilize jars

Wash, rinse and dry thoroughly. Heat the oven to 350°F. Making sure you remove any rubber seals first, place the jars on a tray, then heat the jars for about 20 minutes. Cool a little before handling them—the jars will be very hot.

Jars can also be sterilized by putting them in a pan of boiling water for 10 minutes. Stand them on a trivet so that they are not directly over the heat.

OTHER WAYS OF PRESERVING ALLIUMS

Drying onions

In the past, drying was a popular way of preserving onions, but it is less so now, since onions are available fresh all year round. However, dried onions can make a useful staple ingredient for emergencies. To use dried onions, add them directly to stews or casseroles, or reconstitute them in a little warm water for 10–15 minutes first. Dried shallots may be fried in a little oil over medium heat to produce excellent crisp-fried shallots, which are useful as a garnish for many Thai and Southeast Asian dishes.

1 Peel and thinly slice the onions, then lay them on racks.

2 Leave them in a very low oven 225°F until very dry. This will take anything up to 12 hours. Turn the slices once as they dry.

3 Store the onions in a cloth or paper bag in a dry place or in a jar with a cloth or paper lid to absorb any residual moisture. Shallots may be dried in the same way.

Making roasted garlic purée

This makes a very useful flavoring to have in the refrigerator. It will store for several weeks, as long as you keep the purée covered with at least ½ inch of oil. Add more oil when you remove some purée. As a rough guide, 1 head of garlic should yield about 1–2 tablespoons of purée.

The purée is useful in many dishes. To make a simple sauce for pasta, stir 2–3 tablespoons of the purée into ⅔ cup of heated, bubbling heavy cream, season with salt and pepper to taste and add a little lemon juice and some chopped thyme or basil. This is good with many vegetarian dishes too. The purée is also good in soufflés, omelets and tarts, or simply spread on good bread and eaten with some grilled or baked goat cheese.

Roasted garlic purée

The following quantities make approximately ½ cup purée.

5 large heads garlic
2–3 sprigs thyme or rosemary or both
extra virgin olive oil
salt and ground black pepper

COOK'S TIP

When puréeing this amount of garlic, it is easier to purée the garlic, skins and all, in a food mill. The mill will force through the soft garlic, leaving all the papery skins and debris behind.

Using a dehydrator

If you are planning on drying a lot of onions, it may be worthwhile for you to invest in a domestic dehydrator. They are easy to use and will enable you to dry large amounts of onions quickly and efficiently. They are also useful for drying other vegetables and fruit, as well as being handy for quick-drying fresh herbs. Follow the manufacturer's instructions for timing.

1 Cut a thin slice off the top of each head of garlic.

2 Wrap the garlic in aluminum foil with the herbs and drizzle over 3 tablespoons oil. Bake at 375°F for 50–60 minutes or until the garlic is buttery soft, then cool.

3 Squeeze the garlic out of its skin into a bowl, then mash, beat in the oil and season.

4 Spoon into a sterilized jar. Pour over oil to cover by about ½ inch. Cover and store in the refrigerator for up to 3 weeks.

Freezing

It is not recommended to freeze raw alliums, since they can develop "off flavors" because of the sulphur compounds that are released when they are cut. Sauces that contain raw garlic or onion should also be frozen with caution. With pesto, for instance, prepare and freeze the basil, pine nut and oil paste and only add the garlic and grated cheeses on thawing.

THE RECIPES

With few exceptions, the onion has become an essential part of the cooking of every culture across the globe. However, onions and their relations are often taken for granted and tend to be used simply as the basis for whatever savory dish we are cooking. The wonderful selection of recipes that follow redress the balance in the alliums' favor, and celebrate the onion family not just as kitchen staples, but as star attractions in their own right—from soups and appetizers to meat, poultry and fish dishes to breads and pickles.

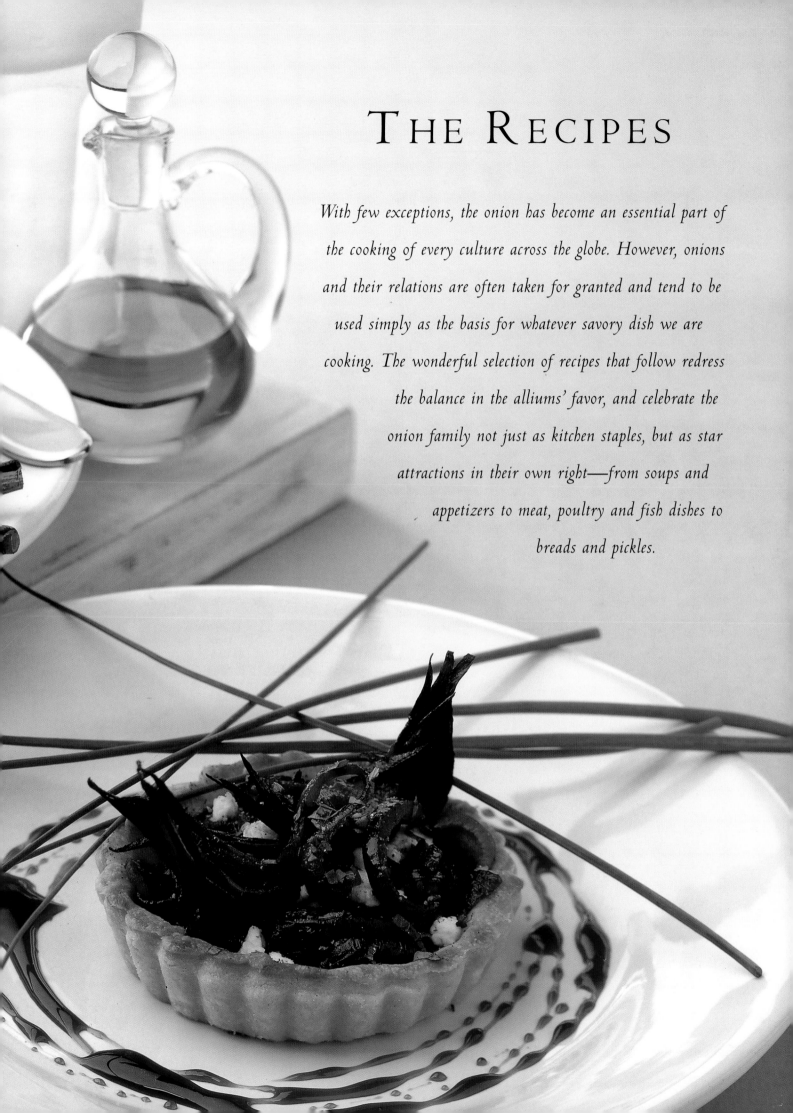

Is there anything more restorative than a steaming bowl of onion soup? Whatever the varying fortunes in alliums' popularity, onions in soups have always been favorites. They are an essential flavoring in good stock, and star in soups as diverse as thick French Onion Soup and velvety, chilled Vichyssoise. Garlic soups cure many ills; thick soupy stews of leeks ward off winter chills and buttery, saffron-scented onion soup is simply delicious to eat. Soups without onions would be hard to imagine.

Soups

SHERRIED ONION AND ALMOND SOUP WITH SAFFRON

THE SPANISH COMBINATION OF ONIONS, SHERRY AND SAFFRON GIVES THIS PALE YELLOW SOUP A BEGUILING FLAVOR THAT IS PERFECT AS THE OPENING COURSE OF A SPECIAL MEAL.

2 Add the saffron threads and cook, uncovered, for 3–4 minutes, then add the ground almonds and cook, stirring constantly, for another 2–3 minutes. Pour in the stock and sherry and stir in 1 teaspoon salt. Season with plenty of black pepper. Bring to a boil, then lower the heat and simmer gently for about 10 minutes.

SERVES FOUR

INGREDIENTS
　3 tablespoons butter
　2 large yellow onions, thinly sliced
　1 small garlic clove, finely chopped
　good pinch of saffron threads
　　(about 12 threads)
　2 ounces blanched almonds, toasted
　　and finely ground
　3 cups good chicken or
　　vegetable stock
　3 tablespoons dry sherry
　salt and ground black pepper
　2 tablespoons sliced almonds,
　　toasted, and chopped fresh parsley
　　to garnish

1 Melt the butter in a heavy saucepan over low heat. Add the onions and garlic, stirring to coat them thoroughly in the butter, then cover the pan and cook very gently, stirring frequently, for 15–20 minutes, until the onions are soft and golden yellow.

VARIATION
This soup is also delicious served chilled. Use olive oil rather than butter and add a little more chicken or vegetable stock to make a slightly thinner soup, then leave to cool and chill for at least 4 hours. Just before serving, taste for seasoning. Float 1–2 ice cubes in each bowl.

3 Process the soup in a blender or food processor until smooth, then return it to the rinsed pan. Reheat slowly, without allowing the soup to boil, stirring occasionally. Taste for seasoning, adding more salt and pepper if desired.

4 Ladle the soup into heated bowls, garnish with the toasted slivered almonds and a little parsley and serve immediately.

SIMPLE CREAM ᴼᶠ ONION SOUP

THIS WONDERFULLY SOOTHING SOUP HAS A DEEP, BUTTERY FLAVOR THAT IS COMPLEMENTED BY CRISP CROUTONS OR SNIPPED CHIVES, SPRINKLED ON JUST BEFORE SERVING.

SERVES FOUR

INGREDIENTS
½ cup unsalted butter
2¼ pounds yellow onions, sliced
1 fresh bay leaf
7 tablespoons dry white vermouth
4 cups good chicken or
  vegetable stock
⅔ cup heavy cream
a little lemon juice (optional)
salt and ground black pepper
croutons or snipped fresh chives,
  to garnish

COOK'S TIP
Adding the second batch of onions gives texture and a lovely buttery flavor to this soup. Make sure the onions do not brown.

1 Melt 6 tablespoons of the butter in a large heavy saucepan. Set about 7 ounces of the onions aside and add the rest to the pan with the bay leaf. Stir to coat in the butter, then cover and cook very gently for about 30 minutes. The onions should be very soft and tender, but not browned.

2 Add the vermouth, increase the heat and boil rapidly until the liquid has evaporated. Add the stock, 1 teaspoon salt and pepper to taste. Bring to a boil, lower the heat and simmer for 5 minutes, then remove from heat.

3 Let the soup cool, then discard the bay leaf and process it in a blender or food processor. Return the soup to the rinsed pan.

4 Meanwhile, melt the remaining butter in another pan and cook the remaining onions slowly, covered, until soft but not browned. Uncover and continue to cook gently until golden yellow.

5 Add the cream to the soup and reheat it gently until hot, but do not let it boil. Taste and adjust the seasoning, adding a little lemon juice if desired. Add the buttery onions and stir for 1–2 minutes, then ladle the soup into bowls. Sprinkle with croutons or snipped chives and serve.

FRENCH ONION SOUP
WITH GRUYÈRE CROÛTES

THIS IS PERHAPS THE MOST FAMOUS OF ALL ONION SOUPS. TRADITIONALLY, IT WAS SERVED AS A SUSTAINING EARLY MORNING MEAL TO THE WORKERS AT LES HALLES MARKET IN PARIS.

SERVES SIX

INGREDIENTS

¼ cup butter
1 tablespoon olive oil
4½ pounds yellow onions, peeled and sliced
1 teaspoon chopped fresh thyme
1 teaspoon sugar
1 tablespoon sherry vinegar
6¼ cups good beef, chicken or duck stock
1½ tablespoons all-purpose flour
⅔ cup dry white wine
3 tablespoons brandy
salt and ground black pepper

For the croûtes

6–12 thick slices day-old French bread or baguette, about 1 inch thick
1 garlic clove, halved
1 tablespoon French mustard
1 cup coarsely grated Gruyère cheese

1 Melt the butter with the oil in a large saucepan. Add the onions and stir to coat them in the fat. Cook over medium heat for 5–8 minutes, stirring once or twice, until the onions begin to soften. Stir in the thyme.

2 Reduce the heat to very low, cover the pan and cook the onions for 20–30 minutes, stirring frequently, until they are very soft and golden yellow.

3 Uncover the pan and increase the heat slightly. Stir in the sugar and cook for 5–10 minutes, until the onions start to brown. Add the sherry vinegar and increase the heat again, then continue cooking, stirring frequently, until the onions turn a deep, golden brown—this could take up to 20 minutes.

COOK'S TIP

The long slow cooking of the onions is the key to success with this soup. If the onions brown too quickly the soup will be bitter.

4 Meanwhile, bring the stock to a boil in another saucepan. Stir the flour into the onions and cook for about 2 minutes, then gradually pour in the hot stock. Add the wine and brandy and season the soup to taste with salt and pepper. Simmer for 10–15 minutes.

5 For the croûtes, preheat the oven to 300°F. Place the slices of bread on a greased baking sheet and bake for 15–20 minutes, until dry and lightly browned. Rub the bread with the cut surface of the garlic and spread with the mustard, then sprinkle the grated Gruyère cheese on the slices.

6 Preheat the broiler to the hottest setting. Ladle the soup into a large flameproof pan or six flameproof bowls. Float the croûtes on the soup, then broil until the cheese melts, bubbles and browns. Serve immediately.

CHILLED GARLIC AND ALMOND SOUP WITH GRAPES

THIS CREAMY CHILLED SUMMER SOUP IS BASED ON AN ANCIENT MOORISH RECIPE FROM ANDALUCIA IN SOUTHERN SPAIN. ALMONDS AND PINE NUTS ARE TYPICAL INGREDIENTS OF THIS REGION.

SERVES SIX

INGREDIENTS
¾ cup blanched almonds
½ cup pine nuts
6 large garlic cloves, peeled
7 ounces good-quality day-old bread,
    crusts removed
3¾–4 cups still mineral water, chilled
½ cup extra virgin olive oil, plus extra
    to serve
1 tablespoon sherry vinegar
2–3 tablespoons dry sherry
9 ounces grapes, peeled, halved
    and seeded
salt and ground white pepper
ice cubes and snipped fresh chives,
    to garnish

1 Roast the almonds and pine nuts together in a dry saucepan over medium heat until they are very lightly browned. Cool, then grind to a powder.

2 Blanch the garlic in boiling water for 3 minutes. Drain and rinse.

3 Soak the bread in 1¼ cups of the water for 10 minutes, then squeeze dry. Process the garlic, bread, nuts and 1 teaspoon salt in a food processor or blender until they form a paste.

4 Gradually blend in the olive oil and sherry vinegar, followed by enough water to make a smooth soup with a creamy consistency.

5 Stir in 2 tablespoons of the sherry. Adjust the seasoning and add more dry sherry to taste. Chill for at least 3 hours, then adjust the seasoning again and stir in a little more chilled water if the soup has thickened. Reserve a few of the grapes for the garnish and stir the remainder into the soup.

6 Ladle the soup into bowls (glass bowls look particularly good) and garnish with ice cubes, the reserved grapes and snipped fresh chives. Serve with additional extra virgin olive oil to drizzle on the soup to taste just before it is eaten.

COOK'S TIPS
• Toasting the nuts slightly accentuates their flavor, but you can omit this step if you prefer a paler soup.
• Blanching the garlic softens its flavor.

VICHYSSOISE

THIS CLASSIC, CHILLED SUMMER SOUP WAS FIRST CREATED IN THE 1920S BY LOUIS DIAT, CHEF AT THE NEW YORK RITZ-CARLTON. HE NAMED IT AFTER VICHY NEAR HIS HOME IN FRANCE. IT IS BASED ON A SIMPLE LEEK AND POTATO SOUP, MADE LUXURIOUSLY VELVETY BY ADDING HEAVY CREAM.

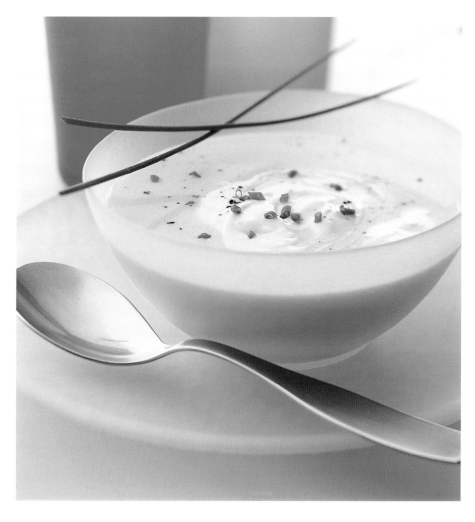

3 Stir in the stock or water, 1 teaspoon salt and pepper to taste. Bring to a boil, then reduce the heat and partly cover the pan. Simmer for 15 minutes or until the potatoes are soft.

4 Cool, then process the soup until smooth in a blender or food processor. Sieve the soup into a bowl and stir in the cream. Taste and adjust the seasoning and add a little ice water if the consistency of the soup seems too thick.

5 Chill the soup for at least 4 hours or until very cold. Taste the chilled soup for seasoning and add a squeeze of lemon juice, if desired. Pour the soup into bowls and sprinkle with snipped chives. Serve immediately.

SERVES FOUR TO SIX

INGREDIENTS
  ¼ cup unsalted butter
  1 pound leeks, white parts only,
    thinly sliced
  3 large shallots, sliced
  9 ounces floury potatoes (such as
    King Edward or Maris Piper), peeled
    and cut into chunks
  4 cups light chicken stock or water
  1¼ cups heavy cream
  ice water (optional)
  a little lemon juice (optional)
  salt and ground black pepper
  snipped fresh chives,
    to garnish

1 Melt the butter in a heavy saucepan and cook the leeks and shallots gently, covered, for 15–20 minutes, until soft but not browned.

2 Add the potatoes and cook, uncovered, for a few minutes.

VARIATIONS
• **Potage Bonne Femme** For this hot leek and potato soup, use 1 chopped onion instead of the shallots and 1 pound potatoes. Halve the amount of heavy cream and reheat it in the puréed soup, adding a little milk if the consistency of the soup seems very thick. Deep-fried shredded leek may be used to garnish the soup instead of snipped fresh chives.
• **Chilled Leek and Sorrel or Watercress Soup** Add about 1 cup shredded sorrel to the soup at the end of cooking. Finish and chill as in the main recipe, then serve the soup garnished with a little pile of finely shredded sorrel. The same amount of watercress can be used in the same way.

CHICKEN AND LEEK SOUP WITH PRUNES AND BARLEY

THIS RECIPE IS BASED ON THE TRADITIONAL SCOTTISH SOUP, COCK-A-LEEKIE. THE UNUSUAL COMBINATION OF LEEKS AND PRUNES IS SURPRISINGLY DELICIOUS.

SERVES SIX

INGREDIENTS
  1 chicken, weighing about
    4¼ pounds
  2 pounds leeks
  1 fresh bay leaf
  a few each fresh parsley stems and
    thyme sprigs
  1 large carrot, thickly sliced
  10 cups chicken or beef stock
  generous ½ cup pearl barley
  14 ounces ready-to-eat prunes
  salt and ground black pepper
  chopped fresh parsley, to garnish

1 Cut the breasts off the chicken and set aside. Place the remaining chicken carcass in a large saucepan. Cut half the leeks into 2-inch lengths and add them to the pan. Tie the bay leaf, parsley and thyme into a bouquet garni and add to the pan with the carrot and the stock. Bring to a boil, then reduce the heat and cover. Simmer gently for 1 hour. Skim off any scum when the water first boils and occasionally during simmering.

2 Add the chicken breasts and cook for another 30 minutes, until they are just cooked. Leave until cool enough to handle, then strain the stock. Reserve the chicken breasts and meat from the chicken carcass. Discard all the skin, bones, cooked vegetables and herbs. Skim as much fat as you can from the stock, then return it to the pan.

3 Meanwhile, rinse the pearl barley thoroughly in a sieve under cold running water, then cook it in a large saucepan of boiling water for about 10 minutes. Drain, rinse well again and drain thoroughly.

4 Add the pearl barley to the stock. Bring to a boil over medium heat, then lower the heat and cook very gently for 15–20 minutes, until the barley is just cooked and tender. Season the soup with 1 teaspoon salt and black pepper.

5 Add the prunes. Slice the remaining leeks and add them to the pan. Bring to a boil, then simmer for 10 minutes or until the leeks are just cooked.

6 Slice the chicken breasts and add them to the soup with the remaining chicken meat, sliced or cut into neat pieces. Reheat if necessary, then ladle the soup into deep plates and sprinkle with chopped parsley.

MEDITERRANEAN LEEK AND FISH SOUP WITH TOMATOES AND GARLIC

THIS CHUNKY SOUP, WHICH IS ALMOST A STEW, MAKES A ROBUST AND WONDERFULLY AROMATIC MEAL IN A BOWL. SERVE IT WITH CRISP-BAKED CROÛTES SPREAD WITH A SPICY GARLIC MAYONNAISE.

SERVES FOUR

INGREDIENTS

  2 tablespoons olive oil
  2 large thick leeks, white and green
    parts separated, both thinly sliced
  1 teaspoon crushed coriander seeds
  good pinch of dried red chile flakes
  11 ounces small salad potatoes,
    thickly sliced
  7-ounce can Italian peeled
    chopped plum tomatoes
  2½ cups fish stock
  ⅔ cup fruity white wine
  1 fresh bay leaf
  1 star anise
  strip of pared orange zest
  good pinch of saffron threads
  1 pound white fish fillets, such as
    monkfish, sea bass, cod or haddock
  1 pound small squid, cleaned
  9 ounces uncooked peeled shrimp
  2–3 tablespoons chopped parsley
  salt and ground black pepper
To serve
  1 loaf French bread, sliced and toasted
  spicy garlic mayonnaise

1 Gently heat the oil in a pan, then add the green part of the leeks, the coriander and the chile flakes, and cook for 5 minutes.

2 Add the potatoes and tomatoes and pour in the stock and wine. Add the bay leaf, star anise, orange zest and saffron.

3 Bring to a boil, reduce the heat and part-cover the pan. Simmer for 20 minutes or until the potatoes are tender. Taste and adjust the seasoning.

4 Cut the fish into chunks. Cut the squid sacs into rectangles and score a criss-cross pattern into them without cutting through.

5 Add the fish to the stew and cook gently for 4 minutes. Add the shrimp and cook for 1 minute. Add the squid and the shredded white part of the leek and cook, stirring occasionally, for 2 minutes.

6 Stir in the chopped parsley and serve with toasted French bread and spicy garlic mayonnaise.

CHICKEN, LEEK AND CELERY SOUP

THIS MAKES A SUBSTANTIAL MAIN COURSE SOUP WITH FRESH CRUSTY BREAD. YOU WILL NEED NOTHING MORE THAN A SALAD AND CHEESE, OR JUST FRESH FRUIT TO FOLLOW.

SERVES FOUR TO SIX

INGREDIENTS
- 3-pound free-range chicken
- 1 small head of celery, trimmed
- 1 onion, coarsely chopped
- 1 fresh bay leaf
- a few fresh parsley stems
- a few fresh tarragon sprigs
- 10 cups cold water
- 3 large leeks
- 5 tablespoons butter
- 2 potatoes, cut into chunks
- ⅔ cup dry white wine
- 2–3 tablespoons light cream (optional)
- salt and ground black pepper
- 3½ ounces pancetta, grilled until crisp, to garnish

1 Cut the breasts off the chicken and set aside. Chop the rest of the chicken carcass into 8–10 pieces and place in a large saucepan.

2 Chop 4–5 of the outer stems of the celery and add them to the pan with the onion. Tie the bay leaf, parsley and tarragon together and add to the pan. Pour in the cold water to cover the ingredients and bring to a boil. Reduce the heat and cover the pan, then simmer for 1½ hours.

3 Remove the chicken and cut off and reserve the meat. Strain the stock, then return it to the pan and boil rapidly until it has reduced to about 6¼ cups.

4 Meanwhile, set about 5 ounces of the leeks aside. Slice the remaining leeks and the remaining celery, reserving any celery leaves. Chop the celery leaves and set aside to garnish the soup.

5 Melt half the butter in a large, heavy saucepan. Add the sliced leeks and celery, cover and cook over low heat for about 10 minutes or until softened but not browned. Add the potatoes, wine and 5 cups of the stock.

6 Season well with salt and pepper, bring to a boil and reduce the heat. Part-cover the pan and simmer the soup for 15–20 minutes or until the potatoes are cooked.

7 Meanwhile, skin the reserved chicken breasts and cut the flesh into small pieces. Melt the remaining butter in a frying pan, add the chicken and fry for 5–7 minutes, until cooked.

8 Thickly slice the remaining leeks, add to the pan and cook, stirring occasionally, for another 3–4 minutes, until just cooked.

9 Process the soup with the cooked chicken from the stock in a blender or food processor. Taste and adjust the seasoning, and add more stock if the soup is very thick.

10 Stir in the cream, if using, and the chicken and leek mixture. Reheat the soup gently. Serve in warmed bowls. Crumble the pancetta on the soup and sprinkle with the chopped celery leaves.

GARLIC AND CILANTRO SOUP

THIS RECIPE IS BASED ON THE WONDERFUL BREAD SOUPS OR AÇORDAS OF PORTUGAL. BEING A SIMPLE SOUP, IT SHOULD BE MADE WITH THE BEST INGREDIENTS—PLUMP GARLIC, CILANTRO, HIGH-QUALITY CRUSTY COUNTRY BREAD AND EXTRA VIRGIN OLIVE OIL.

SERVES SIX

INGREDIENTS

1 ounce cilantro, leaves and stems chopped separately
6¼ cups vegetable or chicken stock, or water
5–6 plump garlic cloves, peeled
6 eggs
10 ounces day-old bread, most of the crust removed and torn into bite-size pieces
salt and ground black pepper
6 tablespoons extra virgin olive oil, plus extra to serve

1 Place the cilantro stems in a saucepan. Add the stock or water and bring to a boil. Lower the heat and simmer for 10 minutes, then process in a blender or food processor and sieve back into the pan.

2 Crush the garlic with 1 teaspoon salt, then stir in ½ cup hot soup. Return the mixture to the pan.

3 Meanwhile, poach the eggs in a frying pan of simmering water for 3–4 minutes, until just set. Use a draining spoon to remove them from the pan and transfer to a warmed plate. Trim off any untidy bits of white.

4 Bring the soup back to a boil and add seasoning. Stir in the chopped cilantro leaves and remove from heat.

5 Place the bread in six soup plates or bowls and drizzle on the oil. Ladle in the soup and stir. Add a poached egg to each bowl and serve immediately, passing olive oil at the table so that it can be drizzled on the soup to taste.

ROASTED GARLIC AND BUTTERNUT SQUASH SOUP WITH TOMATO SALSA

THIS IS A WONDERFUL, RICHLY FLAVORED DISH. A SPOONFUL OF THE HOT AND SPICY TOMATO SALSA GIVES BITE TO THE SWEET-TASTING SQUASH AND GARLIC SOUP.

SERVES FOUR TO FIVE

INGREDIENTS
　　2 garlic bulbs, outer papery
　　　skin removed
　　5 tablespoons olive oil
　　a few fresh thyme sprigs
　　1 large butternut squash, halved
　　　and seeded
　　2 onions, chopped
　　1 teaspoon ground coriander
　　5 cups vegetable or chicken stock
　　2–3 tablespoons chopped fresh
　　　oregano or marjoram
　　salt and ground black pepper
For the salsa
　　4 large ripe tomatoes, halved
　　　and seeded
　　1 red bell pepper, halved and seeded
　　1 large fresh red chile, halved
　　　and seeded
　　2–3 tablespoons extra virgin
　　　olive oil
　　1 tablespoon balsamic vinegar
　　pinch of sugar (optional)

1 Preheat the oven to 425°F. Place the garlic bulbs on a piece of aluminum foil and pour on half the olive oil. Add the thyme sprigs, then fold the foil around the garlic bulbs to enclose them completely. Place the foil parcel on a baking sheet with the butternut squash and brush the squash with 1 tablespoon of the remaining olive oil. Add the tomatoes, red pepper and fresh chile for the salsa.

2 Roast the vegetables for 25 minutes, then remove the tomatoes, pepper and chile. Reduce the temperature to 375°F and cook the squash and garlic for 20–25 more minutes or until the squash is tender.

3 Heat the remaining oil in a large, heavy saucepan and cook the onions and ground coriander gently for about 10 minutes or until softened.

4 Skin the pepper and chile and process in a food processor or blender with the tomatoes and 2 tablespoons olive oil. Stir in the vinegar and seasoning to taste, adding a pinch of sugar, if necessary. Add the remaining oil if you think the salsa needs it.

5 Squeeze the roasted garlic out of its papery skin into the onions and scoop the squash out of its skin, adding it to the pan. Add the stock, 1 teaspoon salt and plenty of black pepper. Bring to a boil and simmer for 10 minutes.

6 Stir in half the oregano or marjoram and cool the soup slightly, then process it in a blender or food processor. Alternatively, press the soup through a fine sieve.

7 Reheat the soup without letting it boil, then taste for seasoning before ladling it into warmed bowls. Top each with a spoonful of salsa and sprinkle on the remaining chopped oregano or marjoram. Serve immediately.

MISO BROTH WITH SCALLIONS AND TOFU

THE JAPANESE EAT MISO BROTH, A SIMPLE BUT HIGHLY NUTRITIOUS SOUP, ALMOST EVERY DAY—IT IS STANDARD BREAKFAST FARE AND IT IS EATEN WITH RICE OR NOODLES LATER IN THE DAY.

SERVES FOUR

INGREDIENTS

- 1 bunch of scallions or
  5 baby leeks
- ½ ounce cilantro
- 3 thin slices fresh ginger root
- 2 star anise
- 1 small dried red chile
- 5 cups dashi stock or vegetable stock
- 8 ounces bok choy or other Asian greens, thickly sliced
- 7 ounces firm tofu, cut into 1-inch cubes
- 4 tablespoons red miso
- 2–3 tablespoons Japanese soy sauce (shoyu)
- 1 fresh red chile, seeded and shredded (optional)

1 Cut the coarse green tops off the scallions or baby leeks and slice the rest of the scallions or leeks finely on the diagonal. Place the coarse green tops in a large saucepan with the cilantro stems, ginger, star anise, dried chile and dashi or vegetable stock.

2 Heat the mixture gently until boiling, then lower the heat and simmer for 10 minutes. Strain, return to the pan and reheat until simmering. Add the green portion of the sliced scallions or leeks to the soup with the bok choy or greens and tofu. Cook for 2 minutes.

3 Mix 3 tablespoons of the miso with a little of the hot soup in a bowl, then stir it into the soup. Taste the soup and add more miso with soy sauce to taste.

4 Coarsely chop the cilantro leaves and stir most of them into the soup with the white part of the scallions or leeks. Cook for 1 minute, then ladle the soup into warmed serving bowls. Sprinkle with the remaining cilantro the fresh red chile, if using, and serve immediately.

COOK'S TIP
Dashi powder is available most Asian stores. Alternatively, make your own by gently simmering 4–6-inch kombu seaweed in 5 cups water for 10 minutes. Do not boil the stock vigorously, as this makes the dashi bitter. Remove the kombu, then add ½ ounce dried bonito flakes and bring to a boil. Strain immediately through a fine sieve.

COCONUT AND SEAFOOD SOUP WITH GARLIC CHIVES

THE LONG LIST OF INGREDIENTS IN THIS THAI-INSPIRED RECIPE COULD MISLEAD YOU INTO THINKING THAT THIS SOUP IS COMPLICATED. IN FACT, IT IS VERY EASY TO PUT TOGETHER.

SERVES FOUR

INGREDIENTS
2½ cups fish stock
5 thin slices fresh galangal or
   fresh ginger root
2 lemongrass stalks, chopped
3 kaffir lime leaves, shredded
1 ounce garlic chives (1 bunch)
½ ounce cilantro
1 tablespoon vegetable oil
4 shallots, chopped
14-fluid-ounce can coconut milk
2–3 tablespoons Thai fish sauce
   (*nam pla*)
3–4 tablespoons Thai green
   curry paste
1 pound large shrimp, peeled
   and deveined
1 pound prepared squid
a little lime juice (optional)
salt and ground black pepper
4 tablespoons crisp fried shallot
   slices, to serve

1 Pour the fish stock into a saucepan and add the slices of galangal or ginger, lemongrass and half the shredded kaffir lime leaves.

2 Reserve a few garlic chives for the garnish, then snip the remainder. Add half the snipped garlic chives to the pan with the cilantro stems. Bring to a boil, reduce the heat and cover the pan, then simmer gently for 20 minutes. Strain the stock.

3 Rinse the pan. Add the oil and shallots. Cook over medium heat for 5–10 minutes, until the shallots are just beginning to brown.

4 Stir in the strained stock, coconut milk, the remaining kaffir lime leaves and 30ml/2 tbsp of the fish sauce. Heat gently until simmering and cook over low heat for 5–10 minutes.

VARIATIONS
• Instead of squid, you could add 14 ounces firm white fish, such as monkfish, cut into small pieces.
• You could also replace the squid with mussels. Steam 1½ pounds closed live mussels in a tightly covered pan for 3–4 minutes or until the shells have opened. Discard any that remain shut, then remove the mussels from their shells.

5 Stir in the curry paste and shrimp, then cook for 3 minutes. Add the squid and cook for another 2 minutes. Add the lime juice, if using, and season, adding more fish sauce to taste.

6 Stir in the remaining chives and the cilantro. Serve in bowls, sprinkled with fried shallots and whole garlic chives.

As we gather around the table, eager to share food with family and friends, the intensely savory smell and flavor of onions make them a good choice to start the meal. Throughout history, onions have been praised for their ability to stimulate the appetite and help us enjoy our food. In this section you'll find a large variety of onion dishes suitable for starting different types of meal and some that are substantial enough to form a light meal on their own with salad and good bread.

Appetizers and Light Meals

SPICED ONION KOFTAS

THESE DELICIOUS INDIAN ONION FRITTERS ARE MADE WITH CHICKPEA FLOUR, OTHERWISE KNOWN AS
GRAM FLOUR OR BESAN. SERVE WITH CHUTNEY OR YOGURT DIP.

SERVES FOUR TO FIVE

INGREDIENTS
  1½ pounds onions, halved and
    thinly sliced
  1 teaspoon salt
  1 teaspoon ground coriander
  1 teaspoon ground cumin
  ½ teaspoon ground turmeric
  1–2 green chiles, seeded and
    finely chopped
  3 tablespoons chopped cilantro
  ¾ cup chickpea flour
  ½ teaspoon baking powder
  vegetable oil, for deep-frying
To serve
  lemon wedges (optional)
  cilantro sprigs
  yogurt and herb dip or yogurt and
    cucumber dip

1 Place the onions in a colander, add the salt and toss. Place on a plate and let stand for 45 minutes, tossing once or twice. Rinse the onions, then squeeze out any excess moisture.

2 Place the onions in a bowl. Add the ground coriander, cumin, turmeric, chiles and cilantro. Mix well.

COOK'S TIPS

• To make a yogurt and herb dip, stir 2 tablespoons each of chopped cilantro and mint into about 1 cup yogurt. Season with salt, ground toasted cumin seeds and a pinch of brown sugar.
• For a cucumber dip, stir half a diced cucumber and 1 seeded and chopped fresh green chile into 1 cup yogurt. Season with salt and cumin.

3 Add the chickpea flour and baking powder, then use your hand to mix all the ingredients thoroughly.

4 Shape the mixture by hand into 12–15 koftas about the size of golf balls.

5 Heat the oil for deep-frying to 350–375°F or until a cube of day-old bread browns in 30–45 seconds. Fry the koftas, 4–5 at a time, until deep golden brown all over. Drain each batch on paper towels and keep warm until all the koftas are cooked. Serve with lemon wedges, cilantro sprigs and a yogurt dip.

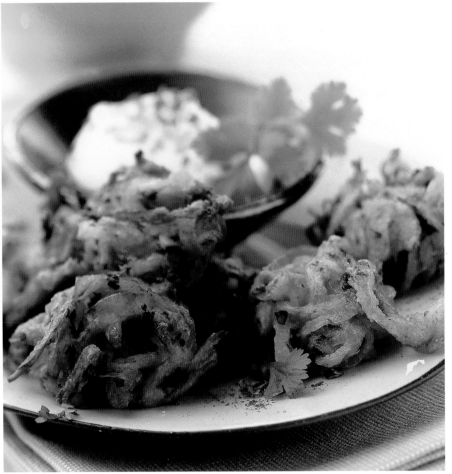

LITTLE ONIONS COOKED WITH WINE, CORIANDER AND OLIVE OIL

IF YOU CAN FIND THE SMALL, FLAT ITALIAN CIPOLLA OR BORETTANE ONIONS, THEY ARE EXCELLENT IN THIS RECIPE—OTHERWISE USE PICKLING ONIONS, SMALL RED ONIONS OR SHALLOTS.

3 Add the currants, reduce the heat and cook gently for 15–20 minutes or until the onions are tender but not falling apart. Use a draining spoon to transfer the onions to a serving dish.

4 Boil the liquid over high heat until it reduces considerably. Taste and adjust the seasoning, if necessary, then pour the reduced liquid over the onions. Sprinkle the oregano on the onions, set aside to cool and then chill them.

5 Just before serving, stir in the grated lemon zest, chopped parsley and toasted pine nuts.

SERVES SIX

INGREDIENTS

 7 tablespoons olive oil
 1½ pounds small onions, peeled
 ⅔ cup dry white wine
 2 bay leaves
 2 garlic cloves, bruised
 1–2 small dried red chiles
 1 tablespoon coriander seeds,
   toasted and lightly crushed
 ½ teaspoon sugar
 a few fresh thyme sprigs
 2 tablespoons currants
 2 teaspoons chopped fresh oregano
 1 teaspoon grated lemon zest
 1 tablespoon chopped fresh
   flat-leaf parsley
 2–3 tablespoons pine nuts, toasted
 salt and ground black pepper

1 Place 2 tablespoons olive oil in a wide saucepan. Add the onions and cook gently over medium heat for about 5 minutes or until they begin to color. Remove from the pan and set aside.

2 Add the remaining oil, the wine, bay leaves, garlic, chiles, coriander, sugar and thyme to the pan. Bring to a boil and cook briskly for 5 minutes. Return the onions to the pan.

COOK'S TIP
Serve this dish as one of several small dishes—an antipasto—perhaps with mustard mayonnaise-dressed celeriac salad and some thinly sliced prosciutto or other air-dried ham.

ROASTED GARLIC WITH GOAT CHEESE, WALNUT AND HERB PÂTÉ

THE COMBINATION OF SWEET, MELLOW ROASTED GARLIC AND GOAT CHEESE IS A CLASSIC ONE. THIS IS PARTICULARLY GOOD MADE WITH THE NEW SEASON'S WALNUTS, SOMETIMES KNOWN AS "WET" WALNUTS, WHICH ARE AVAILABLE IN THE EARLY AUTUMN.

SERVES FOUR

INGREDIENTS

4 large garlic bulbs
4 fresh rosemary sprigs
8 fresh thyme sprigs
4 tablespoons olive oil
sea salt and ground black pepper

For the pâté

7 ounces soft goat cheese
1 teaspoon finely chopped fresh thyme
1 tablespoon chopped fresh parsley
2 ounces shelled walnuts, chopped
1 tablespoon walnut oil (optional)
fresh thyme, to garnish

To serve

4–8 slices sourdough bread
shelled walnuts

1 Preheat the oven to 350°F. Strip the papery skin from the garlic bulbs. Place them in an ovenproof dish large enough to hold them snugly. Tuck in the rosemary and thyme, drizzle on the oil and season to taste.

2 Cover the garlic closely with aluminum foil and bake for 50–60 minutes, basting once. Let cool.

3 Preheat the broiler. To make the pâté, cream the cheese with the thyme, parsley and chopped walnuts. Beat in 1 tablespoon of the cooking oil from the garlic and season to taste, then transfer the pâté to a serving bowl.

4 Brush the sourdough bread with the remaining cooking oil from the garlic, then broil until toasted.

5 Drizzle the walnut oil, if using, onto the goat cheese pâté and grind on some black pepper. Place a bulb of garlic on each plate and serve with the pâté and some toasted bread. Garnish with a little fresh thyme and serve a few freshly shelled walnuts and a little sea salt with each portion.

POTATO AND CHIVE PANCAKES WITH PICKLED HERRING AND ONION RINGS

THESE PANCAKES ARE FULL OF DELICIOUS SCANDINAVIAN FLAVORS. SERVE THEM AS A FIRST COURSE OR AS A LIGHT MAIN COURSE WITH SALAD.. SMALL PANCAKES MAKE EXCELLENT CANAPÉS TO SERVE WITH ICE-COLD SHOTS OF VODKA OR OTHER PRE-DINNER DRINKS.

SERVES SIX

INGREDIENTS
   10 ounces peeled potatoes
   2 eggs, beaten
   ⅔ cup milk
   1½ ounces all-purpose flour
   2 tablespoons snipped fresh chives
   vegetable oil or butter, for greasing
   salt and ground black pepper
For the topping
   2 small red or yellow onions, thinly
      sliced into rings
   4 tablespoons sour cream or
      crème fraîche
   1 teaspoon whole-grain mustard
   1 tablespoon chopped fresh dill
   6 pickled herring fillets
To garnish
   fresh dill sprigs
   fresh chives or chive flowers

1 Cut the potatoes into chunks and cook them in boiling salted water for about 15 minutes or until tender, then drain and mash or sieve to form a smooth purée.

2 Meanwhile prepare the topping. Place the onions in a bowl and cover with boiling water. Set aside for 2–3 minutes, then drain thoroughly and dry on paper towels.

3 Mix the onions with the sour cream or crème fraîche, mustard and chopped dill. Season to taste.

4 Using a sharp knife, cut the pickled herring fillets into 12–18 pieces. Set them aside.

5 Put the potato purée in a bowl and beat in the eggs, milk and flour with a wooden spoon to make a batter. Season to taste with salt and pepper and whisk in the snipped chives.

6 Heat a nonstick frying pan over medium heat and grease it with a little oil or butter. Spoon about 2 tablespoons of batter into the pan to make a pancake, measuring about 3 inches across. Cook for 3–4 minutes, until the underside is set and golden brown. Turn over the pancake and cook the other side for 3–4 minutes, until golden brown. Transfer to a plate and keep warm while you make the remaining pancakes in batches of 3–4. The mixture will make 12 pancakes.

7 Place two pancakes on each of six warmed plates and distribute the pickled herring fillets and onions equally among them. Garnish with dill sprigs, fresh chives and/or chive flowers. Season with black pepper and serve immediately.

DEEP-FRIED SCALLIONS IN BEER BATTER WITH ROMESCO SAUCE

THIS PIQUANT, BUT NOT HOT, SAUCE FROM TARRAGONA IN SPAIN ADMIRABLY CUTS THE RICHNESS OF DEEP-FRIED FOOD, AND IT IS EXCELLENT WITH DEEP-FRIED SCALLIONS IN THEIR CRISP BATTER.

SERVES SIX

INGREDIENTS

3 bunches plump scallions,
   18–24 in all
sea salt and ground black pepper
lemon wedges, to serve
For the batter
2 cups self-rising flour
⅔ cup lager
scant 1 cup ice-cold water
peanut oil, for deep-frying
1 large egg white
½ teaspoon cream of tartar
For the sauce
2–3 large mild dried red chiles, such
   as Spanish *ñoras* or Mexican *anchos*
   or *guajillos*
1 large red bell pepper, halved and
   seeded
2 large tomatoes, halved
   and seeded
4–6 large garlic cloves, unpeeled
5–6 tablespoons olive oil
¼ cup hazelnuts, blanched
4 slices French bread, each about
   ¾ inch thick
1 tablespoon sherry vinegar
squeeze of lemon juice (optional)
chopped fresh parsley, to garnish

1 First, prepare the sauce. Soak the dried chiles in hot water for about 30 minutes. Preheat the oven to 425°F.

2 Place the pepper halves, tomatoes and garlic on a baking sheet and drizzle with 1 tablespoon olive oil.

3 Roast, uncovered, for 30–40 minutes, until the pepper is blistered and blackened and the garlic is soft. Cool slightly, then peel the pepper, tomatoes and garlic.

4 Heat the remaining oil in a small frying pan and fry the hazelnuts until lightly browned, then transfer them to a plate. Fry the bread in the same oil until light brown on both sides, then transfer to the plate with the nuts and let cool. Reserve the oil from cooking.

5 Drain the chiles, discard as many of their seeds as you can, then place them in a food processor. Add the pepper, tomatoes, garlic, hazelnuts and bread with the reserved oil. Add the vinegar and process into a paste. Check the seasoning and thin the sauce with a little more oil or lemon juice, if necessary. Set aside.

6 Trim the roots from the scallions. Trim the leaves to leave the onions 6–7 inches long.

7 To make the batter, sift the flour into a bowl and add a good pinch each of salt and pepper. Make a well in the center, then gradually whisk in the lager, followed by the water. The batter should be the consistency of thick cream, so adjust the volume of water to produce this consistency.

8 Heat the oil for deep-frying to 350°F or until a cube of day-old bread browns in 30–45 seconds. Whisk the egg white with the cream of tartar until stiff, then fold it into the batter.

9 Dip the scallions individually in the batter, drain off the excess and fry them in batches for 4–5 minutes. Drain thoroughly on paper towels and sprinkle with a little sea salt. Keep each batch warm until the next is cooked. Garnish with a little chopped parsley and serve hot with the sauce and lemon wedges.

STILTON-STUFFED MUSHROOMS BAKED IN GARLIC BREAD CRUMBS

SERVE THESE SUCCULENT STUFFED MUSHROOMS WITH CHUNKS OF WARM, CRUSTY BREAD OR FRESH ROLLS TO SOAK UP ALL THEIR DELICIOUS GARLIC-FLAVORED JUICES.

SERVES FOUR

INGREDIENTS
    1 pound chestnut mushrooms
    3 garlic cloves, finely chopped
    7 tablespoons butter, melted
    juice of ½ lemon
    4 ounces Stilton cheese,
      crumbled
    ½ cup walnuts, chopped
    1½ cups fresh white bread crumbs
    1 ounce Parmesan cheese, grated
    2 tablespoons chopped fresh parsley
    salt and ground black pepper

COOK'S TIP
A simple sauce of fromage frais or thick yogurt with some chopped fresh herbs and a little Dijon mustard stirred through goes well with these Stilton-stuffed mushrooms.

1 Preheat the oven to 400°F. Place the mushrooms in an ovenproof dish and sprinkle half the garlic on them. Drizzle with 4 tablespoons of the butter and the lemon juice. Season with salt and pepper and bake for 15–20 minutes. Let cool.

2 Cream the crumbled Stilton with the chopped walnuts and mix in 2 tablespoons of the bread crumbs.

3 Divide the Stilton mixture among the mushrooms.

4 Preheat the broiler. Mix the remaining garlic, bread crumbs and melted butter together. Stir in the Parmesan and parsley and season with pepper. Cover the mushrooms with the bread crumb mixture and broil for about 5 minutes or until crisp and browned. Serve immediately.

SCALLION AND RICOTTA FRITTERS WITH AVOCADO SALSA

THIS FRESH-FLAVORED SALSA SPIKED WITH A LITTLE RED ONION AND CHILE IS EXCELLENT WITH THESE MELT-IN-YOUR-MOUTH HERBED SCALLION FRITTERS.

SERVES FOUR TO SIX

INGREDIENTS
  generous 1 cup ricotta cheese
  1 large egg, beaten
  6 tablespoons self-rising flour
  6 tablespoons milk
  1 bunch scallions, finely sliced
  2 tablespoons chopped cilantro
  sunflower oil, for shallow frying
  salt and ground black pepper
  scant 1 cup crème fraîche, to serve
For the salsa
  2 ripe, but not soft, avocados
  1 small red onion, diced
  grated zest and juice of 1 lime
  1 fresh green or red chile, seeded
    and finely chopped
  8 ounces tomatoes, peeled, seeded
    and diced
  2–3 tablespoons chopped mixed fresh
    mint and cilantro
  pinch of sugar
  1–2 teaspoons Thai fish sauce
    (*nam pla*)
To garnish
  cilantro sprigs
  lime wedges

2 Beat the ricotta until smooth, then beat in the egg and flour, followed by the milk to make a smooth, thick batter. Beat in the scallions and cilantro. Season well with pepper and a little salt.

3 Heat a little oil in a nonstick frying pan over a medium heat. Add spoonfuls of the mixture to make fritters about 3 inches across and fry for about 4–5 minutes on each side, until set and browned. The mixture makes 12 fritters.

4 Taste the salsa and adjust the seasoning, adding more lime juice and/or sugar to taste. Serve the fritters immediately, with the salsa and a dollop of crème fraîche. Garnish with cilantro sprigs and lime wedges.

VARIATION
The fritters are also good served with thinly sliced smoked salmon.

1 Make the salsa first. Peel, pit and dice the avocados. Place in a bowl with the red onion, lime zest and juice. Add chile to taste, the tomatoes, mint and cilantro. Season with salt, pepper, sugar and Thai fish sauce. Mix well and set aside for 30 minutes.

MUSSELS <u>IN</u> GARLIC BUTTER

GARLIC AND HERB BUTTER IS A CLASSIC TREATMENT FOR SNAILS IN BURGUNDY BUT BECAME VERY POPULAR IN THE 1960s WITH MUSSELS, AND MAKES A DELICIOUS FIRST COURSE.

SERVES FOUR

INGREDIENTS

    4½ pounds mussels, scrubbed
    2 large shallots, finely chopped
    scant 1 cup dry white wine
    ½ cup unsalted butter,
     softened
    2–3 garlic cloves, finely chopped
    grated zest of 1 lemon
    4 tablespoons finely chopped mixed
     herbs, such as parsley, chervil,
     tarragon and chives
    1 cup fresh white bread crumbs
    salt and ground black pepper
    lemon wedges, to serve

1 Check that all the mussels are closed after cleaning and discard any that remain open when sharply tapped.

2 Place the shallots and wine in a large saucepan and bring to a boil. Throw in the mussels and cover tightly. Cook over high heat for 4–5 minutes, shaking the pan vigorously 2–3 times.

3 The mussels should be cooked and gaping open. Discard any that do not open after 5 minutes' cooking. Drain, reserving the cooking liquid.

4 Discard the top (empty) half of each shell. Place the mussels in a large roasting pan or heatproof dish.

5 Pour the cooking liquid into a clean saucepan and boil it vigorously until reduced to about 3 tablespoons. Remove from heat and let cool.

6 Cream the butter with the shallots from the reduced liquid, the garlic, lemon zest and herbs. Season well and chill until firm.

7 Distribute the flavored butter among the mussels. Sprinkle with the cooking liquid, then sprinkle the bread crumbs on top.

8 Preheat the broiler and position the rack about 4 inches below the heat. Broil the mussels until the butter is bubbling and the bread crumbs are golden and crisp. Serve immediately, with wedges of lemon.

TAPENADE WITH QUAIL'S EGGS AND CRUDITÉS

TAPENADE IS A SOCIABLE START TO A MEAL. SERVE WITH HARD-BOILED QUAIL'S EGGS AND VEGETABLE CRUDITÉS, AND LET EVERYONE HELP THEMSELVES.

SERVES SIX

INGREDIENTS
    2 cups pitted black olives
    2 large garlic cloves, peeled
    1 tablespoon salted capers, rinsed
    6 canned or bottled anchovy
        fillets, drained
    2 ounces good-quality canned tuna
    1–2 teaspoons cognac (optional)
    1 teaspoon chopped fresh thyme
    2 tablespoons chopped fresh parsley
    2–4 tablespoons extra virgin
        olive oil
    a dash of lemon juice
    2 tablespoons crème fraîche or
        fromage frais (optional)
    12–18 quail's eggs
    ground black pepper
For the crudités
    bunch of scallions, halved
        if large
    bunch of radishes, trimmed
    bunch of baby fennel, trimmed and
        halved if large, or 1 large fennel
        bulb, cut into thin wedges
To serve
    French bread
    unsalted butter
    sea salt

1 Process the olives, garlic, capers, anchovies and tuna in a food processor or blender. Blend in the cognac, if using, the thyme, parsley and enough olive oil to make a paste. Season to taste with pepper and a dash of lemon juice. Stir in the crème fraîche or fromage frais, if using, and transfer to a serving bowl.

2 Place the quail's eggs in a saucepan, cover with cold water and bring to a boil. Cook for only 2 minutes, then immediately drain and plunge the eggs into ice water to stop them from cooking further and to make them easier to shell.

3 When the eggs are cold, carefully part-shell them.

4 Arrange the tapenade with the eggs and crudités and serve, offering French bread, unsalted butter and sea salt to accompany them.

COOK'S TIPS
• Crème fraîche or fromage frais softens the flavor of the olives for a milder tapenade.
• In Provence, where tapenade comes from, it is traditional to serve it with crudités of celery, fennel and tomato.
• Tapenade is also delicious spread on thin slices of toasted French bread and served as an appetizer with pre-dinner drinks. It may be garnished with chopped hard-boiled egg.

RED ONION AND MUSHROOM TARTLETS WITH GOAT CHEESE

CRISP AND SAVORY, THESE ATTRACTIVE LITTLE TARTS ARE DELICIOUS SERVED WITH A FEW MIXED SALAD LEAVES DRIZZLED WITH A GARLIC-INFUSED FRENCH DRESSING.

SERVES SIX

INGREDIENTS

    4 tablespoons olive oil
    2 tablespoons butter
    4 red onions, thinly sliced
    1 teaspoon brown sugar
    1 tablespoon balsamic vinegar
    1 tablespoon soy sauce
    7 ounces button mushrooms,
      thinly sliced
    1 garlic clove, finely chopped
    ½ teaspoon chopped fresh tarragon
    2 tablespoons chopped fresh parsley
    9-ounce goat cheese
      log (*chèvre*)
    salt and ground black pepper
    mixed salad leaves,
      to serve
For the pastry
    1¾ cups all-purpose flour
    pinch of cayenne pepper
    7 tablespoons butter
    ½ cup freshly grated Parmesan
      cheese
    3–4 tablespoons ice water

1 First, make the pastry. Sift the flour and cayenne into a bowl, add the butter, then rub in with the fingertips until the mixture looks like bread crumbs.

2 Stir in the grated Parmesan, then bind the pastry with the ice water, adding just enough to give a firm dough. Press the pastry together into a ball, then wrap it in plastic wrap and chill for at least 45 minutes.

3 Heat 1 tablespoon of the oil and half the butter in a heavy frying pan, then add the onions, cover and cook gently for 15 minutes, stirring occasionally.

4 Uncover the pan, increase the heat slightly and sprinkle in the brown sugar. Cook, stirring frequently, until the onions begin to caramelize and brown. Add the vinegar and soy sauce and cook briskly until the liquid evaporates. Season to taste, then set aside.

5 Heat another 2 tablespoons of the oil and the remaining butter in a saucepan, then add the mushrooms and garlic and cook fairly briskly for 5–6 minutes, until the mushrooms are browned and cooked.

6 Set a few mushrooms and onion rings aside then stir the rest of the mushrooms into the onions with the tarragon and parsley. Adjust the seasoning to taste. Preheat the oven to 375°F.

7 Roll out the pastry and use to line 4-inch tartlet pans, preferably loose-bottomed and metal. Prick the pastry shells with a fork and line the sides with strips of aluminum foil. Bake for 10 minutes remove the foil and bake for another 5–7 minutes or until the pastry is lightly browned and cooked. Remove from the oven and increase the temperature to 400°F.

8 Remove the pastry shells from the pans and arrange them on a baking sheet. Distribute the onion mixture equally among the pastry shells. Cut the goat cheese into 6 equal slices and place 1 slice on each tartlet. Add a few reserved mushrooms and onion slices to each tartlet, drizzle with the remaining oil and season with pepper.

9 Return the tartlets to the oven and bake for 5–8 minutes or until the goat cheese is just beginning to turn brown. Serve with mixed salad leaves.

CHICKEN LIVER PÂTÉ <u>WITH</u> GARLIC

THIS SMOOTH, GARLICKY PÂTÉ IS WICKEDLY INDULGENT BUT ABSOLUTELY DELICIOUS. IT IS IDEAL AS A FIRST COURSE, WITH TOAST AND SOME SMALL CORNICHONS. IT IS ALSO GOOD WITH CONFIT OF SLOW-COOKED ONIONS.

SERVES SIX TO EIGHT

INGREDIENTS

1 cup unsalted butter
14 ounces chicken livers, chopped
3–4 tablespoons Madeira
3 large shallots, chopped
2 large garlic cloves, finely chopped
1 teaspoon finely chopped fresh thyme
pinch of ground allspice
2 tablespoons heavy cream (optional)
salt and ground black pepper
small fresh bay leaves or fresh thyme
   sprigs, to garnish

VARIATIONS

• Cognac, Armagnac or port can be used instead of the Madeira.
• Use duck livers instead of chicken and add ½ teaspoon grated orange zest.

1 Melt 6 tablespoons butter in a small saucepan over low heat, then let it bubble gently until it is clear. Pour off the clarified butter into a bowl.

2 Melt 3 tablespoons butter in a frying pan and fry the chicken livers for 4–5 minutes, until browned.

3 Add the Madeira and set it on fire, then scrape the contents of the pan into a food processor or blender.

4 Melt 2 tablespoons butter in the pan over low heat and cook the shallots for 5 minutes, until soft. Add the garlic, thyme and allspice and cook for another 2–3 minutes. Add this mixture to the livers with the remaining butter and cream, if using, then process until smooth.

5 Add about 1½ teaspoons each of salt and pepper and more Madeira to taste. Scrape the pâté into a serving dish and place a few bay leaves or thyme sprigs on top. Melt the clarified butter, if necessary, then pour it onto the pâté. Cool and chill for 4 hours or overnight.

COOK'S TIP
The flavor of the pâté deepens and matures on chilling, so it is best if you make it a day before it is needed.

BAGNA CAUDA

THIS HOT GARLIC DIP FROM PIEDMONT IN NORTHERN ITALY IS OUTRAGEOUSLY RICH, AS IT CONTAINS OLIVE OIL, BUTTER AND CREAM. LITERALLY TRANSLATED, THE NAME MEANS "A HOT BATH," AND IN PIEDMONT IT IS TRADITIONALLY EATEN TO CELEBRATE THE END OF THE GRAPE HARVEST.

2 Place the olive oil in a small saucepan over very low heat, then add the rosemary and sliced or chopped garlic. Keep the heat low for about 5 minutes so that the flavor of the garlic permeates the oil, but do not let the garlic brown.

3 Add the anchovies, remove the rosemary, and cook for 3–5 minutes, mashing the anchovies into the oil with a wooden spoon. Keep the heat low to ensure that the garlic does not brown.

4 When the anchovies have broken down completely, add the butter and cream and whisk gently until the butter has melted. Season to taste with a little pepper.

5 Pour the mixture into a fondue pan or small earthenware container and stand this over very low heat to keep the bagna cauda warm. Surround with the bread, vegetables and shrimp for dipping and serve immediately.

SERVES FOUR

INGREDIENTS

⅔ cup extra virgin olive oil
2-inch sprig fresh rosemary
6 garlic cloves, thinly sliced or finely chopped
2-ounce can anchovy fillets, drained and chopped
7 tablespoons unsalted butter
5 tablespoons heavy cream (optional)
ground black pepper
To serve
a selection of vegetables, such as new potatoes, baby artichokes, cardoons, cauliflower florets, fennel, celery, baby carrots
crusty bread
large cooked shrimp

1 Prepare the serving ingredients you have chosen for dipping according to type. Cook them if necessary—new potatoes and baby artichokes, for example—and cut the bread and large vegetables into small portions.

VARIATIONS

• In Piedmont they sometimes add a little very finely shaved white truffle. Add this at the very end to appreciate the wonderful aroma of the truffle.
• The rosemary is not traditional, but the slight bitterness it imparts cuts the rich sauce. Omit it if you prefer.
• Omit the cream for a stronger-tasting, less rich dip, and use a light olive oil from Provence or Liguria instead.

LEEK, SAFFRON AND MUSSEL TARTS

SERVE THESE VIVIDLY COLORED LITTLE TARTS AS A FIRST COURSE, WITH A FEW SALAD LEAVES, SUCH AS WATERCRESS, ARUGULA AND FRISÉE. ALTERNATIVELY, COOK THE FILLING IN ONE 9-INCH TART SHELL AND SERVE IT AS A MAIN COURSE WITH SALAD AND FRESH BREAD.

2 Soak the saffron in the hot water for 10 minutes. Fry the leeks in the oil in a large saucepan over medium heat for 6–8 minutes, until softened and beginning to brown. Add the pepper strips and cook for another 2 minutes.

3 Bring a 1-inch depth of water to a rolling boil in a large saucepan and add 2 teaspoons salt. Discard any open mussels that do not shut when tapped sharply, then throw the rest into the pan. Cover and cook over high heat, shaking the pan occasionally, for 3–4 minutes or until the mussels open. Discard any mussels that do not open. Shell the mussels.

SERVES SIX

INGREDIENTS
   12 ounces shortcrust pastry, thawed
      if frozen
   large pinch of saffron threads (about
      15 threads)
   1 tablespoon hot water
   2 large leeks, sliced
   2 tablespoons olive oil
   2 large yellow bell peppers, halved,
      seeded, broiled and peeled, then
      cut into strips
   2 pounds mussels, scrubbed and
      beards removed
   2 large eggs
   1¼ cups light cream
   2 tablespoons finely chopped
      fresh parsley
   salt and ground black pepper
   salad leaves, to serve

1 Preheat the oven to 375°F. Roll out the pastry and use to line 4-inch tartlet pans, 1 inch deep. Prick the bottoms and line the sides with strips of aluminum foil. Bake for 10 minutes. Remove the foil and bake for another 5–8 minutes, until lightly colored. Remove from the oven. Reduce the temperature to 350°F.

4 Beat the eggs, cream and saffron liquid together. Season well with salt and pepper and whisk in the parsley.

5 Arrange the leeks, peppers and mussels in the pastry shells, add the egg mixture and bake for 20–25 minutes, until risen and just firm. Serve immediately with salad leaves.

BAKED EGGS EN COCOTTE
WITH WILD MUSHROOMS AND CHIVES

*THESE SIMPLE, BUT UTTERLY DELICIOUS, BAKED EGGS MAKE A SPLENDID START TO A LIGHT MEAL OR
AN EXCELLENT DISH FOR BRUNCH. SERVE WITH HOT, BUTTERED WHOLE-WHEAT TOAST.*

SERVES FOUR TO SIX

INGREDIENTS
  5 tablespoons butter
  2 shallots, finely chopped
  1 small garlic clove, finely chopped
  9 ounces mixed mushrooms,
    finely chopped
  1 tablespoon lemon juice
  1 teaspoon chopped fresh tarragon
  2 tablespoons crème fraîche
  2 tablespoons snipped fresh chives
  4–6 eggs
  salt and ground black pepper
  whole chives, to garnish
  buttered whole-wheat toast, to serve

COOK'S TIP
The eggs may also be cooked by standing
the dishes in a covered frying pan
containing 1 inch boiling water. Cook
over medium heat for 8–10 minutes.

1 Melt 4 tablespoons of the butter in a
saucepan over medium-low heat and
cook the shallots and garlic gently,
stirring occasionally, for 5 minutes, until
softened but not browned.

2 Increase the heat and add the
mushrooms, then cook briskly, stirring
frequently, until the mushrooms lose
their moisture and begin to brown.

3 Stir in the lemon juice and tarragon
and continue to cook over medium
heat, stirring occasionally, until the
mushrooms absorb the liquid. Stir in
half the crème fraîche and half the
snipped chives and season to taste.

4 Preheat the oven to 375°F. Distribute
the mushroom mixture equally among
4–6 large ramekins or small ovenproof
dishes of about ⅔–¾ cup capacity.
Sprinkle the remaining snipped chives
onto the mushrooms.

5 Break an egg into each dish, add a
dab of crème fraîche and season to
taste with black pepper. Dot with the
remaining butter and bake in the center
of the oven for 10–15 minutes or until
the whites of the eggs are set and the
yolks cooked to your liking.

6 Serve immediately, garnished with
fresh chives and accompanied by lots
of hot, buttered whole-wheat toast.

LEEK TERRINE WITH RED BELL PEPPERS

THIS PRESSED LEEK TERRINE LOOKS VERY PRETTY WHEN SLICED AND SERVED ON INDIVIDUAL PLATES WITH THE DRESSING DRIZZLED ON AND AROUND THE SLICES.

SERVES SIX TO EIGHT

INGREDIENTS
    4 pounds slender leeks
    4 large red bell peppers, halved
        and seeded
    1 tablespoon extra virgin olive oil
    2 teaspoons balsamic vinegar
    1 teaspoon ground roasted
        cumin seeds
    salt and ground black pepper
For the dressing
    ½ cup extra virgin olive oil
    1 garlic clove,
        bruised and peeled
    1 teaspoon Dijon mustard
    1 teaspoon soy sauce
    1 tablespoon balsamic vinegar
    pinch of sugar
    ½–1 teaspoon ground roasted
        cumin seeds
    1–2 tablespoons chopped mixed fresh
        basil and flat-leaf parsley

COOK'S TIP
It is easier to slice the terrine if you leave the plastic wrap on and use a very sharp knife or an electric carving knife. Use a spatula to transfer the slices to the plates, then remove the plastic wrap.

1 Line a 9-inch-long terrine or loaf pan with plastic wrap, leaving the ends overhanging the pan. Cut the leeks to the same length as the pan.

2 Cook the leeks in boiling salted water for 5–7 minutes, until just tender. Drain thoroughly and let cool, then squeeze out as much water as possible from the leeks and let them drain on a clean dish towel.

3 Broil the red peppers, skin-side facing up, until the skin blisters and blackens. Place in a bowl, cover and let sit for 10 minutes. Peel the peppers and cut the flesh into long strips, then place them in a bowl and add the oil, balsamic vinegar and ground roasted cumin. Season to taste with salt and pepper and toss well.

4 Layer the leeks and strips of red pepper in the lined pan, alternating the layers so that the white of the leeks in one row is covered by the green of the next row. Season the leeks with a little more salt and pepper.

5 Cover with the overhanging plastic wrap. Top with a plate and weigh it down with heavy food cans. Chill for several hours or overnight.

6 To make the dressing, place the oil, garlic, mustard, soy sauce and vinegar in a bowl and mix thoroughly. Season and add the sugar. Add ground cumin to taste and let stand for several hours. Discard the garlic and add the fresh herbs to the dressing.

7 Unmold the terrine and cut it into thick slices. Put 1–2 slices on each plate, drizzle with dressing and serve.

GRILLED LEEK AND ZUCCHINI SALAD WITH FETA AND MINT

SERVED ON CRISP, SWEET LETTUCE, THIS MAKES A DELICIOUS SUMMERY APPETIZER. TRY TO OBTAIN GENUINE SHEEP'S MILK FETA FOR THE BEST FLAVOR AND TEXTURE.

SERVES SIX

INGREDIENTS

12 slender, baby leeks
6 small zucchini
6 tablespoons extra virgin olive oil
finely shredded zest and juice
  of ½ lemon
1–2 garlic cloves, finely chopped
½ fresh red chile, seeded and diced
pinch of sugar (optional)
½ cup black olives, pitted and
  roughly chopped
2 tablespoons chopped fresh mint
5 ounces feta cheese, sliced
  or crumbled
salt and ground black pepper
fresh mint leaves, to garnish
crisp lettuce leaves, to serve

1 Bring a large saucepan of salted water to a boil. Add the leeks and cook for 2–3 minutes. Drain, refresh under cold water, then squeeze out excess water and let drain.

2 Cut the zucchini in half lengthwise. Place in a colander, adding 1 teaspoon salt to the layers, and let drain for 45 minutes. Rinse and dry thoroughly on paper towels.

3 Heat the broiler. Toss the leeks and zucchini in 2 tablespoons of the oil. Broil the leeks for 2–3 minutes on each side and the zucchini for about 5 minutes on each side. Cut the leeks into serving pieces and place them in a shallow dish with the zucchini.

4 Place the remaining oil in a small bowl and whisk in the lemon zest, 1 tablespoon of the lemon juice, the garlic, chile and a pinch of sugar, if using. Season to taste with salt and pepper. Add more lemon juice to taste.

5 Pour the dressing onto the leeks and zucchini. Stir in the olives and mint, then set aside to marinate for a few hours, turning the vegetables in the dressing once or twice. If the salad has been marinated in the refrigerator, remove it 30 minutes before serving and bring back to room temperature.

6 Add the feta cheese just before serving. Serve with crisp lettuce leaves or spoon the salad onto the leaves arranged on individual serving plates and garnish with fresh mint leaves.

BRAISED BABY LEEKS IN RED WINE WITH AROMATICS

CORIANDER SEEDS AND OREGANO LEND A GREEK FLAVOR TO THIS DISH OF BRAISED LEEKS. SERVE IT AS AN HORS D'OEUVRE OR AS A PARTNER FOR BAKED WHITE FISH.

3 Add the leeks. Bring back to a boil, reduce the heat and cover the pan. Cook gently for 5 minutes. Uncover and simmer gently for another 5–8 minutes, until the leeks are just tender when tested with the tip of a sharp knife.

4 Use a draining spoon to transfer the leeks to a serving dish. Boil the juices rapidly until reduced to about 5–6 tablespoons. Add salt and pepper to taste and pour the liquid onto the leeks. Let cool.

5 The leeks can be left to stand for several hours. If you chill them, bring them back to room temperature again before serving. Sprinkle chopped oregano or marjoram on the leeks just before serving them.

SERVES SIX

INGREDIENTS

    12 baby leeks or 6 thick leeks
    1 tablespoon coriander seeds,
      lightly crushed
    2-inch piece cinnamon stick
    ½ cup olive oil
    3 fresh bay leaves
    2 strips pared orange zest
    5–6 fresh or dried oregano sprigs
    1 teaspoon sugar
    ⅔ cup fruity red wine
    2 teaspoons balsamic or sherry vinegar
    2 tablespoons coarsely chopped fresh
      oregano or marjoram
    salt and ground black pepper

1 Leave baby leeks whole, but cut thick ones into 2–3-inch lengths.

2 Place the coriander seeds and cinnamon in a pan wide enough to hold all the leeks in a single layer. Cook over medium heat for 2–3 minutes, until the spices are fragrant, then stir in the oil, bay leaves, orange zest, oregano, sugar, wine and vinegar. Bring to a boil and simmer for 5 minutes.

GRILLED SCALLIONS <u>AND</u> ASPARAGUS <u>WITH</u> PROSCIUTTO

THIS IS A GOOD CHOICE OF FIRST COURSE AT THE BEGINNING OF SUMMER, WHEN BOTH SCALLIONS AND ASPARAGUS ARE AT THEIR BEST. THE SLIGHT SMOKINESS OF THE GRILLED VEGETABLES GOES VERY WELL WITH THE SWEETNESS OF THE AIR-DRIED HAM.

<u>SERVES FOUR TO SIX</u>

INGREDIENTS
  2 bunches plump scallions
  (about 24)
  1¼ pounds asparagus
  3–4 tablespoons olive oil
  4 teaspoons balsamic vinegar
  8–12 slices prosciutto or San
  Daniele ham
  2 ounces Pecorino cheese
  sea salt and ground black pepper
  extra virgin olive oil, to serve

COOK'S TIP
The scallions can be cooked on a cast-iron ridged grill pan. If more convenient, the asparagus can be roasted at 400°F for 15 minutes.

1 Trim the root, outer papery skin and tops off the scallions.

2 Cut off and discard the woody ends of the asparagus and use a vegetable peeler to peel the bottom 3 inches of the spears.

3 Heat the broiler. Toss the scallions and asparagus in 2 tablespoons of the oil. Place on 2 baking sheets and season.

4 Broil the asparagus for 5 minutes on each side, until just tender when tested with the tip of a sharp knife. Protect the tips with aluminum foil if they seem to char too much. Broil the scallions for 3–4 minutes on each side, until tinged with brown. Brush both vegetables with more oil when you turn them.

5 Distribute the vegetables among 4–6 plates. Season with pepper and drizzle on the vinegar. Lay 2–3 slices of prosciutto on each plate and shave the Pecorino on the top. Serve more extra virgin olive oil for drizzling on at the table.

FLASH-FRIED SQUID WITH PAPRIKA AND GARLIC

THESE QUICK-FRIED SQUID ARE GOOD SERVED WITH A DRY SHERRY OR MANZANILLA AS AN APPETIZER OR AS A TAPAS. ALTERNATIVELY, SERVE THEM ON A BED OF SALAD LEAVES AND OFFER WARM BREAD AS AN ACCOMPANIMENT FOR A MORE SUBSTANTIAL FIRST COURSE.

SERVES SIX TO EIGHT AS AN APPETIZER,
FOUR AS A FIRST COURSE

INGREDIENTS
    1¼ pounds very small squid, cleaned
    6 tablespoons olive oil, plus extra
    1 red chile, seeded and
      finely chopped
    2 teaspoons Spanish mild smoked
      paprika (*pimentón*)
    2 tablespoons all-purpose flour
    2 garlic cloves, finely chopped
    1 tablespoon sherry vinegar
    1 teaspoon grated lemon zest
    2–3 tablespoons finely chopped
      fresh parsley
salt and ground black pepper

1 Choose small squid that are no longer than 4 inches. Cut the body sacs into rings and cut the tentacles into bite-size pieces.

2 Place the squid in a bowl and add 2 tablespoons of the oil, half the chile and the paprika. Season with a little salt and some pepper, cover and marinate for 2–4 hours in the refrigerator.

COOK'S TIPS
• Make sure the wok or pan is very hot, as the squid should cook for only 1–2 minutes: any longer and it will begin to toughen.
• Smoked paprika, known as *pimentón* in Spain, has a wonderful smoky flavor. If you cannot find it, use mild paprika.

3 Toss the squid in the flour and divide it into 2 batches. Heat the remaining oil in a preheated wok or deep frying pan over high heat until very hot. Add the first batch of squid and stir-fry for 1–2 minutes or until the squid becomes opaque and the tentacles have curled.

4 Sprinkle in half the garlic. Stir, then turn out onto a plate. Repeat with the second batch, adding more oil if needed.

5 Sprinkle on the sherry vinegar, lemon zest, remaining chile and parsley. Season and serve hot or cool.

A little onion will often take a salad into new realms. But raw onion needs some discretion: use red onions or scallions for their mild, sweet flavor. Onions also make some of the most delicious cooked salads. Try lightly blanched leeks or grilled onions, mixed with herby, mustardy dressings. Cheese, from mild mozzarella to salty feta, makes a great addition. And don't restrict chives to pretty garnishes—they pack a surprising punch of flavor in dressings for salads with potatoes, beets or egg.

Salads

WARM POTATO SALAD <u>WITH</u> BACON <u>AND</u> SHALLOT DRESSING

THIS WARM SALAD MAKES A FINE ACCOMPANIMENT FOR GRILLED SAUSAGES OR SMOKED MACKEREL. TARRAGON VINEGAR AND MUSTARD WITH TARRAGON OR FINES HERBES ARE GOOD IN THE DRESSING.

<u>SERVES SIX</u>

INGREDIENTS

2 pounds salad potatoes (waxy variety)
6 tablespoons olive oil
7 ounces bacon, cut into strips
3 shallots, chopped
1 small garlic clove, finely chopped
2 tablespoons white wine vinegar
2 tablespoons dry white vermouth or white wine
1 teaspoon French mustard
3–4 tablespoons chopped fresh herbs, such as chervil, parsley and tarragon
1 tablespoon snipped fresh chives
salt and ground black pepper
whole chives, to garnish

1 Cook the potatoes in boiling, salted water for 15–20 minutes, until tender. Drain, cool a little, then peel. Slice the potatoes directly into a bowl and add 3 tablespoons of the oil. Season with pepper to taste. Stir to coat the potatoes, then set aside.

2 Heat another 2 tablespoons of the oil in a frying pan. Fry the bacon until crisp and lightly browned, then add the shallots and cook, stirring constantly, for 2–3 minutes. Add the garlic and cook for another 1 minute. Scrape the contents of the pan over the potatoes and stir to mix.

3 Return the pan to the heat. Add the vinegar and vermouth or wine and reduce a little, then stir in the mustard. Immediately pour this mixture onto the potatoes. Add most of the mixed herbs and stir to mix.

4 Spoon the salad into a large serving bowl or individual bowls. Drizzle the remaining oil on top and sprinkle with the remaining herbs and the chives. Garnish with whole chives, then serve immediately.

LEEK <u>AND</u> ROASTED RED PEPPER SALAD <u>WITH</u> GOAT CHEESE

THE CONTRASTING TEXTURES OF SILKY, ROASTED PEPPERS, SOFT CHEESE AND SLIGHTLY CRISP LEEKS MAKES THIS SALAD EXTRA DELICIOUS. THIS IS A GOOD FIRST COURSE SERVED WITH CRUSTY BREAD.

3 Halve and seed the peppers, then grill them, skin-side facing up, until the skin is blackened and blistered. Place them in a bowl, cover and let stand for 10 minutes, so that they soften in their own steam. Remove the skin and cut the flesh into strips, then mix with the leeks and thyme, adding pepper to taste.

4 Make the dressing by shaking all the ingredients together in a jar, adding seasoning to taste. Pour the dressing onto the salad and chill it for several hours. Bring the salad back to room temperature before serving.

SERVES SIX

INGREDIENTS
  4 ½-inch thick slices goat cheese log
    (*chèvre*)
  1 cup fine dry white bread crumbs
  1½ pounds young slender
    leeks, trimmed
  1 tablespoon olive oil
  2 large red bell peppers
  few sprigs fresh thyme, chopped
  vegetable oil, for shallow-frying
  3 tablespoons chopped fresh
    flat-leaf parsley
  salt and ground black pepper
For the dressing
  5 tablespoons extra virgin olive oil
  1 small garlic clove, finely chopped
  1 teaspoon Dijon mustard, plain or
    flavored with herbes de Provence
  1 tablespoon red wine vinegar

1 Remove any skin from the cheese and roll the slices in the bread crumbs, pressing them in so that the cheese is well coated. Chill the cheese for 1 hour.

2 Cook the leeks in boiling salted water for 3–4 minutes. Drain and cut into 3–4-inch lengths and toss in the oil, adding seasoning to taste. Broil the leeks for 3–4 minutes on each side.

5 When ready to serve, heat a shallow layer of vegetable oil in a nonstick frying pan and fry the goat cheeses quickly until golden brown on each side. Drain them on paper towels and cool slightly, then cut into bite-size pieces. Toss the cheese and parsley into the salad and serve immediately.

Grilled Onion and Eggplant Salad with Garlic and Tahini Dressing

This is a deliciously smoky salad that balances sweet and sharp flavors. It makes a good filling for pita bread, with some crisp lettuce and sweet, ripe tomatoes.

SERVES SIX

INGREDIENTS

   3 eggplant, cut into ½-inch
    thick slices
   1½ pounds round, not flat, onions,
    thickly sliced
   5–6 tablespoons olive oil
   1 teaspoon powdered sumac (optional)
   3 tablespoons roughly chopped
    flat-leaf parsley
   3 tablespoons pine nuts, toasted
   salt and ground black pepper
For the dressing
   2 garlic cloves, crushed
   ⅔ cup light tahini
   juice of 1–2 lemons
   3–4 tablespoons water

1 Place the eggplant on a rack or in a colander and sprinkle generously with salt. Leave for 45–60 minutes, then rinse thoroughly under cold running water and pat dry with paper towels.

2 Thread the onions onto skewers or place them in an oiled wire grill cage.

COOK'S TIPS
• Sumac is a Mediterranean spice with a sharp, lemony taste. Buy it ready-ground at Middle Eastern stores, good healthfood stores or gourmet stores.
• Tahini is a thick, smooth, oily paste made from sesame seeds. It is also available at Middle Eastern stores and healthfood stores and at some supermarkets.

3 Brush the eggplant and onions with about 3 tablespoons of the oil and grill for 6–8 minutes on each side. Brush with more oil, if necessary, when you turn the vegetables. The vegetables should be browned and soft when cooked. The onions may need a little longer than the eggplant.

4 Arrange the vegetables on a serving dish and sprinkle with the sumac, if using, and season with salt and pepper to taste. Sprinkle with the remaining oil if they seem dry.

5 For the dressing, crush the garlic in a mortar with a pinch of salt and gradually work in the tahini. Gradually work in the juice of 1 lemon, followed by the water. Taste and add more lemon juice if you think the dressing needs it. Thin with more water, if necessary, so that the dressing is fairly runny.

6 Drizzle the dressing on the salad and let sit for 30–60 minutes, then sprinkle with the chopped parsley and pine nuts. Serve immediately at room temperature, not chilled.

BEET AND RED ONION SALAD

THIS SALAD LOOKS ESPECIALLY ATTRACTIVE WHEN MADE WITH A MIXTURE OF RED AND YELLOW BEETS.
TRY IT WITH ROAST BEEF OR COOKED HAM, AS IT TASTES EXCELLENT WITH THESE RICH MEATS.

SERVES SIX

INGREDIENTS

- 1¼ pounds small beets
- 5 tablespoons water
- 4 tablespoons olive oil
- scant 1 cup walnut or pecan halves
- 1 teaspoon sugar, plus a little extra for the dressing
- 2 tablespoons walnut oil
- 1 tablespoon sherry vinegar or balsamic vinegar
- 1 teaspoon soy sauce
- 1 teaspoon grated orange zest
- ½ teaspoon ground roasted coriander seeds
- 1–2 teaspoons orange juice
- 1 red onion, halved and very thinly sliced
- 1–2 tablespoons chopped fresh fennel
- 3 ounces watercress or mizuna leaves
- handful of baby red chard or beet leaves (optional)
- salt and ground black pepper

3 Meanwhile, heat 1 tablespoon of the olive oil in a small frying pan and cook the walnuts or pecans until they begin to brown. Add the sugar and cook, stirring, until the nuts begin to caramelize. Season with ½ teaspoon salt and lots of pepper, then turn the nuts out onto a plate and let cool.

4 In a bowl, whisk together the remaining olive oil, the walnut oil, sherry or balsamic vinegar, soy sauce, orange zest and ground roasted coriander to make the dressing. Season with salt and pepper to taste and add a pinch of sugar. Whisk in orange juice to taste.

5 Separate the red onion slices into half-rings and add them to the strips of beet. Add the dressing and toss thoroughly to mix.

6 When ready to serve, toss the salad with the fennel, watercress or mizuna and red chard or beet leaves, if using. Transfer to individual bowls or plates and sprinkle on the caramelized nuts. Serve immediately.

1 Preheat the oven to 350°F. Place the beets in an ovenproof dish just large enough to hold them in a single layer and add the water. Cover tightly and cook for 1–1½ hours or until they are just tender.

2 Cool, then peel the beets, then slice them or cut them into strips and toss with 1 tablespoon of the olive oil. Transfer to a bowl and set aside.

Moroccan Orange, Onion and Olive Salad

This is a refreshing salad to follow a rich main dish, such as a Moroccan tagine of lamb, or to lighten any spicy meal. It is also delicious with cold roast duck.

SERVES SIX

INGREDIENTS
  5 large oranges
  scant 1 cup black olives
  1 red onion, thinly sliced
  1 large fennel bulb, thinly sliced,
    feathery tops reserved
  1 tablespoon chopped fresh mint,
    plus a few extra sprigs
  1 tablespoon chopped cilantro, plus a
    few extra sprigs
  ½ teaspoon orange flower water
For the dressing
  4 tablespoons olive oil
  2 teaspoons lemon juice
  ½ teaspoon ground toasted
    coriander seeds
  salt and ground black pepper

1 Peel the oranges with a sharp knife, making sure you remove all the white pith, and cut them into ¼-inch slices. Remove any seeds and work over a bowl to catch all the orange juice. Set the juice aside.

2 Pit the olives, if desired. In a bowl, toss the orange slices, onion and fennel together with the olives, chopped mint and cilantro.

3 Make the dressing. In a bowl or jug, whisk together the olive oil, 1 tablespoon of the reserved fresh orange juice and the lemon juice. Add the ground toasted coriander seeds and season to taste with a little salt and pepper. Whisk thoroughly to mix.

4 Toss the dressing into the salad and let stand for 30–60 minutes.

5 Drain off any excess dressing and place the salad on a serving dish. Sprinkle on the herbs and fennel tops and the orange flower water.

Tomato, Mozzarella and Red Onion Salad with Basil and Caper Dressing

Sweet tomatoes and the heady scent of basil capture the essence of summer in this simple salad. Vine-ripened tomatoes usually have the best flavor.

SERVES FOUR

INGREDIENTS
  5 large ripe tomatoes, peeled,
    if desired
  2 buffalo mozzarella cheeses,
    drained and sliced
  1 small red onion, chopped
For the dressing
  ½ small garlic clove, peeled
  ½ ounce fresh basil
  2 tablespoons chopped fresh
    flat-leaf parsley
  5 teaspoons small salted
    capers, rinsed
  ½ teaspoon mustard
  5–6 tablespoons extra virgin olive oil
  1–2 teaspoons balsamic vinegar
  salt and ground black pepper
For the garnish
  fresh basil leaves
  fresh parsley sprigs

1 First, make the dressing. Put the garlic, basil, parsley, half the capers and the mustard in a food processor or blender and process briefly to chop. Then, with the motor running, gradually pour in the olive oil through the feeder tube to make a smooth purée with a dressing consistency. Add the balsamic vinegar to taste and season with ground black pepper.

2 Slice the tomatoes. Arrange the tomato and mozzarella slices on a plate. Sprinkle on the onion and season with a little pepper.

3 Drizzle the dressing on the salad, then sprinkle a few basil leaves, parsley sprigs and the remaining capers on top as a garnish. Let sit for 10–15 minutes before serving.

SALAD OF ROASTED SHALLOTS AND BUTTERNUT SQUASH WITH FETA CHEESE

THIS IS ESPECIALLY GOOD SERVED WITH A GRAIN OR STARCHY SALAD, BASED ON RICE OR COUSCOUS, FOR EXAMPLE. SERVE PLENTY OF GOOD BREAD TO MOP UP THE JUICES.

SERVES FOUR TO SIX

INGREDIENTS
    5 tablespoons olive oil
    1 tablespoon balsamic vinegar, plus a
      little extra, if desired
    1 tablespoon sweet soy sauce
    12 ounces shallots, peeled but
      left whole
    3 fresh red chiles
    1 butternut squash, peeled, seeded
      and cut into chunks
    1 teaspoon finely chopped fresh thyme
    ½ ounce flat-leaf parsley
    1 small garlic clove, finely chopped
    3 ounces walnuts, chopped
    5 ounces feta cheese
    salt and ground black pepper

1 Preheat the oven to 400°F. Beat the oil, vinegar and soy sauce together in a large bowl, then season with salt and pepper.

2 Toss the shallots and 2 of the chiles in the oil mixture and turn into a large roasting pan or ovenproof dish. Roast for 15 minutes, stirring once or twice.

3 Add the butternut squash and roast for another 30–35 minutes, stirring once, until the squash is tender and browned. Remove from the oven, stir in the chopped thyme and set the vegetables aside to cool.

4 Chop the parsley and garlic together and mix with the walnuts. Seed and finely chop the remaining chile.

5 Stir the parsley, garlic and walnut mixture into the vegetables. Add chopped chile to taste and adjust the seasoning, adding a little extra balsamic vinegar, if desired. Crumble the feta and add to the salad. Transfer to a serving dish and serve immediately.

POTATO <u>AND</u> MUSSEL SALAD <u>WITH</u> SHALLOT <u>AND</u> CHIVE DRESSING

SHALLOT AND CHIVES IN A CREAMY DRESSING ADD BITE TO THIS SALAD OF POTATO AND SWEET MUSSELS. SERVE WITH A BOWL OF FULL-FLAVORED WATERCRESS AND PLENTY OF WHOLE-WHEAT BREAD.

SERVES FOUR

INGREDIENTS

1½ pounds salad potatoes
2¼ pounds mussels, scrubbed and
  beards removed
scant 1 cup dry white wine
½ ounce flat-leaf parsley, chopped
salt and ground black pepper
snipped fresh chives or chive flowers,
  to garnish
For the dressing
7 tablespoons mild olive oil
1–2 tablespoons white wine vinegar
1 teaspoon Dijon mustard
1 large shallot, very finely chopped
1 tablespoon snipped fresh chives
3 tablespoons heavy cream
pinch of sugar (optional)

1 Cook the potatoes in boiling, salted water for 15–20 minutes or until tender. Drain, cool, then peel. Slice the potatoes into a bowl and toss with 2 tablespoons of the oil for the dressing.

2 Discard any open mussels that do not close when sharply tapped. Bring the white wine to a boil in a large, heavy saucepan. Add the mussels, cover and boil vigorously, shaking the pan occasionally, for 3–4 minutes, until the mussels have opened. Discard any mussels that have not opened after 5 minutes' cooking. Drain and shell the mussels, reserving the cooking liquid.

3 Boil the reserved cooking liquid until reduced to about 3 tablespoons. Strain this through a fine sieve over the potatoes and toss to mix.

4 For the dressing, whisk together the remaining oil, 1 tablespoon vinegar, the mustard, shallot and chives.

5 Add the cream and whisk again to form a thick dressing. Adjust the seasoning, adding more vinegar and/or a pinch of sugar to taste.

6 Toss the mussels with the potatoes, then mix in the dressing and chopped parsley. Serve sprinkled with extra snipped chives or chive flowers separated into florets.

COOK'S TIP
Potato salads, such as this one, should not be chilled if at all possible, as the cold alters the texture of the potatoes and of the creamy dressing. For the best flavor and texture, serve this salad just cool or at room temperature.

LEEK AND FENNEL SALAD WITH SPICY TOMATO DRESSING

THIS IS AN EXCELLENT SALAD TO MAKE IN THE EARLY AUTUMN WHEN YOUNG LEEKS ARE AT THEIR BEST AND RIPE TOMATOES ARE FULL OF FLAVOR. SERVE WITH GOOD BREAD AS AN APPETIZER OR SERVE TO ACCOMPANY SIMPLY GRILLED WHITE FISH FOR A MAIN COURSE.

SERVES SIX AS AN APPETIZER

INGREDIENTS

   1½ pounds leeks
   2 large fennel bulbs
   ½ cup extra virgin olive oil
   2 shallots, chopped
   ⅔ cup dry white wine or white
     vermouth
   1 teaspoon fennel seeds, crushed
   6 fresh thyme sprigs
   2–3 bay leaves
   good pinch of dried red chile flakes
   12 pounds tomatoes, peeled, seeded
     and diced
   1 teaspoon sun-dried tomato
     paste (optional)
   good pinch of sugar (optional)
   ¾ cup small black olives
   salt and ground black pepper

2 Trim the fennel bulbs, reserving any feathery tops for the garnish and cut the bulbs either into thin slices or into thicker wedges, according to taste.

3 Cook the fennel in the reserved cooking water for about 5 minutes, then drain thoroughly and toss with 2 tablespoons of the olive oil. Season to taste with black pepper.

6 Add the diced tomatoes and cook briskly for 5–8 minutes or until reduced and thickened.

7 Add the tomato paste, if using, and adjust the seasoning, adding a good pinch of sugar if you think the dressing needs it.

1 Cook the leeks in boiling salted water for 4–5 minutes. Use a draining spoon to remove the leeks and place them in a colander to drain thoroughly and cool. Reserve the cooking water in the pan. Squeeze out excess water and cut the leeks into 3-inch lengths.

COOK'S TIP
When buying fennel, look for rounded bulbs; they have a better shape for this dish. The flesh should be crisp and white, with no signs of bruising. Avoid specimens with broken leaves or with brown or dried out patches.

4 Heat a ridged cast-iron grill pan. Arrange the leeks and fennel on the pan and cook until tinged deep brown, turning once. Remove the vegetables from the pan, place in a large shallow dish and set aside.

5 Place the remaining olive oil, the shallots, white wine or vermouth, crushed fennel seeds, thyme, bay leaves and chile flakes in a large saucepan and bring to a boil over medium heat. Lower the heat and simmer for 10 minutes.

8 Pour the dressing onto the leeks and fennel, toss to mix and let cool. The salad may be made several hours in advance and kept in the refrigerator, but bring it back to room temperature before serving.

9 When ready to serve, stir the salad then sprinkle the chopped fennel tops and black olives on top.

LEEK SALAD WITH ANCHOVIES, EGGS AND PARSLEY

CHOPPED HARD-BOILED EGGS AND COOKED LEEKS ARE A CLASSIC COMBINATION IN FRENCH-STYLE SALADS. THIS ONE MAKES A GOOD FIRST COURSE, WITH SOME CRUSTY BREAD, OR A LIGHT MAIN DISH THAT CAN BE FINISHED WITH A TOMATO SALAD AND/OR A POTATO SALAD.

3 To make the dressing, whisk the mustard with the vinegar. Gradually whisk in the oil, followed by the cream. Stir in the shallot, then season to taste with salt, pepper and a pinch of sugar, if desired.

4 Leave the leeks whole or thickly slice them, then place in a serving dish. Pour most of the dressing on them and stir to mix. Leave for at least 1 hour or until ready to serve, bringing them back to room temperature first, if necessary.

SERVES FOUR

INGREDIENTS

   1½ pounds thin or baby
    leeks, trimmed
   2 large or 3 medium eggs
   2 ounces good-quality anchovy
    fillets in olive oil, drained
   ½ ounce flat-leaf parsley, chopped
   a few black olives, pitted
    (optional)
   salt and ground black pepper
For the dressing
   1 teaspoon Dijon mustard
   1 tablespoon tarragon vinegar
   5 tablespoons olive oil
   2 tablespoons heavy cream
   1 small shallot, very finely
    chopped
   pinch of sugar (optional)

1 Cook the leeks in boiling salted water for 3–4 minutes. Drain, plunge into cold water, then drain again. Squeeze out excess water, then pat dry.

2 Place the eggs in a saucepan of cold water, bring to a boil and cook for 6–7 minutes. Drain, plunge into cold water, then shell and chop the eggs.

5 Arrange the anchovies on the leeks, then sprinkle the eggs and parsley on top. Drizzle on the remaining dressing, season with black pepper and dot with a few olives, if using. Serve immediately.

COOK'S TIP
Make sure the leeks are well drained and squeezed of excess water or they will dilute the dressing and spoil the flavor.

PARSLEY AND ARUGULA SALAD WITH BLACK OLIVE AND GARLIC DRESSING

BEING LIGHT BUT FULL OF FLAVOR, THIS MAKES A WELL-ROUNDED FIRST COURSE; IT IS ALSO GOOD SERVED ALONGSIDE RARE ROAST BEEF. USE THE BEST PARMESAN CHEESE—PARMIGIANO REGGIANO—TO ENSURE THAT THIS SALAD IS SPECIAL.

SERVES SIX

INGREDIENTS
1 garlic clove, halved
4 ounces good white bread, cut into ½-inch thick slices
3 tablespoons olive oil, plus extra for shallow frying
3 ounces arugula leaves
3 ounces baby spinach
1 ounce flat-leaf parsley, leaves only
3 tablespoons salted capers, rinsed and dried
1½ ounces Parmesan cheese, pared into shavings
For the dressing
5 teaspoons black olive paste
1 garlic clove, finely chopped
1 teaspoon Dijon mustard
5 tablespoons olive oil
2 teaspoons balsamic vinegar
ground black pepper

1 First, make the dressing. Whisk the black olive paste, garlic and mustard together in a bowl. Gradually whisk in the olive oil, then the vinegar. Adjust the seasoning with black pepper—the dressing should be sufficiently salty.

2 Heat the oven to 375°F. Rub the halved garlic clove on the bread and cut or tear the slices into bite-size croutons. Toss them in the oil and place on a small baking sheet. Bake for 10–15 minutes, stirring once, until golden brown. Cool on paper towels.

3 Mix the arugula, spinach and parsley in a large salad bowl.

4 Heat a shallow layer of olive oil in a frying pan. Add the capers and fry briefly until crisp. Scoop out right away and drain on paper towels.

5 Toss the dressing and croutons into the salad and divide it among 6 bowls or plates. Sprinkle the Parmesan shavings and the fried capers on top and serve immediately.

COOK'S TIP
Use a swivel-action or fixed-blade vegetable peeler to cut thin shavings from a block of Parmigiano Reggiano—some supermarkets sell tubs of ready-shaved cheese. It is easier to make shavings if you choose a relatively young cheese rather than an older, drier and much harder Parmesan.

LENTIL <u>AND</u> SPINACH SALAD <u>WITH</u> ONION, CUMIN <u>AND</u> GARLIC

THIS WONDERFUL, EARTHY SALAD IS GREAT FOR A PICNIC OR WITH GRILLED FOOD. IT IMPROVES WITH STANDING AND IS AT ITS BEST SERVED AT ROOM TEMPERATURE RATHER THAN CHILLED.

<u>SERVES SIX</u>

INGREDIENTS
  1 cup Puy lentils
  1 fresh bay leaf
  1 celery stalk
  fresh thyme sprig
  2 tablespoons olive oil
  1 onion or 3–4 shallots,
    finely chopped
  2 teaspoons crushed toasted
    cumin seeds
  14 ounces young spinach
  salt and ground black pepper
  2–3 tablespoons chopped fresh
    parsley, plus a few extra sprigs
For the dressing
  5 tablespoons extra virgin olive oil
  1 teaspoon Dijon mustard
  3–5 teaspoons red wine vinegar
  1 small garlic clove, finely chopped
  ½ teaspoon finely grated lemon zest

1 Rinse the lentils and place them in a large saucepan. Add plenty of water to cover. Tie the bay leaf, celery and thyme into a bundle and add to the pan, then bring to a boil. Reduce the heat so that the water boils steadily. Cook the lentils for 30–45 minutes, until just tender. Do not add salt at this stage, as it toughens the lentils.

2 Meanwhile, to make the dressing, mix the oil, mustard, 3 teaspoons vinegar, the garlic and lemon zest, and season well with salt and pepper.

3 Thoroughly drain the lentils and turn them into a bowl. Add most of the dressing and toss well, then set the lentils aside, stirring occasionally.

COOK'S TIP
Named after the town of Puy in France, these small, grayish-green lentils are considered to have the best and most distinctive flavor. They keep both their shape and color well when cooked, making them ideal for salads.

4 Heat the oil in a deep frying pan and cook the onion or shallots over low heat for 4–5 minutes, until they are beginning to soften. Add the cumin and cook for 1 minute.

5 Add the spinach and season to taste, cover and cook for 2 minutes. Stir, then cook again briefly until wilted.

6 Stir the spinach into the lentils and let the salad cool. Bring back to room temperature if necessary. Stir in the remaining dressing and chopped parsley. Adjust the seasoning, adding extra red wine vinegar if necessary.

7 Turn the salad onto a serving platter and sprinkle on some parsley sprigs.

BEAN SALAD <u>WITH</u> TUNA <u>AND</u> RED ONION

THIS MAKES A GREAT FIRST COURSE OR EVEN A LIGHT MAIN COURSE IF SERVED WITH A GREEN SALAD, SOME GARLIC MAYONNAISE AND PLENTY OF WARM, CRUSTY BREAD.

SERVES FOUR

INGREDIENTS

1⅓ cups dried haricot
  or cannellini beans, soaked
  overnight in cold water
1 bay leaf
7–9 ounces fine green
  beans, trimmed
1 large red onion, very thinly sliced
3 tablespoons chopped fresh
  flat-leaf parsley
7–9 ounces good-quality canned tuna
  in olive oil, drained
7 ounces cherry tomatoes, halved
salt and ground black pepper
a few onion rings, to garnish

For the dressing

6 tablespoons extra virgin olive oil
1 tablespoon tarragon vinegar
1 teaspoon tarragon mustard
1 garlic clove, finely chopped
1 teaspoon grated lemon zest
a little lemon juice
pinch of sugar (optional)

1 Drain the beans and bring them to a boil in fresh water with the bay leaf added. Boil rapidly for 10 minutes, then reduce the heat and boil steadily for 1–1½ hours, until tender. The cooking time depends on the age of the beans. Drain well. Discard the bay leaf.

3 Blanch the beans in plenty of boiling water for 3–4 minutes. Drain, refresh under cold water and drain thoroughly again.

5 Flake the tuna into large chunks with a knife and toss it into the beans with the tomato halves.

2 Meanwhile, place all the dressing ingredients other than the lemon juice and sugar in a bowl and whisk until mixed. Season to taste with salt, pepper, lemon juice and a pinch of sugar, if desired. Let stand.

4 Place both types of beans in a bowl. Add half the dressing and toss to mix. Stir in the onion and half the chopped parsley, then season to taste with salt and pepper.

6 Arrange the salad on four individual plates. Drizzle the remaining dressing on the salad and sprinkle the remaining chopped parsley on top. Garnish with a few onion rings and serve immediately, at room temperature.

THAI SHRIMP SALAD WITH GARLIC DRESSING AND FRIZZLED SHALLOTS

IN THIS INTENSELY FLAVORED SALAD, SWEET SHRIMP AND MANGO ARE PARTNERED WITH A SWEET-AND-SOUR GARLIC DRESSING HEIGHTENED WITH THE HOT TASTE OF CHILE. THE CRISP FRIZZLED SHALLOTS ARE A TRADITIONAL ADDITION TO THAI SALADS.

SERVES FOUR TO SIX

INGREDIENTS
  1½ pounds medium-size shrimp, shelled and deveined with tails on
  finely shredded zest of 1 lime
  ½ fresh red chile, seeded and finely chopped
  2 tablespoons olive oil, plus extra for brushing
  1 ripe but firm mango
  2 carrots, cut into long thin shreds
  4-inch piece cucumber, sliced
  1 small red onion, halved and thinly sliced
  a few sprigs of cilantro
  a few sprigs of fresh mint
  3 tablespoons roasted peanuts, roughly chopped
  4 large shallots, thinly sliced and fried until crisp in 2 tablespoons peanut oil
  salt and ground black pepper
For the dressing
  1 large garlic clove, chopped
  2–3 teaspoons sugar
  juice of 2 limes
  1–2 tablespoons Thai fish sauce (*nam pla*)
  1 red chile, seeded
  1–2 teaspoons light rice vinegar

1 Place the shrimp in a glass or china dish and add the lime zest and chile. Season with salt and pepper and spoon the oil on them. Toss to mix and let marinate for 30–40 minutes.

2 For the dressing, place the garlic in a mortar with 2 teaspoons sugar and pound until smooth, then work in the juice of 1½ limes and 1 tablespoon of the Thai fish sauce.

3 Transfer the dressing to a bowl. Finely chop half the chile and add it to the dressing. Taste the dressing and add more sugar, lime juice, fish sauce and the rice vinegar to taste.

COOK'S TIP
To devein shrimp, make a shallow cut down the back of the shrimp using a small, sharp knife. Using the tip of the knife, lift out the thin, black vein, then rinse the shrimp thoroughly under cold, running water.

4 Peel and pit the mango, then cut it into very fine strips.

5 Toss together the mango, carrots, cucumber and onion, and half the dressing. Arrange the salad on individual plates or in bowls.

6 Heat a ridged, cast-iron grill pan or heavy frying pan until very hot. Brush with a little oil, then sear the shrimp for 2–3 minutes on each side, until they turn pink and are patched with brown on the outside. Arrange the shrimp on the salads.

7 Sprinkle the remaining dressing on the salads and add the sprigs of cilantro and mint. Finely shred the remaining chile and sprinkle it on the salads with the peanuts and crisp-fried shallots. Serve immediately.

BEEF AND GRILLED SWEET POTATO SALAD WITH SHALLOT AND HERB DRESSING

THIS SALAD MAKES A GOOD MAIN DISH FOR A SUMMER BUFFET, ESPECIALLY IF THE BEEF HAS BEEN CUT INTO FORK-SIZE STRIPS. IT IS ABSOLUTELY DELICIOUS WITH A SIMPLE POTATO SALAD AND SOME PEPPERY LEAVES, SUCH AS WATERCRESS, MIZUNA OR ARUGULA.

SERVES SIX TO EIGHT

INGREDIENTS
- 1¾-pound fillet of beef
- 1 teaspoon black peppercorns, crushed
- 2 teaspoons chopped fresh thyme
- 4 tablespoons olive oil
- 1 pound orange-fleshed sweet potato, peeled
- salt and ground black pepper

For the dressing
- 1 garlic clove, chopped
- ½ ounce flat-leaf parsley
- 2 tablespoons chopped cilantro
- 1 tablespoon small salted capers, rinsed
- ½–1 fresh green chile, seeded and chopped
- 2 teaspoons Dijon mustard
- 2–3 teaspoons white wine vinegar
- 5 tablespoons extra virgin olive oil
- 2 shallots, finely chopped

1 Roll the beef fillet in the crushed peppercorns and thyme, then set aside to marinate for a few hours. Preheat the oven to 400°F.

2 Heat half the olive oil in a heavy frying pan. Add the beef and brown it all over, turning frequently, to seal it. Place on a baking sheet and cook for 10–15 minutes.

3 Remove the beef from the oven, and cover with aluminum foil, then let rest for 10–15 minutes.

4 Meanwhile, preheat the broiler. Cut the sweet potatoes into ½-inch slices. Brush with the remaining olive oil, season to taste with salt and pepper, and broil for 5–6 minutes on each side, until tender and browned. Cut the sweet potato slices into strips and place them in a bowl.

5 Cut the beef into slices or strips and toss with the sweet potato, then set the bowl aside.

6 For the dressing, process the garlic, parsley, cilantro, capers, chile, mustard and 2 teaspoons of the vinegar in a food processor or blender until chopped. With the motor still running, gradually pour in the oil to make a smooth dressing. Season the dressing with salt and pepper and add more vinegar, to taste. Stir in the shallots.

7 Toss the dressing into the sweet potatoes and beef and let stand for up to 2 hours before serving.

EGG AND BACON CAESAR SALAD

CAESAR CARDINI INVENTED THE CLASSIC CAESAR SALAD IN 1924 AT HIS RESTAURANT IN TIJUANA, JUST SOUTH OF THE UNITED STATES BORDER. THE ESSENTIALS ARE GOOD, SWEET ROMAINE LETTUCE, CRISP GARLIC CROUTONS AND A CREAMY MAYONNAISE-LIKE DRESSING.

3 Meanwhile, for the dressing, bring a saucepan of water to a boil and add the egg, then boil it for 90 seconds. Plunge the egg into cold water and shell it into a food processor or blender.

4 Add the garlic and anchovy fillets and process to mix. With the motor still running, gradually add the olive oil in a thin stream. When all the oil is incorporated and the dressing is creamy, add 2–3 teaspoons lemon juice or wine vinegar and season to taste with salt and pepper.

5 Trim the lettuces, cutting into quarters or separating the larger lettuces into leaves. Place in a large salad bowl.

SERVES SIX AS AN APPETIZER OR
FOUR AS A LIGHT MAIN COURSE

INGREDIENTS
  3 ½-inch thick slices white bread
  3 tablespoons olive oil
  1 large garlic clove,
    finely chopped
  2 Romaine lettuces
  12–18 quail's eggs
  4 ounces thinly sliced San Daniele or
    Serrano ham
  1½–2 ounces Parmesan
    cheese, grated
  salt and ground black pepper
For the dressing
  1 large egg
  1–2 garlic cloves, chopped
  4 anchovy fillets in oil, drained
  ½ cup olive oil
  lemon juice or white wine vinegar

1 Preheat the oven to 375°F. Cut the bread into bite-size squares or chunks and toss them with the oil and garlic. Season to taste with salt and pepper.

2 Turn out onto a baking sheet. Bake for 10–14 minutes, stirring once or twice, until golden brown all over.

6 Place the quail's eggs in a saucepan, cover with cold water, then bring to a boil and boil for 2 minutes. Plunge the eggs into cold water, then part-shell them. Broil the ham for 2–3 minutes on each side or until crisp.

7 Toss the dressing into the lettuce with 1 ounce of the Parmesan. Add the croutons. Cut the quail's eggs in half and add them to the salad. Crumble the ham into large pieces and sprinkle it on the salad with the remaining cheese. Serve immediately.

Flavor-packed onions make superb partners for the delicate flavors of seafood. They are essential in pickled fish dishes, as an aromatic bed for baked fish and in stuffings for mackerel, snapper and trout. Garlic complements seafood—think of mussels in garlic bread crumbs. Aioli, the rich garlic mayonnaise from Provence, is wonderful with salt cod and Mediterranean fish stews. On the milder side, leeks and chives are perfect with fine-flavored seafood such as sole and scallops.

Fish and Shellfish

CEVICHE WITH RED ONION, AVOCADO AND SWEET POTATO

CEVICHE IS A SOUTH AMERICAN DISH OF FISH MARINATED IN CITRUS JUICE AND ONION, WHICH HAS A SIMILAR EFFECT TO COOKING, MAKING THE FISH OPAQUE AND FIRM IN TEXTURE.

SERVES SIX AS AN APPETIZER

INGREDIENTS
1¼–1½ pounds white fish
    fillets, skinned
1 red onion, thinly sliced
pinch of dried red chile flakes
grated zest of 1 small lime and
    juice of 5 limes
1–1¼ pounds sweet potatoes
5 tablespoons mild olive oil
3–5 teaspoons rice vinegar
½–1 teaspoon sugar
½ teaspoon ground toasted
    cumin seeds
½–1 fresh red or green chile, seeded
    and finely chopped
1 large or 2 small avocados, peeled,
    pitted and sliced
8 ounces peeled cooked shrimp
3 tablespoons chopped cilantro
2 tablespoons roasted peanuts,
    chopped
salt and ground black pepper

1 Cut the fish into strips or chunks. Put half the onion in a glass dish and lay the fish on top. Sprinkle on the dried red chile flakes and pour in the lime juice. Cover and chill for 2–3 hours, spooning the lime juice onto the fish once or twice. Drain, and discard the onion.

2 Steam or boil the sweet potatoes for 20–25 minutes or until just tender. Peel and slice, or cut into wedges.

3 Place the oil in a bowl and whisk in the rice vinegar and sugar to taste, then add the cumin, season, and whisk in the fresh chile and grated lime zest.

4 In a glass bowl, toss together the fish, sweet potatoes, avocado slices, shrimp and most of the cilantro, and the dressing.

5 Toss in the remaining half of the sliced red onion. Sprinkle with the remaining cilantro and the peanuts and serve immediately.

COOK'S TIP
Choose orange-fleshed sweet potatoes if you can for this dish.

MOUCLADE

THIS IS A TRADITIONAL DISH OF MUSSELS COOKED WITH SHALLOTS, GARLIC AND SAFFRON FROM THE WEST ATLANTIC COAST OF FRANCE. IT TASTES AS SUPERB AS IT LOOKS.

SERVES SIX

INGREDIENTS

4½ pounds fresh mussels, scrubbed
  and beards removed
9 ounces shallots, finely chopped
1¼ cups medium white wine, such as
  Vouvray
generous pinch of saffron threads
  (about 12 threads)
6 tablespoons butter
2 celery stalks, finely chopped
1 teaspoon fennel seeds,
  lightly crushed
2 large garlic cloves, finely chopped
1 cup fish or vegetable stock
1 bay leaf
pinch of cayenne pepper
2 large egg yolks
⅔ cup heavy cream
juice of ½–1 lemon
2–3 tablespoons chopped
  fresh parsley
salt and ground black pepper

1 Discard any mussels that do not shut when tapped sharply.

2 Place 2 tablespoons of the shallots with the wine in a wide saucepan and bring to a boil. Add half the mussels and cover, then boil rapidly for 1 minute, shaking the pan once. Remove all the mussels, discarding any that remain closed. Repeat with the remaining mussels. Remove the top half-shell from each mussel. Strain the cooking liquid through a fine sieve into a bowl and stir in the saffron, then set aside.

3 Melt 4 tablespoons of the butter in a heavy saucepan. Add the remaining shallots and celery and cook over low heat, stirring occasionally, for 5–6 minutes, until softened but not browned. Add the fennel seeds and half of the garlic, then cook for another 2–3 minutes.

4 Pour in the reserved mussel liquid, bring to a boil and then simmer for 5 minutes before adding the stock, bay leaf and cayenne. Season with salt and pepper to taste, then simmer, uncovered, for 5–10 minutes.

5 Beat the egg yolks with the cream, then whisk in a ladleful of the hot liquid followed by the juice of ½ lemon. Whisk this mixture back into the sauce. Cook over very low heat, without allowing it to boil, for 5–10 minutes, until slightly thickened. Taste for seasoning and add more lemon juice if necessary.

6 Stir the remaining garlic, butter and most of the parsley into the sauce with the mussels and reheat for 30–60 seconds. Distribute the mussels among 6 soup plates and ladle on the sauce. Sprinkle with the remaining parsley and serve.

Salt Cod Fritters with Aioli

Aioli is a fiercely garlicky, olive oil mayonnaise from Provence in the south of France and is a traditional accompaniment to salt cod.

SERVES SIX

INGREDIENTS

    1 pound salt cod
    1¼ pounds floury potatoes
    1¼ cups milk
    6 scallions, finely chopped
    2 tablespoons extra virgin olive oil
    2 tablespoons chopped fresh parsley
    juice of ½ lemon, to taste
    2 eggs, beaten
    4 tablespoons all-purpose flour
    1⅓ cups dry white bread crumbs
    vegetable oil, for shallow-frying
    salt and ground black pepper
    lemon wedges and salad,
       to serve
For the aioli
    2 large garlic cloves
    2 egg yolks
    1¼ cups olive oil
    lemon juice, to taste

1 Soak the salt cod in cold water for 24–36 hours, changing the water 5–6 times. The cod should swell as it rehydrates, and a tiny piece should not taste unpleasantly salty when tried. Drain well.

2 Cook the potatoes, unpeeled, in a saucepan of boiling salted water for about 20 minutes, until tender. Drain, then peel and mash the potatoes.

3 Poach the cod very gently in the milk with half the scallions for 10–15 minutes or until it flakes easily. Remove the cod and flake it with a fork into a bowl, discarding bones and skin.

4 Add 4 tablespoons mashed potatoes to the flaked cod and beat with a wooden spoon. Work in the olive oil, then gradually add the remaining potato. Beat in the remaining scallions and the parsley. Season with lemon juice and pepper to taste—the mixture may need a little salt. Beat in 1 egg, then chill the mixture until firm.

5 Shape the mixture into 12–18 small round cakes. Coat them in flour, then dip them in the remaining egg and coat with the bread crumbs. Chill until ready to fry.

COOK'S TIPS
• Try to find a thick, creamy white piece of salt cod, preferably cut from the middle of the fish rather than the tail and fin ends. Avoid thin, yellowish salt cod, as it will be too dry and salty.
• Mash potatoes by hand, never in a food processor, as it makes them gluey.
• Aioli traditionally has a sharp bite from the raw garlic. However, if you prefer a milder flavor, blanch the garlic once or twice in boiling water for about 3 minutes each time before using it.

6 Meanwhile, make the aioli. Place the garlic and a good pinch of salt in a mortar and pound into a paste with a pestle. Using a small whisk or a wooden spoon, gradually work in the egg yolks.

7 Add the olive oil, a drop at a time, until about half is incorporated. When the sauce is as thick as soft butter, beat in 1–2 teaspoons lemon juice, then continue adding oil until the aioli is very thick. Adjust the seasoning, adding lemon juice to taste.

8 Heat about ¾-inch depth of oil in a large, heavy frying pan. Add the fritters and cook over medium-high heat for about 4 minutes. Turn them over and cook for another 4 minutes on the other side, until crisp and golden. Drain on crumpled paper towels, then serve with the aioli, lemon wedges and salad leaves.

SHELLFISH AND SCALLION SKEWERS WITH TARTAR SAUCE

IF YOU MAKE THESE SKEWERS QUITE SMALL, THEY ARE GOOD AS A CANAPÉ TO SERVE AT A COCKTAIL PARTY OR BEFORE DINNER, WITH THE TARTAR SAUCE OFFERED AS A DIP.

MAKES NINE

INGREDIENTS

   1½ pounds monkfish tail, filleted, skinned and membrane removed
   1 bunch thick scallions
   5 tablespoons olive oil
   1 garlic clove, finely chopped
   1 tablespoon lemon juice
   1 teaspoon dried oregano
   2 tablespoons chopped fresh flat-leaf parsley
   12–18 small scallops or large shrimp
   1½ cups fine fresh bread crumbs
   salt and ground black pepper
For the tartar sauce
   2 egg yolks
   1¼ cups olive oil, or vegetable oil and olive oil mixed
   1–2 tablespoons lemon juice
   1 teaspoon French mustard, preferably tarragon mustard
   1 tablespoon chopped gherkin or pickled cucumber
   1 tablespoon chopped capers
   2 tablespoons chopped fresh flat-leaf parsley
   2 tablespoons snipped fresh chives
   1 teaspoon chopped fresh tarragon

2 Whisk in 1 tablespoon lemon juice, then a little more oil. Stir in all the mustard, gherkin or cucumber, capers, parsley, chives and tarragon. Add more lemon juice and seasoning to taste.

4 Mix the bread crumbs and remaining parsley. Toss the seafood and scallions in the mixture to coat. Soak 9 bamboo skewers in cold water.

1 First, make the tartar sauce. Whisk the egg yolks and a pinch of salt. Whisk in the oil, a drop at a time at first. When about half the oil is incorporated, add it in a thin stream, whisking constantly. Stop when the mayonnaise is very thick.

3 Cut the monkfish into 18 pieces and cut the scallions into 18 pieces about 2–2½ inches long. Mix the oil, garlic, lemon juice, oregano and half the parsley with seasoning. Add the monkfish, scallops or shrimp and scallions, then marinate for 15 minutes.

5 Preheat the broiler. Drain the skewers and thread the monkfish, scallops or shrimp and scallions onto them. Drizzle with a little marinade, then broil for 5–6 minutes, turning once and drizzling on the marinade, until the fish is just cooked. Serve immediately with the tartar sauce.

MARINATED RED MULLET <u>WITH</u> ONION, BELL PEPPER <u>AND</u> EGGPLANT

SNAPPER, SEA BREAM OR TILAPIA ARE ALL GOOD ALTERNATIVES TO MULLET IN THIS RECIPE, BASED ON A SPANISH WAY OF COOKING FISH EN ESCABECHE *BY FIRST FRYING IT, THEN MARINATING IT.*

SERVES SIX

INGREDIENTS
- 1½ teaspoons mild Spanish paprika, preferably Spanish smoked *pimentón*
- 3 tablespoons all-purpose flour
- ½ cup olive oil
- 6 red mullet, each weighing about 11 ounces, filleted
- 2 eggplant, sliced or cut into long wedges
- 2 red or yellow bell peppers, seeded and thickly sliced
- 1 large red onion, thinly sliced
- 2 garlic cloves, sliced
- 1 tablespoon sherry vinegar
- juice of 1 lemon
- brown sugar, to taste
- 1 tablespoon chopped fresh oregano
- 18–24 black olives
- 3 tablespoons chopped fresh flat-leaf parsley
- salt and ground black pepper

3 Add another 2 tablespoons oil to the pan and cook the peppers and onion gently for 6–8 minutes, until softened but not browned. Add the garlic and remaining paprika, then cook for another 2 minutes. Stir in the sherry vinegar and lemon juice with 2 tablespoons water and heat until simmering. Season to taste with a pinch of sugar.

4 Stir in the oregano and olives, then spoon onto the fish. Set aside to cool, then cover and marinate in the refrigerator for several hours or overnight.

5 About 30 minutes before serving, bring the fish and vegetables back to room temperature. Stir in the parsley just before serving.

1 Mix 1 teaspoon of the paprika with the flour and season well with salt and pepper. Heat half the oil in a large frying pan. Dip the fish into the flour, turning to coat both sides, and fry for 4–5 minutes, until browned on each side. Place the fish in a glass or china dish suitable for marinating it.

2 Add 2 tablespoons of the remaining oil to the pan and fry the eggplant until softened and browned. Drain on paper towels and add to the fish.

BROILED SOLE WITH CHIVE AND LEMONGRASS BUTTER

CHIVES ARE AT THEIR BEST WHEN BARELY COOKED, AND THEY MAKE A DELICIOUS BUTTER TO SERVE WITH SIMPLE BROILED FISH. SOLE IS THE IDEAL CHOICE, BUT HALIBUT, TURBOT AND SWORDFISH ARE ALSO GOOD. SERVE WITH STEAMED NEW POTATOES AND A SIMPLE VEGETABLE ACCOMPANIMENT.

SERVES FOUR

INGREDIENTS
- ½ cup unsalted butter, softened, plus extra melted butter
- 1 teaspoon minced lemongrass
- pinch of finely grated lime zest
- 1 kaffir lime leaf, very finely shredded (optional)
- 3 tablespoons snipped chives or chopped chive flowers, plus extra chives or chive flowers to garnish
- ½–1 teaspoon Thai fish sauce
- 4 sole, skinned
- salt and ground black pepper
- lemon or lime wedges, to serve

COOK'S TIP
Finer white fish fillets, such as plaice, can be cooked in this way, but reduce the cooking time slightly.

1 Cream the butter with the lemongrass, lime zest, lime leaf, if using, and chives or chive flowers. Season to taste with Thai fish sauce, salt and pepper.

2 Chill the butter mixture to firm it for a short while, then form it into a roll and wrap in aluminum foil, plastic wrap or waxed paper. Chill until firm. Preheat the broiler.

3 Brush the fish with a little melted butter. Place it on a broiler pan and season. Broil for about 5 minutes on each side, until firm and just cooked. Meanwhile, cut the chilled butter into thin slices. Serve the fish topped with slices of the butter. Serve immediately, garnished with chives. Pass lemon or lime wedges with the fish.

SEARED TUNA STEAKS WITH RED ONION SALSA

RED ONIONS ARE IDEAL FOR THIS SALSA, NOT ONLY FOR THEIR MILD AND SWEET FLAVOR, BUT ALSO BECAUSE THEY LOOK SO APPETIZING. SALAD, RICE OR BREAD AND A BOWL OF THICK YOGURT FLAVORED WITH CHOPPED FRESH HERBS ARE GOOD ACCOMPANIMENTS.

SERVES FOUR

INGREDIENTS

4 tuna steaks, each weighing about
  6–7 ounces
1 teaspoon cumin seeds, toasted
  and crushed
pinch of dried red chile flakes
grated zest and juice of 1 lime
2–4 tablespoons extra virgin
  olive oil
salt and ground black pepper
lime wedges and cilantro sprigs, to
  garnish
For the salsa
1 small red onion,
  finely chopped
7 ounces red or yellow cherry
  tomatoes, roughly chopped
1 avocado, peeled, pitted
  and chopped
2 kiwi fruit, peeled and chopped
1 fresh red chile, seeded and
  finely chopped
½ ounce cilantro, chopped
6 fresh mint sprigs, leaves
  only, chopped
1–2 teaspoons Thai fish sauce
  (*nam pla*)
about 1 teaspoon brown sugar

1 Wash the tuna steaks and pat dry. Sprinkle with half the cumin, the dried chile, salt, pepper and half the lime zest. Rub in 2 tablespoons of the oil and set aside in a glass or china dish for about 30 minutes.

2 Meanwhile, make the salsa. Mix the onion, tomatoes, avocado, kiwi fruit, fresh chile, chopped cilantro and mint. Add the remaining cumin, the rest of the lime zest and half the lime juice. Add Thai fish sauce and sugar to taste. Set aside for 15–20 minutes, then add more Thai fish sauce, lime juice and olive oil if desired.

3 Heat a ridged, cast iron grill pan. Cook the tuna, allowing about 2 minutes on each side for rare tuna or a little longer for medium.

4 Serve the tuna steaks garnished with lime wedges and cilantro sprigs. Serve the salsa separately or spoon onto the plates with the tuna.

PISSALADIÈRE

THIS FAMOUS ONION AND ANCHOVY DISH IS A TRADITIONAL MARKET FOOD IN NICE IN SOUTHERN FRANCE. IT CAN BE MADE USING EITHER SHORTCRUST PASTRY OR, AS HERE, YEASTED DOUGH, SIMILAR TO A PIZZA CRUST. EITHER WAY, IT IS MOST DELICIOUS EATEN LUKEWARM RATHER THAN PIPING HOT.

SERVES SIX

INGREDIENTS
2¼ cups all-purpose flour, plus extra
   for dusting
⅓ cup fine polenta or semolina
1 teaspoon salt
¾ cup lukewarm water
1 teaspoon active dry yeast
1 teaspoon sugar
2 tablespoons extra virgin olive oil
For the topping
4–5 tablespoons extra virgin
   olive oil
6 large sweet Spanish onions,
   thinly sliced
2 large garlic cloves, thinly sliced
1 teaspoon chopped fresh thyme,
   plus several sprigs
1 fresh rosemary sprig
1–2 2-ounce cans anchovies in
   olive oil
2–3 ounces small black olives,
   preferably small Niçoise olives
salt and ground black pepper

1 Mix the flour, polenta or semolina and salt in a large mixing bowl. Pour half the water into a bowl. Add the yeast and sugar, then set in a warm place for 10 minutes, until frothy. Pour the yeast mixture into the flour mixture with the remaining water and the olive oil.

2 Using your hands, mix all the ingredients together to form a dough, then turn out and knead for 5 minutes, until smooth, springy and elastic.

3 Return the dough to the clean, floured bowl and place it in a plastic bag or cover with oiled plastic wrap, then set the dough aside at room temperature for 30–60 minutes to rise and double in bulk.

4 Meanwhile, start to prepare the topping. Heat 3 tablespoons of the olive oil in a large, heavy saucepan and add the sliced onions. Stir well to coat the onions in the oil, then cover the pan and cook over very low heat, stirring occasionally, for 20-30 minutes. (Use a heat-diffuser mat to keep the heat low, if possible.)

5 Add a little salt to taste and the garlic, chopped thyme and rosemary sprig. Stir well and continue cooking for another 15–25 minutes or until the onions are soft and deep golden yellow but not browned at all. Uncover the pan for the last 5–10 minutes if the onions seem very wet. Remove and discard the rosemary. Set the onions aside to cool.

6 Preheat the oven to 425°F. Roll out the dough thinly and use to line a large baking sheet, about 12 × 9–10 inches. Taste the onions for seasoning before spreading them on the dough.

7 Drain the anchovies, cut them in half lengthwise and arrange them in a lattice pattern on the onions. Sprinkle the olives and thyme sprigs on top of the pissaladière and drizzle on the remaining olive oil. Bake for about 20–25 minutes or until the dough is browned and cooked. Season with pepper and serve warm, cut into slices.

VARIATIONS
• Shortcrust pastry can be used instead of yeast dough: bake it blind for 10–15 minutes before adding the filling.
• If you enjoy anchovies, try spreading about 4 tablespoons anchovy purée (*anchoïade*) on the crust before adding the onions. Alternatively, spread black olive paste on the crust.

JANSSON'S TEMPTATION

A TRADITIONAL SWEDISH FAVORITE, THIS RICH GRATIN IS DELICIOUS. AS FOOD WRITER JANE GRIGSON POINTED OUT, THE NAME PROBABLY DOES NOT REFER TO A SPECIFIC JANSSON BUT MEANS "EVERYONE'S TEMPTATION," AS JANSSON IS A COMMON SWEDISH SURNAME.

SERVES FOUR TO SIX

INGREDIENTS
¼ cup butter
2 pounds potatoes (preferably Estima or Desirée)
2 large sweet Spanish onions, sliced
2 2-ounce cans anchovies in olive oil, drained
scant 2 cups whipping cream
a little milk (optional)
salt and ground black pepper

2 Using a sharp knife, carefully cut the potatoes into fine matchstick strips.

3 Toss the potato strips with salt and freshly ground black pepper and put half of them in the prepared ovenproof dish.

1 Preheat the oven to 400°F. Use 1 tablespoon of the butter to grease a 6¼-cup ovenproof dish.

4 Lay half of the onions on top of the potatoes, season with black pepper and dot with butter. Lay the anchovies on top of the onions, then add the rest of the sliced onions and top with the remaining potatoes.

5 Mix the cream with 2 tablespoons cold water and pour this on the potatoes. Add a little milk, if necessary, to bring the liquid to just below the top of the final layer of potatoes.

6 Dot the potatoes with the remaining butter, then cover with aluminum foil and bake for 1 hour.

7 Reduce the heat to 350°F and uncover the dish. Bake for another 40–50 minutes or until the potatoes are tender and brown.

COOK'S TIPS
• Cover the gratin with aluminum foil for the first half of cooking so that the potatoes don't brown or dry out too much. If using whole, salted anchovies they will need to be boned. If they are very salty, soak in a little milk for 30 minutes before using.
• Serve with small glasses of chilled schnapps and cold beer for an authentic Swedish flavor.

BAKED MONKFISH WITH POTATOES AND GARLIC

THIS SIMPLE SUPPER DISH CAN BE MADE WITH OTHER FISH. TARTAR SAUCE OR A THICK VINAIGRETTE FLAVORED WITH CHOPPED GHERKINS AND HARD-BOILED EGG ARE DELICIOUS ACCOMPANIMENTS.

SERVES FOUR

INGREDIENTS
  2¼ pounds waxy potatoes, cut
    into chunks
  ¼ cup butter
  2 onions, thickly sliced
  4 garlic cloves
  few fresh thyme sprigs
  2–3 fresh bay leaves
  scant 2 cups vegetable or fish stock,
    plus 3 tablespoons
  2 pounds monkfish tail
    in one piece, skin and
    membrane removed
  2–3 tablespoons white wine
  1 cup fresh white bread crumbs
  ½ ounce fresh parsley,
    chopped
  1 tablespoon olive oil
  salt and ground black pepper

1 Preheat the oven to 375°F. Put the chunks of potato in an ovenproof dish. Melt half the butter in a large frying pan and cook the onions gently for 5–6 minutes. Add the onions to the potatoes and mix.

2 Slice 2–3 of the garlic cloves and add to the potatoes with the thyme and bay leaves, and season with salt and freshly ground black pepper.

3 Pour the main batch of stock onto the potatoes and bake, stirring once or twice, for 50–60 minutes, until the potatoes are just tender.

4 Nestle the monkfish into the potatoes and season with salt and pepper. Bake for 10–15 minutes. Mix the 3 tablespoons stock with the wine and use to baste the monkfish 2–3 times during cooking.

5 Finely chop the remaining garlic. Melt the remaining butter and toss it with the bread crumbs, chopped garlic, most of the chopped parsley and seasoning. Spoon onto the monkfish, pressing down gently with the back of a spoon.

6 Drizzle the olive oil on the crumb-covered fish, return the dish to the oven and bake for a final 10–15 minutes, until the bread crumbs are crisp and golden and all the liquid has been absorbed. Sprinkle the remaining parsley on the potatoes and serve immediately.

SALMON EN PAPILLOTE <u>WITH</u> LEEKS <u>AND</u> YELLOW BELL PEPPERS

COOKING FISH "EN PAPILLOTE" MAKES A LOT OF SENSE, ENSURING THAT THE FISH RETAINS ITS FLAVOR WHILE IT COOKS IN ITS STEAMY PARCEL WITH AROMATIC INGREDIENTS SUCH AS LEEKS AND HERBS. IT IS ALSO EXCELLENT WHEN ENTERTAINING, AS THE PARCELS MAY BE PREPARED AHEAD OF COOKING.

<u>SERVES SIX</u>

INGREDIENTS

  1½ tablespoons peanut oil
  2 yellow bell peppers, seeded and
    thinly sliced
  1½-inch piece fresh ginger root,
    peeled and finely shredded
  1 large fennel bulb, finely sliced,
    feathery tops chopped and reserved
  1 green chile, seeded and
    finely shredded
  2 large leeks, cut into 4-inch lengths
    and shredded lengthwise
  2 tablespoons snipped chives
  2 teaspoons light soy sauce
  6 portions salmon fillet, each
    weighing 5–6 ounces, skinned
  2 teaspoons toasted sesame oil
  salt and ground black pepper

1 Heat the oil in a large nonstick frying pan and cook the peppers, ginger and fennel for 5–6 minutes, until they are softened but not browned. Add the chile and leeks and cook for another 2–3 minutes. Stir in half the chives and the soy sauce with seasoning to taste. Set aside to cool.

2 Preheat the oven to 375°F. Cut 14-inch circles of baking parchment or aluminum foil. Divide the vegetable mixture between the 6 circles and place a portion of salmon on each pile of vegetables. Drizzle with sesame oil and sprinkle with the remaining chives and the chopped fennel tops. Season with salt and pepper.

3 Fold the paper or foil over to enclose the fish, rolling and twisting the edges together to seal the parcels. Place the parcels on a baking sheet and bake for 15–20 minutes, until the parcels are puffed up and, if made with paper, lightly browned. Transfer the parcels to warmed individual plates and serve immediately.

BACON-WRAPPED TROUT WITH OATMEAL AND ONION STUFFING

THIS STUFFING IS BASED ON A SCOTTISH SPECIALTY, A MIXTURE OF OATMEAL AND ONIONS CALLED SKIRLIE. HERRING CAN BE COOKED IN THE SAME WAY. THIS IS VERY GOOD WITH SLICES OF COOKED POTATOES, BRUSHED WITH OLIVE OIL AND BROILED UNTIL GOLDEN ON EACH SIDE.

SERVES FOUR

INGREDIENTS
   10 strips bacon
   3 tablespoons butter or bacon fat
   1 onion, finely chopped
   1 cup oatmeal
   2 tablespoons chopped fresh parsley
   2 tablespoons snipped fresh chives
   4 trout, about 12 ounces each,
      gutted and boned
   juice of ½ lemon
   salt and ground black pepper
   watercress, cherry tomatoes and
   lemon wedges, to serve
For the herb mayonnaise
   6 watercress sprigs
   1 tablespoon snipped fresh chives
   2 tablespoons roughly chopped
      parsley
   6 tablespoons lemon mayonnaise
   2 tablespoons fromage frais or
      crème fraîche
   ½–1 teaspoon tarragon mustard

3 Wash and dry the trout, then stuff with the oatmeal mixture. Wrap each fish in 2 strips of bacon and place in an ovenproof dish. Dot with the remaining butter and sprinkle with the lemon juice. Bake for 20–25 minutes, until the bacon browns and crisps a little.

4 Meanwhile, make the mayonnaise. Place the watercress, chives and parsley in a sieve and pour boiling water on them. Drain, rinse under cold water, and drain well on paper towels.

5 Purée the herbs in a mortar with a pestle. (This is easier than using a food processor for this small amount.) Stir the puréed herbs into the lemon mayonnaise together with the fromage frais or crème fraîche. Add tarragon mustard to taste and stir to combine.

6 When cooked, transfer the trout to warmed serving plates and serve immediately with watercress, tomatoes and lemon wedges, accompanied by the herb mayonnaise.

1 Preheat oven to 375°F. Chop 2 of the bacon strips. Melt 2 tablespoons of the butter or bacon fat in a large frying pan and cook the bacon briefly. Add the finely chopped onion and fry gently for 5–8 minutes, until softened.

2 Add the oatmeal and cook until the oatmeal darkens and absorbs the fat, but do not let it overbrown. Stir in the parsley, chives and seasoning. Cool.

SEARED SCALLOPS WITH CHIVE SAUCE ON LEEK AND CARROT RICE

SCALLOPS ARE ONE OF THE MOST DELICIOUS SHELLFISH. HERE THEY ARE PARTNERED WITH A DELICATE CHIVE SAUCE AND A PILAF OF WILD AND WHITE RICE WITH SWEET LEEKS AND CARROTS.

SERVES FOUR

INGREDIENTS

- 12–16 shelled scallops
- 3 tablespoons olive oil
- ⅓ cup wild rice
- 5 tablespoons butter
- 4 carrots, cut into long thin strips
- 2 leeks, cut into thick, diagonal slices
- 1 small onion, finely chopped
- ⅔ cup long-grain rice
- 1 fresh bay leaf
- scant 1 cup white wine
- scant 2 cups fish stock
- 4 tablespoons heavy cream
- a little lemon juice
- 5 teaspoons snipped fresh chives
- 2 tablespoons chervil sprigs
- salt and ground black pepper

1 Lightly season the scallops, brush with 1 tablespoon of the olive oil and set aside.

2 Cook the wild rice in plenty of boiling water for about 30 minutes, until tender, then drain.

3 Melt half the butter in a small frying pan and cook the carrots fairly gently for 4–5 minutes. Add the leeks and fry for another 2 minutes. Season with salt and pepper and add 2–3 tablespoons water, then cover and cook for a few more minutes. Uncover and cook until the liquid has reduced. Set aside off the heat.

4 Melt half the rest of the butter with 1 tablespoon of the remaining oil in a heavy saucepan. Add the onion and fry for 3–4 minutes, until softened but not browned.

5 Add the long-grain rice and bay leaf and cook, stirring constantly, until the rice looks translucent and the grains are coated with oil.

6 Pour in half the wine and half the stock. Season with ½ teaspoon salt and bring to a boil. Stir, then cover and cook very gently for 15 minutes or until the liquid is absorbed and the rice is cooked and tender.

7 Reheat the carrots and leeks gently, then stir them into the long-grain rice with the wild rice. Add seasoning to taste, if necessary.

8 Meanwhile, pour the remaining wine and stock into a small saucepan and boil rapidly until reduced by half.

COOK'S TIP

Choose fresh, rather than frozen, scallops as the frozen ones tend to exude water on cooking. Scallops need only the briefest cooking at high heat, just until they turn opaque and brown on each side, so have the pan very hot. Although some people avoid eating the orange-colored coral, it is delicious and many people consider it to be the best bit.

9 Heat a heavy frying pan over high heat. Add the remaining butter and oil. Sear the scallops for 1–2 minutes on each side, then set aside and keep warm.

10 Pour the reduced stock into the pan and heat until bubbling, then add the cream and boil until thickened. Season with lemon juice, salt and pepper. Stir in the chives and scallops.

11 Stir the chervil into the rice and pile it on plates. Arrange the scallops on top and spoon the sauce on the rice.

CHINESE-STYLE STEAMED FISH

THIS IS A CLASSIC CHINESE WAY OF COOKING WHOLE FISH, WITH GARLIC, SCALLIONS, GINGER AND BLACK BEANS. THE FISH MAKES A SPLENDID CENTERPIECE FOR A CHINESE MEAL OR IT CAN BE SERVED MORE SIMPLY, WITH BOILED RICE AND SOME STIR-FRIED CHINESE GREENS.

SERVES FOUR TO SIX

INGREDIENTS

   2 sea bass, grey mullet or trout, each
      weighing about 1½–1¾ pounds
   1½ tablespoons salted black beans
   ½ teaspoon sugar
   2 tablespoons finely shredded
      fresh ginger root
   4 garlic cloves, thinly sliced
   2 tablespoons Chinese rice wine or
      dry sherry
   2 tablespoons light soy sauce
   4–6 scallions, finely shredded or
      sliced diagonally
   3 tablespoons peanut oil
   2 teaspoons sesame oil

1 Wash the fish inside and out under cold running water, then pat them dry on paper towels. Using a sharp knife, slash 3–4 deep cross shapes on each side of each fish.

2 Mash half the black beans with the sugar in a small bowl and then stir in the remaining whole beans.

3 Place a little ginger and garlic inside the cavity of each fish and then lay them on a plate or dish that will fit inside a large steamer. Rub the bean mixture into the fish, especially into the slashes, then sprinkle the remaining ginger and garlic on top. Cover and chill for 30 minutes.

4 Place the steamer over a pan of boiling water. Sprinkle the rice wine or sherry and half the soy sauce on the fish and steam them for 15–20 minutes or until just cooked.

5 Sprinkle the remaining soy sauce and scallions on the fish.

6 In a small saucepan, heat the peanut oil until smoking, then trickle it on the scallions. Sprinkle with the sesame oil and serve immediately.

SEAFOOD LAKSA

A LAKSA IS A MALAYSIAN STEW OF FISH, POULTRY, MEAT OR VEGETABLES WITH NOODLES. AUTHENTIC LAKSAS ARE OFTEN VERY HOT AND ARE COOLED BY THE COCONUT MILK AND THE NOODLES. IF YOU PREFER A SPICY VERSION, ADD A LITTLE CHILI POWDER INSTEAD OF SOME OF THE PAPRIKA.

SERVES FOUR TO FIVE

INGREDIENTS
    3 medium-hot fresh red
      chiles, seeded
    4–5 garlic cloves
    1 teaspoon mild paprika
    2 teaspoons fermented shrimp
      paste (*trassi*)
    1½ tablespoons chopped fresh ginger
      root or galangal
    9 ounces small red shallots
    1 ounce cilantro (preferably with
      roots)
    3 tablespoons peanut oil
    1 teaspoon fennel seeds, crushed
    2 fennel bulbs, cut into thin wedges
    2½ cups fish stock
    11 ounces thin vermicelli
      rice noodles
    scant 2 cups coconut milk
    juice of 1–2 limes
    2–3 tablespoons Thai fish sauce
      (*nam pla*)
    1 pound firm white fish fillet, such
      as monkfish, halibut or snapper
    1 pound large shrimp (about 20),
      shelled and deveined
    small bunch of fresh holy basil or
      ordinary basil
    2 scallions, thinly sliced

1 Process the chiles, garlic, paprika, shrimp paste, ginger or galangal and 2 shallots into a paste in a food processor, blender or spice grinder. Remove the roots and stems from the cilantro and add them to the paste; chop and reserve the cilantro leaves. Add 1 tablespoon of the oil to the paste and process again until fairly smooth.

2 Heat the remaining oil in a large saucepan. Add the remaining shallots, the fennel seeds and fennel wedges. Cook until lightly browned, then add 3 tablespoons of the paste and stir-fry for 1–2 minutes. Pour in the fish stock and bring to a boil. Reduce the heat and simmer for 8–10 minutes.

3 Meanwhile, cook the vermicelli rice noodles according to the package instructions. Drain and set aside.

4 Add the coconut milk and the juice of 1 lime to the pan of shallots. Stir in 2 tablespoons of the fish sauce. Bring to a simmer and taste, adding a little more spice paste, lime juice or fish sauce as necessary.

5 Cut the fish into chunks and add to the pan. Cook for 2–3 minutes, then add the shrimp and cook until they turn pink. Chop most of the basil and add to the pan with the reserved cilantro.

6 Divide the noodles among 4–5 wide bowls, then ladle in the stew. Sprinkle with scallions and the remaining whole basil leaves. Serve immediately.

We add onions to marinades, to stews and casseroles, to roasts and braises, and we cook them in countless ways to accompany simply cooked meat or poultry. Certain classics stand out: lamb studded with garlic, steak topped with deep-fried onions and the Cantonese mixture of garlic, black beans and scallions with beef. Imagine liver without onions, Thai curries without garlic or sausages and mashed potatoes without onion gravy. In fact, it is hard to think of many meat and poultry recipes in which onions aren't an essential ingredient.

Meat and Poultry

GIGOT BOULANGÈRE

LAMB COOKED IN THE STYLE OF THE BAKER'S WIFE (LA BOULANGÈRE) IS A CLASSIC OF FRENCH PROVINCIAL COOKING. ONE OF THE BEST-KNOWN AND BEST-LOVED PAIRINGS OF LAMB AND GARLIC, THIS IS A TROUBLE-FREE AND DELICIOUS CHOICE FOR SUNDAY LUNCH.

4 Pour in the hot stock and add a little hot water, if necessary, to bring the liquid to just below the level of the potatoes. Dot with the remaining butter, cover them with aluminum foil and cook in the oven for 40 minutes. Increase the oven temperature to 400°F.

5 Meanwhile, cut the rest of the garlic into slivers. Make slits all over the lamb with a narrow, sharp knife and insert slivers of garlic and sprigs of thyme or rosemary into the slits. Season the lamb well with salt and pepper.

6 Uncover the potatoes and scatter a few rosemary or thyme sprigs over them. Rest a roasting rack or ovenproof cooling rack over the dish and place the lamb on it. Rub the olive oil on the meat, then return the dish to the oven. Cook, turning the lamb once or twice, for 1½–1¾ hours, depending on how well done you prefer lamb. Let the lamb rest for 20 minutes in a warm place (in the switched-off oven, for example) before carving.

SERVES SIX

INGREDIENTS

¼ cup butter, plus extra
  for greasing
4–6 garlic cloves
2 yellow onions, thinly sliced
12–18 small fresh thyme or
  rosemary sprigs
2 fresh bay leaves
4 pounds red potatoes, thinly sliced
scant 2 cups hot lamb or
  vegetable stock
4½-pound leg of lamb
2 tablespoons olive oil
salt and ground black pepper

1 Preheat the oven to 375°F. Use a little butter to grease a large ovenproof dish, about 2½ inches deep. Finely chop half the garlic and sprinkle a little on the prepared dish.

2 Fry the onions in 2 tablespoons of the butter for 5–8 minutes, until softened. Roughly chop half the thyme or rosemary and crush the bay leaves.

3 Arrange a layer of potatoes in the dish, season and sprinkle with half the remaining chopped garlic, rosemary or thyme, 1 bay leaf and the onions. Add the remaining potatoes, chopped garlic and herbs.

LAMB BURGERS <u>WITH</u> RED ONION <u>AND</u> TOMATO RELISH

A SHARP-SWEET RED ONION RELISH WORKS WELL WITH BURGERS BASED ON MIDDLE-EASTERN STYLE LAMB. SERVE WITH PITA BREAD AND TABBOULEH OR WITH FRIES AND A CRISP GREEN SALAD.

SERVES FOUR

INGREDIENTS

3 tablespoons bulghur wheat
1¼ pounds lean ground lamb
1 small red onion, finely chopped
2 garlic cloves, finely chopped
1 green chile, seeded and
 finely chopped
1 teaspoon ground toasted
 cumin seeds
½ teaspoon ground sumac
½ ounce chopped fresh
 flat-leaf parsley
2 tablespoons chopped fresh mint
olive oil, for frying
salt and ground black pepper
For the relish
2 red bell peppers, halved and seeded
2 red onions, cut into ¼-inch
 thick slices
5–6 tablespoons extra virgin olive oil
12 ounces cherry tomatoes, chopped
½–1 fresh red or green chile, seeded
 and finely chopped (optional)
2 tablespoons chopped fresh mint
2 tablespoons chopped fresh parsley
1 tablespoon chopped fresh oregano
 or marjoram
½–1 teaspoon each ground toasted
 cumin seeds
½–1 teaspoon sumac
juice of ½ lemon
sugar, to taste

1 Pour ⅔ cup hot water on the bulghur wheat in a bowl and let stand for 15 minutes, then drain in a sieve and squeeze out the excess moisture.

2 Place the bulghur in a bowl and add the lamb, onion, garlic, chile, cumin, sumac, parsley and mint. Mix the ingredients thoroughly by hand, then season with 1 teaspoon salt and plenty of black pepper and mix again. Form the mixture into 8 small burgers and set aside while you make the relish.

3 Broil the peppers, skin side up, until the skin chars and blisters. Place in a bowl, cover and let stand for 10 minutes. Peel off the skin, dice the peppers finely and place in a bowl.

4 Brush the onions with 1 tablespoon oil and broil for 5 minutes on each side, until browned. Cool, then chop.

5 Add the onions, tomatoes and chile to taste, the mint, parsley, oregano or marjoram and ½ teaspoon each of the cumin and sumac to the peppers. Stir in 4 tablespoons of the remaining oil and 1 tablespoon of the lemon juice. Season with salt, pepper and sugar and let stand for 20–30 minutes.

6 Heat a heavy frying pan or a ridged, cast-iron grill pan over high heat and grease lightly with olive oil. Cook the burgers for 5–6 minutes on each side or until just cooked in the center.

7 While the burgers are cooking, taste the relish and adjust the seasoning, adding more salt, pepper, sugar, oil, chile, cumin, sumac and lemon juice to taste. Serve the burgers immediately as they are cooked, with the relish.

Lamb Stew <u>with</u> Baby Onions <u>and</u> New Potatoes

This fresh lemon-seasoned stew is finished with an Italian mixture of chopped garlic, parsley and lemon zest known as gremolata, the traditional topping for osso bucco.

SERVES SIX

INGREDIENTS

   2¼ pounds boneless shoulder of
     lamb, trimmed of fat and cut into
     2-inch cubes
   1 garlic clove, finely chopped
   finely grated zest of ½ lemon and
     juice of 1 lemon
   6 tablespoons olive oil
   3 tablespoons all-purpose flour
   1 large onion, sliced
   5 anchovy fillets in olive oil,
     drained
   ½ teaspoon sugar
   1¼ cups fruity white wine
   2 cups lamb stock or half stock and
     half water
   1 fresh bay leaf
   fresh thyme sprig
   fresh parsley sprig
   1¼ pounds small new potatoes
   9 ounces shallots, peeled but
     left whole
   3 tablespoons heavy cream (optional)
   salt and ground black pepper
For the gremolata
   1 garlic clove, finely chopped
   finely shredded zest of ½ lemon
   3 tablespoons chopped fresh
     flat-leaf parsley

1 Mix the lamb with the garlic and the zest and juice of ½ lemon. Season with pepper and mix in 1 tablespoon olive oil, then let marinate for 12–24 hours.

2 Drain the lamb, reserving the marinade, and pat the lamb dry with paper towels. Preheat the oven to 350°F.

COOK'S TIP

A mezzaluna (double-handled, half-moon shaped, curved chopping blade) makes a very good job of chopping gremolata ingredients. If using a food processor or electric chopper, take care not to overprocess the mixture as it is easy to grind the ingredients into a paste.

3 Heat 2 tablespoons olive oil in a large, heavy frying pan. Season the flour with salt and pepper and toss the lamb in it to coat, shaking off any excess. Seal the lamb on all sides in the hot oil. Do this in batches, transferring each batch of lamb to an ovenproof saucepan or a flameproof casserole as you brown it. You may need to add an extra 1 tablespoon olive oil to the pan.

4 Reduce the heat, add another 1 tablespoon oil to the pan and cook the onion gently over very low heat, stirring frequently, for 10 minutes, until softened and golden but not browned. Add the anchovies and sugar and cook, mashing the anchovies into the soft onion with a wooden spoon.

5 Add the reserved marinade, increase the heat a little and cook for 1–2 minutes, then pour in the wine and stock or stock and water, and bring to a boil. Simmer gently for about 5 minutes, then pour onto the lamb.

6 Tie the bay leaf, thyme and parsley together and add to the lamb. Season with salt and pepper, then cover tightly and cook for 1 hour. Stir the potatoes into the casserole and cook for another 20 minutes.

7 Meanwhile, to make the gremolata, chop all the ingredients together finely. Place in a dish, cover and set aside.

8 Heat the remaining oil in a frying pan and brown the shallots on all sides, then stir them into the lamb. Cover and cook for another 30–40 minutes, until the lamb is tender. Transfer the lamb and vegetables to a dish and keep warm. Discard the herbs.

9 Boil the cooking juices to reduce and concentrate them, then add the cream, if using, and simmer for 2–3 minutes. Adjust the seasoning, adding a little lemon juice to taste. Pour this sauce on the lamb, scatter the gremolata on top and serve immediately.

LAMB SMOTHERED IN ONIONS AND NORTH AFRICAN SPICES

THIS IS A WONDERFUL WAY OF COOKING A LEG OR SHOULDER OF LAMB, FIRST BY MARINATING IT IN YOGURT WITH NORTH AFRICAN SPICES, THEN BY COVERING WITH SLICED ONIONS AND POT-ROASTING. SERVE A COUSCOUS PILAF AND YOGURT FLAVORED WITH GARLIC AS ACCOMPANIMENTS.

SERVES SIX

INGREDIENTS
    4½-pound leg or shoulder of lamb
    2 tablespoons olive oil
    2 large onions, halved and
        thinly sliced
    3 fresh bay leaves
    1¼ cups water
    1¼ pounds prepared butternut or
        onion squash, peeled, seeded and
        cut into thick chunks or wedges
    2–3 green or red bell peppers,
        seeded and cut into thick slices
    chopped cilantro, to serve
For the spice paste
    1 tablespoon cumin seeds
    1 tablespoon coriander seeds
    1-inch piece cinnamon stick
    1½ teaspoons paprika
    good pinch of saffron threads
    1 green chile, seeded and chopped
    2 garlic cloves, chopped
    ½ ounce cilantro, chopped
    2 tablespoons fresh mint, chopped
    3 tablespoons extra virgin olive oil
    grated zest and juice of 1 lemon
    1 cup plain yogurt
    salt and ground black pepper

1 First prepare the spice paste. Set
1 teaspoon each of the cumin and
coriander seeds aside and toast the
remainder separately in a small dry pan
until they are aromatic. Take care not to
overcook the spices or cook them too
quickly or they will taste bitter.

2 Grind the toasted spices with the
cinnamon in a spice or coffee grinder.
Then process them with all the paste
ingredients, other than the yogurt, in a
food processor or blender to make a
paste. Season with salt and pepper.

3 Use a sharp knife to make deep slits
all over the lamb, then rub the spice
paste all over, forcing it into the slits.
Place the lamb in a roasting pan and
rub the yogurt all over. Cover and
marinate for several hours, preferably
overnight, turning once or twice.

4 Preheat the oven to 350°F. Scrape
the marinade off the meat and reserve.
Heat a large roasting pan and brown the
lamb all over. Remove it and set aside.
Add the oil and cook the onions for
6–8 minutes, until softened. Coarsely
grind the reserved coriander and cumin
seeds, add to the onions and cook for
2–3 minutes. Transfer the onions to
a plate.

5 Add the marinade to the pan with the
bay leaves and water. Bring to a boil.
Return the lamb to the pan and turn it
in the liquid. Cover with the onions, then
cover the dish tightly with aluminum foil
and cook for 1¾–2 hours, until tender.
Baste the lamb occasionally and add a
little more water if the dish seems dry.
Remove the lamb and onions, cover
and keep warm. Increase the oven
temperature to 400°F.

6 Add the squash and peppers to the
pan and toss in the lamb juices. Roast,
uncovered, for 30–35 minutes, stirring
once or twice, until the squash is tender.
Return the lamb for the last 15 minutes.

7 Transfer the lamb and vegetables to
a warmed serving dish and sprinkle on
the cilantro. Serve immediately, cut into
thick slices.

GARLIC <u>AND</u> CHILI MARINATED BEEF <u>WITH</u> CORN-CRUSTED ONION RINGS

FRUITY, SMOKY AND MILD MEXICAN CHILES COMBINE WELL WITH GARLIC IN THIS MARINADE FOR STEAK. POLENTA MAKES A CRISP COATING FOR THE ACCOMPANYING FRIED ONION RINGS.

SERVES FOUR

INGREDIENTS
¾ ounce large mild dried red chiles
(such as *mulato* or *pasilla*)
2 garlic cloves, plain or smoked,
finely chopped
1 teaspoon ground toasted
cumin seeds
1 teaspoon dried oregano
4 tablespoons olive oil
4 6–8-ounce steaks
(rump or rib-eye)
salt and ground black pepper
For the onion rings
2 onions, sliced into rings
1 cup milk
¾ cup coarse cornmeal (polenta)
½ teaspoon dried red chile flakes
1 teaspoon ground toasted
cumin seeds
1 teaspoon dried oregano
vegetable oil,
for deep-frying

3 Wash and dry the steaks, rub the chili paste all over them and let marinate for up to 12 hours.

4 For the onion rings, soak the onions in the milk for 30 minutes. Mix the cornmeal, chile, cumin and oregano and season with salt and pepper.

5 Heat the oil for deep-frying to 325–350°F or until a cube of day-old bread turns brown in about a minute.

6 Drain the onion rings and dip each one into the cornmeal mixture, coating it thoroughly. Fry for 2–4 minutes, until browned and crisp. Do not overcrowd the pan, but cook in batches. Lift the onion rings out of the pan with a slotted spoon and drain on paper towels.

7 Heat a cast-iron grill pan. Season the steaks with salt and grill for about 4 minutes on each side for medium; reduce or increase this time according to how rare or well-done you like steak. Serve the steaks with the onion rings.

1 Cut the stems from the chiles and discard the seeds. Toast the chiles in a dry frying pan for 2–4 minutes, until they give off their aroma. Place the chiles in a bowl, cover with warm water and let soak for 20–30 minutes. Drain and reserve the water.

2 Process the chiles into a paste with the garlic, cumin, oregano and oil in a food processor. Add a little soaking water, if needed. Season with pepper.

STIR-FRIED BEEF AND MUSHROOMS WITH GARLIC, BLACK BEANS AND SCALLIONS

THE COMBINATION OF GARLIC AND SALTED BLACK BEANS IS A CLASSIC CANTONESE SEASONING FOR BEEF. SERVE RICE AND SIMPLE BRAISED CHINESE GREENS AS ACCOMPANIMENTS.

SERVES FOUR

INGREDIENTS

    2 tablespoons soy sauce
    2 tablespoons Chinese rice wine or
      dry sherry
    2 teaspoons cornstarch
    2 teaspoons sesame oil
    1-pound fillet or rump steak,
      trimmed of fat
    12 dried shiitake mushrooms
      (Chinese black mushrooms)
    1½ tablespoons salted black beans
    1 teaspoon sugar
    ½ cup peanut oil
    4 garlic cloves, thinly sliced
    1-inch piece fresh ginger root, cut
      into fine strips
    7 ounces open cap
      mushrooms, sliced
    1 bunch scallions,
      sliced diagonally
    1 fresh red chile, seeded and
      finely shredded
    salt and ground black pepper

1 In a bowl large enough to hold the meat, mix half the soy sauce, half the rice wine or sherry, half the cornstarch and all the sesame oil with 1 tablespoon cold water until smooth. Add a good pinch of salt and pepper.

2 Cut the beef into very thin slices, no more than ¼ inch thick. Add the slices to the cornstarch mixture and rub the mixture into the beef with your fingers. Set aside for 30 minutes.

3 Pour boiling water onto the dried mushrooms and soak for 25 minutes. Drain, reserving 3 tablespoons of the soaking water. Remove and discard the hard stems and cut the caps in half.

4 Using a fork mash the black beans with the sugar in a small bowl. Stir the remaining cornstarch, soy sauce and rice wine or sherry together in another small bowl.

5 Heat the oil in a wok until very hot, then stir-fry the beef for 30–45 seconds, until just brown. Use a draining spoon to transfer it to a plate. Pour off some oil to leave about 3 tablespoons in the wok.

6 Add the garlic and ginger, stir-fry for 1 minute, then add the shiitake and fresh mushrooms and stir-fry for 2 minutes. Set aside a few tablespoons of the green part of the scallions, then add the rest to the wok. Stir, add the mashed black beans and stir-fry for another 1–2 minutes.

7 Stir the beef back into the mixture in the wok, then add 3 tablespoons of the shiitake soaking water. Let the mixture bubble. Stir the cornstarch mixture to mix it well, pour it into the wok, stirring, and simmer until the sauce thickens. Sprinkle the chile and reserved scallions on the beef and serve.

BEEF CARBONADE

THIS RICH, DARK STEW OF BEEF COOKED SLOWLY WITH LOTS OF ONIONS, GARLIC AND BEER IS A CLASSIC CASSEROLE FROM THE NORTH OF FRANCE AND NEIGHBORING BELGIUM.

3 Reduce the heat and return the onions to the pan. Add the garlic, cook briefly, then add the beer or ale, water and sugar. Tie the thyme and bay leaf together and add to the pan with the celery. Bring to a boil, stirring, then season with salt and pepper.

4 Pour the sauce over the beef and mix well. Cover tightly, then place in the oven for 2½ hours. Check the beef once or twice to make sure that it is not too dry, adding a little water, if necessary. Test for tenderness, allowing an extra 30–40 minutes if necessary.

SERVES SIX

INGREDIENTS
 3 tablespoons vegetable oil or
  beef dripping
 3 onions, sliced
 3 tablespoons all-purpose flour
 ½ teaspoon mustard powder
 2¼ pounds stewing beef (shin or
  chuck), cut into large cubes
 2–3 garlic cloves, finely chopped
 1¼ cups dark beer or ale
 ⅔ cup water
 1 teaspoon dark brown sugar
 1 fresh thyme sprig
 1 fresh bay leaf
 1 piece celery stalk
 salt and ground black pepper
For the topping
 ½ cup butter
 1 garlic clove, crushed
 1 tablespoon Dijon mustard
 3 tablespoons chopped fresh parsley
 6–12 slices baguette

1 Preheat the oven to 325°F. Heat 2 tablespoons of the oil or dripping in a frying pan and cook the onions over low heat until softened. Remove from the pan and set aside.

2 Meanwhile, mix the flour and mustard and season. Toss the beef in the flour. Add the remaining oil or dripping to the pan and heat over high heat. Brown the beef all over, then transfer it to a casserole.

5 To make the topping, cream the butter with the garlic, mustard and 2 tablespoons of the parsley. Spread the butter thickly on the bread. Increase the oven temperature to 375°F. Taste and season the casserole, then arrange the bread slices, buttered side facing up, on top. Bake for 20–25 minutes, until the bread is browned and crisp. Sprinkle the remaining parsley on top and serve immediately.

CALF'S LIVER WITH SLOW-COOKED ONIONS, MARSALA AND SAGE

LIVER AND ONIONS IS AN INTERNATIONAL FAVORITE, FROM BRITISH LIVER WITH ONION GRAVY TO THE FAMOUS VENETIAN DISH OF FEGATO ALLA VENEZIANA. INSPIRED BY ITALIAN COOKING, THIS DISH IS GOOD SERVED WITH POLENTA, EITHER SOFT, OR SET AND BROILED.

SERVES FOUR

INGREDIENTS

3 tablespoons olive oil, plus extra for shallow frying
2 tablespoons butter
1¼ pounds mild onions, thinly sliced
small bunch of fresh sage leaves
2 tablespoons chopped fresh parsley, plus a little extra to garnish
½ teaspoon sugar
1 tablespoon balsamic vinegar
2 tablespoons all-purpose flour
1½-pound calf's liver, thinly sliced
⅔ cup Marsala
salt and ground black pepper

1 Heat half the oil with half the butter in a large, wide, heavy saucepan and cook the onions, covered, over very low heat for 30 minutes. Stir once or twice.

2 Chop 5 of the sage leaves and add them to the pan with the parsley, a pinch of salt, the sugar and balsamic vinegar. Cook, uncovered and stirring frequently, until very tender and golden. Taste for seasoning and add salt and pepper as necessary.

3 Heat a shallow layer of olive oil in a frying pan and fry the remaining sage leaves for 15–30 seconds, then drain them on paper towels.

4 Heat the remaining butter and oil together in a frying pan over high heat. Season the flour, then dip the liver in it and fry it quickly for about 2 minutes on each side until browned but still pink in the middle. Use a draining spoon to transfer the liver to warm plates and keep warm.

5 Immediately add the Marsala to the pan and let it bubble fiercely until reduced to a few tablespoons of sticky glaze. Distribute the onions on the liver and spoon on the Marsala juices. Sprinkle on the fried sage leaves and extra parsley and serve immediately.

VARIATION
Chicken liver and onion bruschetta Cook the onions as above, replacing the sage with 1 teaspoon chopped thyme. Fry 14 ounces trimmed chicken livers in 2 tablespoons butter and 1 tablespoon oil until browned but still pink in the center. Flame the chicken livers with 3 tablespoons cognac, and add 5 ounces seeded, skinned grapes (optional). Heat the grapes through, then toss into the cooked onions. Heap onto thick slices of toasted country bread rubbed with oil and garlic or onto slices of broiled polenta. Serve sprinkled with chopped fresh parsley.

BAKED STUFFED ONIONS
WITH TOMATO SAUCE

*THESE ARE IDEAL COMFORT FOOD FOR SUPPER ON COLD WINTER EVENINGS. SERVE WITH BUTTERED
CABBAGE AND RICE OR THICK SLICES OF BREAD TO MOP UP THE SAUCE.*

SERVES EIGHT

INGREDIENTS
  8 onions, each about 3½ inches
    in diameter, peeled but left whole
  4 tablespoons olive oil
  ½ teaspoon ground allspice
  2 ounces pancetta or bacon, chopped
  9 ounces ground pork
  2 cups fresh bread crumbs
  3 tablespoons chopped fresh parsley
  1 tablespoon chopped fresh oregano
  ½ teaspoon ground cinnamon
  5 tablespoons water
  2 tablespoons butter
For the tomato sauce
  2 tablespoons olive oil
  1 garlic clove, finely chopped
  ½ teaspoon ground allspice
  14-ounce can chopped tomatoes
  small piece of cinnamon stick
  1 fresh bay leaf
  1 tablespoon chopped fresh oregano
  2 tablespoons heavy cream
  ¼–½ teaspoon harissa or other
    chili paste
  pinch of brown sugar (optional)
  salt and ground black pepper

1 Place the onions in a large saucepan,
pour in water to cover and bring to a
boil. Reduce the heat and simmer for
10–15 minutes. Drain and cool.

2 Cut a small cap off the top of each
onion, then use a small, sharp knife
and a teaspoon to hollow out the
centers, leaving a shell of 2–3 layers.

3 Stand the onion shells in a large
ovenproof dish and patch any holes in
their bottoms with pieces of onion. Chop
the flesh removed from the centers and
set aside 3 tablespoons for the sauce.
Heat 2 tablespoons of the oil in a frying
pan and cook the chopped onion over
low heat until just beginning to brown.
Add the allspice and cook for a little
longer. Remove and set aside.

4 Fry the pancetta or bacon in the pan
until the fat melts, then add the pork
and fry until it is beginning to brown.
Preheat the oven to 375°F.

5 Place 1½ cups of the bread crumbs
in a bowl and add the cooked onions,
pork, half the parsley, the oregano and
the ground cinnamon. Season well and
mix to form a stuffing.

6 Fill the onions with the stuffing.
Spoon the water around the onions and
dot the butter on top of them. Cover with
aluminum foil and bake for 30 minutes.

7 To make the sauce, heat the oil and
cook the reserved onion and the garlic
until soft and just beginning to brown.
Add the allspice and fry for 2 minutes,
then add the tomatoes, cinnamon stick,
bay leaf and oregano. Cook, uncovered,
for 15–20 minutes.

8 Remove the cinnamon and bay leaf.
Process the sauce in a blender or food
processor until smooth. Add
3–4 tablespoons water to thin to a
pouring consistency. Add the cream with
seasoning, harissa and sugar to taste.

9 Pour the sauce around the onions
and use it to baste them. Cover the
dish and bake for 20–25 minutes, then
uncover and baste again. Mix the
remaining bread crumbs and parsley.
Sprinkle the crumbs on the onions, then
drizzle with the remaining 2 tablespoons
of oil. Return the dish to the oven
and bake for 15–20 minutes, until
the topping is browned and crisp.
Serve immediately.

BRAISED PORK CHOPS WITH ONION AND MUSTARD SAUCE

THE PIQUANT SAUCE ADDS PUNCH AND EXTRA FLAVOR TO THIS SIMPLE SUPPER DISH. SERVE IT WITH CELERIAC AND MASHED POTATOES AND A GREEN VEGETABLE, SUCH AS BROCCOLI OR CABBAGE.

SERVES FOUR

INGREDIENTS

4 pork loin chops, at least
  ¾ inch thick
2 tablespoons all-purpose flour
3 tablespoons olive oil
2 Spanish onions, thinly sliced
2 garlic cloves, finely chopped
1 cup dry cider
⅔ cup vegetable, chicken or pork
  stock
generous pinch of brown sugar
2 fresh bay leaves
6 fresh thyme sprigs
2 strips lemon zest
½ cup heavy cream
2–3 tablespoons whole-grain mustard
2 tablespoons chopped fresh parsley
salt and ground black pepper

1 Preheat the oven to 400°F. Trim the chops of excess fat. Season the flour with salt and pepper and use to coat the chops. Heat 2 tablespoons of the oil in a frying pan and brown the chops on both sides, then transfer them to an ovenproof dish.

2 Add the remaining oil to the pan and cook the onions over fairly low heat until they soften and begin to brown at the edges. Add the garlic and cook for 2 more minutes.

3 Stir in any leftover flour, then gradually stir in the cider and stock. Season well with salt and pepper and add the brown sugar, bay leaves, thyme sprigs and lemon zest. Bring the sauce to a boil, stirring constantly, then pour onto the chops.

4 Cover and cook for 20 minutes. Reduce the heat to 350°F and continue cooking for another 30–40 minutes. Remove the aluminum foil for the last 10 minutes of the cooking time. Remove the chops from the dish and keep warm, covered with foil.

5 Put the remaining contents of the dish into a saucepan or, if the dish is flameproof, place it over direct heat. Discard the herbs and lemon zest, then bring to a boil.

6 Add the cream and continue to boil, stirring constantly. Taste for seasoning, adding a pinch more sugar if necessary. Finally, stir in the mustard to taste and pour the sauce onto the braised chops. Sprinkle with the chopped parsley and serve immediately.

VARIATION
For a less rich sauce, omit the cream and purée the sauce in a blender. Reheat, thinning with a little extra stock if necessary, then adjust the seasoning and add mustard to taste. This will produce a sharper tasting sauce that will need less mustard.

ROAST PORK WITH SAGE AND ONION STUFFING

SAGE AND ONION MAKE A CLASSIC STUFFING FOR ROAST PORK, DUCK AND TURKEY, WITH THE SAGE COUNTERACTING THE FATTINESS OF THE RICH MEATS. SERVE WITH APPLESAUCE AND ROAST POTATOES.

SERVES SIX TO EIGHT

INGREDIENTS
- 3–3½-pound boneless loin of pork
- 4 tablespoons fine, dry bread crumbs
- 2 teaspoons chopped fresh sage
- 1½ tablespoons all-purpose flour
- 1¼ cups cider
- ⅔ cup water
- 1–2 teaspoons crab apple or red currant jelly
- salt and ground black pepper
- sprigs of thyme, to garnish

For the stuffing
- 2 tablespoons butter
- 2 ounces bacon, finely chopped
- 2 large onions, finely chopped
- 1½ cups fresh white bread crumbs
- 2 tablespoons chopped fresh sage
- 1 teaspoon chopped fresh thyme
- 2 teaspoons finely grated lemon zest
- 1 small egg, beaten

1 Preheat the oven to 425°F. Make the stuffing first. Melt the butter in a heavy pan and fry the bacon until it begins to brown, then add the onions and cook gently until they soften, but do not let brown. Mix with the bread crumbs, sage, thyme, lemon zest and egg, then season well with salt and pepper.

2 Cut the rind off the pork in one piece and score it well. Cooking the rind separately makes crisper crackling than leaving it on the pork.

3 Place the pork fat-side down and season. Add a layer of stuffing, then roll up and tie neatly.

4 Lay the rind on the pork and rub in 1 teaspoon salt. Roast for 2–2½ hours, basting with the pork fat once or twice. Reduce the temperature to 375ºF after 20 minutes. Shape the remaining stuffing into balls and add to the roasting pan for the last 30 minutes.

5 Remove the rind from the pork. Increase the oven temperature to 425°F and roast the rind for another 20–25 minutes, until crisp.

6 Mix the dry bread crumbs and sage and press them into the fat. Cook the pork for 10 minutes, then cover and set aside in a warm place for 15–20 minutes.

7 Remove all but 2–3 tablespoons of the fat from the roasting pan and place it on the stove to make gravy. Stir in the flour, followed by the cider and water. Bring to a boil and then cook gently for 10 minutes. Strain the gravy into a clean pan, add the crab apple or red currant jelly, and cook for another 5 minutes. Adjust the seasoning.

8 Serve the pork cut into thick slices and the crisp crackling cut into strips with the cider gravy, garnished with thyme.

PORK CASSEROLE <u>WITH</u> ONIONS, CHILI <u>AND</u> DRIED FRUIT

INSPIRED BY SOUTH AMERICAN COOKING, A MOLE—PASTE—OF CHILE, SHALLOTS AND NUTS IS ADDED TO THIS CASSEROLE OF PORK AND ONIONS. PART OF THE MOLE IS ADDED AT THE END OF COOKING TO RETAIN ITS FRESH FLAVOR. SERVE WITH RICE AND A GREEN SALAD.

SERVES SIX

INGREDIENTS

1½ tablespoons all-purpose flour
2¼-pound shoulder or leg of pork,
   cut into 2-inch cubes
3–4 tablespoons olive oil
2 large onions, chopped
2 garlic cloves,
   finely chopped
2½ cups fruity white wine
7 tablespoons water
4 ounces prunes
4 ounces dried apricots
grated zest and juice of
   1 small orange
pinch of brown sugar (optional)
2 tablespoons chopped fresh parsley
½–1 fresh green chile, seeded and
   finely chopped (optional)
salt and ground black pepper
For the mole
3 *ancho* chiles and 2 *pasilla* chiles
   (or other varieties of large, medium-
   hot dried red chiles)
2 tablespoons olive oil
2 shallots, chopped
2 garlic cloves, chopped
1 fresh green chile, seeded
   and chopped
2 teaspoons ground coriander
1 teaspoon mild Spanish paprika
   or *pimentón*
½ cup blanched almonds,
   toasted
1 tablespoon chopped fresh oregano
   or ½ teaspoon dried oregano

1 Make the mole paste first. Toast the dried chiles in a dry frying pan over low heat for 1–2 minutes, until they are aromatic, then soak them in warm water for 30 minutes.

2 Drain the chiles, reserving the soaking water, and discard their stems and seeds. Preheat the oven to 325°F.

3 Heat the oil in a small frying pan and fry the shallots, garlic, fresh green chile and ground coriander over very low heat for 5 minutes.

4 Transfer the shallot mixture to a food processor or blender and add the drained chiles, paprika or *pimentón*, almonds and oregano. Process the mixture, adding 3–4 tablespoons of the chile soaking liquid to make a workable paste.

5 Season the flour with salt and black pepper, then use to coat the pork. Heat 3 tablespoons of the olive oil in a large, heavy frying pan and fry the pork, stirring frequently, until sealed on all sides. Transfer the pork cubes to a flameproof casserole.

6 If necessary, add the remaining oil to the frying pan and cook the onions and garlic gently for 8–10 minutes, stirring occasionally.

7 Add the wine and water to the frying pan. Cook for 2 minutes. Stir in half the mole paste, bring back to a boil and bubble for a few seconds before pouring onto the pork.

8 Season lightly with salt and pepper and stir to mix, then cover and cook for 1½ hours.

9 Increase the oven temperature to 350°F. Stir in the prunes, apricots and orange juice. Test the seasoning, adding the brown sugar if necessary, cover and cook for another 30–45 minutes.

10 Place the casserole over direct heat and stir in the remaining mole paste. Simmer, stirring once or twice, for 5 minutes. Serve sprinkled with the orange zest, chopped parsley and fresh chile, if using.

LEEKS BAKED WITH HAM, CREAM AND MINT

CHOOSE LEEKS THAT ARE NOT TOO THICK FOR THIS VERY EASY BUT DELICIOUS SUPPER DISH.
SERVE GOOD BREAD TO MOP UP THE SAUCE AND A GREEN SALAD TO REFRESH THE PALATE.

SERVES FOUR

INGREDIENTS

8–12 slender leeks
8–12 large, medium-thick slices
  Parma or Serrano ham
1 tablespoon butter
1 cup freshly grated Parmesan
  cheese
1 cup heavy cream
1 tablespoon chopped fresh mint
pinch of cayenne pepper
3 tablespoons fine white
  bread crumbs
salt and ground black pepper

1 Trim the leeks so that they are all the same size. Bring a large saucepan of lightly salted water to a boil, add the leeks and cook for 5–8 minutes. Test the leeks with the tip of a sharp knife to check if they are cooked. Drain, reserving 4 tablespoons of the cooking water. Squeeze the excess water out of the leeks. Preheat the oven to 375°F.

VARIATIONS

• Arrange the leeks on a bed of 12 ounces ripe tomatoes, peeled, seeded and finely chopped.
• Wrap the cooked leeks in fried, but not crisp, bacon. Then pour on a cheese sauce made with equal amounts of the reserved cooking water and milk. Season the sauce to taste with Dijon mustard, grated Cheddar cheese and a little nutmeg. Sprinkle on freshly grated Parmesan and fine white bread crumbs and bake as above.
• Wrap 8 raw, slender leeks in slices of pancetta or prosciutto, then fry gently in 2 tablespoons butter for 5 minutes. Add 6 tablespoons white wine and some sprigs of thyme and season to taste with salt and pepper. Cover and cook very gently for 15–20 minutes, until the leeks are cooked. Remove the leeks from the pan, increase the heat and add 4 tablespoons heavy cream, then bubble to make a sauce. Adjust the seasoning and pour on the leeks. Sprinkle with a little chopped parsley before serving.

2 Wrap each leek in a slice of ham. Butter an ovenproof gratin dish just large enough to hold the leeks in one layer and arrange the leeks in it. Season to taste with salt and pepper and sprinkle half the grated Parmesan cheese on the leeks.

3 Mix the cream, cooking water and mint. Season with salt, pepper and cayenne and pour onto the leeks. Sprinkle the bread crumbs and the remaining Parmesan on top. Bake for 30–35 minutes, until bubbling and browned. Serve immediately.

BOILED HAM WITH ONION AND CAPER SAUCE

ONIONS AND CAPERS MAKE A PIQUANT SAUCE THAT IS TRADITIONAL WITH BOILED MUTTON, BUT IT IS ALSO DELICIOUS WITH BOILED HAM. SERVE WITH SMALL NEW POTATOES, SAUTÉED WITH BUTTER AND A LITTLE GARLIC, AND FAVA BEANS TO MAKE A SPLENDID MEAL.

SERVES SIX

INGREDIENTS
4–4½-pound ham,
  soaked if necessary
4 cloves
1 onion, quartered
1 large carrot, sliced
1 celery stalk
1 fresh bay leaf
fresh thyme sprig
2 tablespoons Dijon mustard
3–4 tablespoons sugar
For the sauce
¼ cup butter
8 ounces onions, chopped
¼ cup all-purpose flour
1 cup milk
1 fresh bay leaf
2 tablespoons small salted capers,
  rinsed and roughly chopped
2 tablespoons chopped fresh
  parsley (optional)
1–2 tablespoons Dijon mustard
salt and ground black pepper

1 Place the ham in a large saucepan and cover with cold water. Bring to a boil and simmer for 5 minutes. Drain, rinse, then return the meat to the pan and cover with fresh water. Stick the cloves into the onion and add to the pan with the carrot. Tie the celery, bay leaf and thyme together and add to the pan. Bring to a boil, then part-cover and simmer very gently for 25 minutes per 1 pound.

2 Preheat the oven 400°F. Drain the ham or bacon, reserving 2 cups of the cooking liquid. Place the ham in a roasting pan and strip off and discard the skin. Spread the mustard on the fat and press the sugar all over the ham.

3 Cook for 20–25 minutes, until glazed and browned. Keep warm, covered in aluminum foil, until ready to serve.

4 Start making the sauce just before the ham has finished boiling. Melt 3 tablespoons of the butter in a saucepan and cook the onions very gently, half-covered, for 20 minutes, until soft and yellow but not browned. Stir occasionally.

5 Stir in the flour and cook, stirring constantly, for 2–3 minutes. Gradually stir in 1¼ cups of the hot reserved cooking liquid. Cook until the sauce is thick and smooth, then gradually stir in the milk. Add the bay leaf and cook very gently for 20–25 minutes, stirring frequently.

6 Gradually stir in a little more of the reserved cooking liquid to make a sauce of pouring consistency and cook for another 5 minutes. Remove the bay leaf. Stir in the chopped capers and parsley, if using. Add 1 tablespoon mustard, then taste for seasoning. Add salt, pepper and more mustard to taste. Stir in the remaining butter and serve immediately with the sliced meat.

VEAL IN A WHEAT BEER SAUCE WITH ONIONS AND CARROTS

WHEAT BEERS ARE MADE IN BAVARIA, BELGIUM AND NORTHERN FRANCE, WHERE THEY ARE KNOWN AS BIÈRES BLANCHES OR WHITE BEERS. THE SLIGHT BITTERNESS THAT THE BEER GIVES THE SAUCE IN THIS DELECTABLE STEW IS MATCHED BY THE SWEETNESS OF THE CARAMELIZED ONIONS AND CARROTS.

SERVES FOUR

INGREDIENTS

3 tablespoons all-purpose flour
2 pounds boned shoulder or leg of
  veal, cut into 2-inch cubes
5 tablespoons butter
3 shallots, finely chopped
1 celery stalk
fresh parsley sprig
2 fresh bay leaves
1 teaspoon sugar, plus a
  good pinch
scant 1 cup wheat beer
scant 2 cups veal stock
20–25 large silverskin onions or
  small pickling onions
1 pound carrots,
  thickly sliced
2 large egg yolks
7 tablespoons heavy cream
a little lemon juice (optional)
2 tablespoons chopped fresh parsley
salt and ground black pepper

3 Replace the veal. Tie the celery, parsley and 1 bay leaf together in a bundle, then add them to the pan with a good pinch of sugar. Increase the heat, pour in the beer and let bubble briefly before pouring in the stock. Season, bring to a boil, then cover and simmer gently, stirring once or twice, for 40–50 minutes or until the veal is cooked and tender.

4 Meanwhile, melt the remaining butter in another frying pan and add the onions, then fry them over low heat until golden all over. Use a draining spoon to remove the onions from the pan and set aside.

5 Add the carrots and turn to coat them in the butter remaining from the onions. Stir in 1 teaspoon sugar, a pinch of salt, the remaining bay leaf and enough water to cover the carrots. Bring to a boil and cook, uncovered, for 10–12 minutes.

6 Return the onions to the pan with the carrots and continue to cook until all but a few tablespoons of the liquid has evaporated and the onions and carrots are tender and slightly caramelized. Keep warm.

7 Use a draining spoon to transfer the veal to a bowl and discard the celery and herb bundle.

8 Beat the egg yolks and cream together in another bowl, then beat in a ladleful of the hot, but not boiling, carrot liquid. Return this mixture to the pan and cook over very low heat without boiling, stirring constantly, until the sauce has thickened a little.

9 Add the veal to the sauce, add the onions and carrots and reheat slightly until thoroughly warmed through. Taste and adjust the seasoning, adding a little lemon juice, if necessary, then serve immediately, sprinkled with the parsley.

1 Season the flour and dust the veal in it. Heat 2 tablespoons of the butter in a deep, lidded frying pan, add the veal and quickly seal it on all sides. The veal should be golden but not dark brown. Use a draining spoon to remove the veal from the pan and set aside.

2 Reduce the heat, add another 1 tablespoon butter to the pan and cook the shallots gently for 5–6 minutes, until soft and yellow.

CHICKEN WITH FORTY CLOVES OF GARLIC

THIS DISH DOES NOT HAVE TO BE MATHEMATICALLY EXACT, SO DO NOT WORRY IF YOU HAVE 35 OR EVEN 50 CLOVES OF GARLIC—THE IMPORTANT THING IS THAT THERE SHOULD BE LOTS. THE SMELL THAT EMANATES FROM THE OVEN AS THE CHICKEN AND GARLIC COOK IS INDESCRIBABLY DELICIOUS.

3 Sprinkle in 1 teaspoon flour and cook for 1 minute. Add the port or wine. Tuck in the whole heads of garlic and the peeled cloves with the herb sprigs. Pour on the remaining oil and season to taste with salt and pepper.

4 Mix the main batch of flour with sufficient water to make a firm dough. Roll it out into a long sausage and press it around the rim of the casserole, then press on the lid, folding the dough up and over it to create a tight seal. Cook for 1½ hours.

5 To serve, lift off the lid to break the seal and remove the chicken and whole garlic to a serving platter and keep warm. Remove and discard the herb sprigs, then place the casserole on the stove and whisk to combine the garlic cloves with the juices. Add the crème fraîche, if using, and a little lemon juice to taste. Process the sauce in a food processor or blender or press through a sieve if smoother results are desired. Serve the garlic purée with the chicken.

SERVES FOUR TO FIVE

INGREDIENTS
    5–6 whole heads of garlic
    1 tablespoon butter
    3 tablespoons olive oil
    4–4½-pound chicken
    1¼ cups all-purpose flour,
      plus 1 teaspoon
    5 tablespoons white port, Pineau
      de Charentes or other white,
      fortified wine
    2–3 fresh tarragon or rosemary sprigs
    2 tablespoons crème fraîche (optional)
    few drops of lemon juice (optional)
    salt and ground black pepper

1 Separate 3 of the heads of garlic into cloves and peel them. Remove the first layer of papery skin from the remaining heads of garlic and cut off the tops to expose the cloves, if desired, or leave them whole. Preheat the oven to 350°F.

2 Heat the butter and 1 tablespoon of the olive oil in a flameproof casserole that is just large enough to take the chicken and garlic. Add the chicken and cook over medium heat, turning frequently, for 10–15 minutes, until it is browned all over.

CHICKEN BAKED WITH SHALLOTS, GARLIC AND FENNEL

THIS IS A VERY SIMPLE AND DELICIOUS WAY TO COOK CHICKEN. IF YOU HAVE TIME, LEAVE THE CHICKEN TO MARINATE FOR A FEW HOURS FOR THE BEST FLAVOR.

SERVES FOUR

INGREDIENTS

3½–4-pound chicken, cut into
  8 pieces
9 ounces shallots, peeled
1 head garlic, separated into cloves
  and peeled
4 tablespoons extra virgin olive oil
3 tablespoons tarragon vinegar
3 tablespoons white wine or
  vermouth (optional)
1 teaspoon fennel seeds, crushed
2 bulbs fennel, cut into wedges,
  feathery tops reserved
⅔ cup heavy cream
1 teaspoon red currant jelly
1 tablespoon tarragon mustard
sugar (optional)
2 tablespoons chopped fresh
  flat-leaf parsley
salt and ground black pepper

1 Place the chicken pieces, shallots and all but one of the garlic cloves in a flameproof dish or roasting pan. Add the oil, vinegar, wine or vermouth, if using, and fennel seeds. Season with pepper, then set aside to marinate for 2–3 hours.

2 Preheat the oven to 375°F. Add the fennel to the chicken, season with salt and stir to mix.

3 Cook the chicken in the oven for 50–60 minutes, stirring once or twice. The chicken juices should run clear, not pink, when the thick thigh meat is pierced with a skewer.

4 Transfer the chicken and vegetables to a serving dish and keep them warm. Skim off some of the fat and bring the cooking juices to a boil, then pour in the cream. Stir, scraping up all the delicious juices. Whisk in the red currant jelly followed by the mustard. Check the seasoning, adding a little sugar, if desired.

5 Chop the remaining garlic clove with the feathery fennel tops and mix with the parsley. Pour the sauce on the chicken and sprinkle the chopped garlic and herb mixture on top. Serve immediately.

COOK'S TIPS
• If possible, use the fresh new season's garlic for this dish, as it is plump, moist and full of flavor. Purple-skinned garlic is considered by many cooks to have the best flavor.
• The cut surfaces of fennel quickly discolor, so do not prepare it much in advance of using it. If you must prepare it beforehand, then put the wedges into a bowl of cold water acidulated with a little lemon juice.

COQ AU VIN

THIS IS A FAMOUS BURGUNDIAN RECIPE THAT IS GARNISHED WITH LITTLE ONIONS AND MUSHROOMS.
IT WAS THE HEIGHT OF FASHION IN THE 1960s, AND IT IS BACK IN VOGUE AGAIN.

SERVES FOUR

INGREDIENTS

1 celery stalk
1 fresh bay leaf
fresh thyme sprig
1 bottle full-bodied red wine
  (Shiraz or Zinfandel
  would be good)
2½ cups good chicken stock
¼ cup butter
2 tablespoons olive oil
24 small pickling onions
4-ounce piece of bacon or
  unsmoked pancetta, cut
  into lardons
3 tablespoons all-purpose flour
5-pound chicken, jointed
  into 8 pieces
3 tablespoons cognac
2 garlic cloves, chopped
1 tablespoon tomato paste
piece of fresh pork skin, about
  6-inch square (optional)
9 ounces button mushrooms
2 tablespoons chopped fresh parsley
salt and ground black pepper
croutons, to garnish (optional)

1 Tie the celery, bay leaf and thyme together in a bundle and place in a saucepan. Pour in the wine and stock and simmer, uncovered, for 15 minutes.

2 Melt 1 tablespoon of the butter with half the olive oil in a heavy frying pan and brown 16 of the onions all over. Use a draining spoon to transfer the onions to a plate.

3 Add the bacon or pancetta and cook until browned, then set aside.

COOK'S TIP
For a really good flavor, complete the casserole up to the end of step 5, then cool and leave in the refrigerator overnight. Next day, skim off the excess fat from the top of the casserole and reheat gently on the stove for about 20 minutes before finishing steps 6–11.

4 Meanwhile, season 2 tablespoons of the flour with salt and pepper. Dust the chicken with the seasoned flour and fry them in the fat remaining in the pan over medium heat, turning frequently, for about 10 minutes or until golden brown all over.

5 Pour in the cognac and carefully set it on fire using a long match or taper. When the flames have died down, remove the chicken from the pan and set aside.

6 Chop the remaining onions. Add another 1 tablespoon of the butter to the frying pan and fry the chopped onions with the garlic over medium heat, stirring frequently, for 5 minutes, until softened and just turning brown. Preheat the oven to 375°F.

7 Add the wine and stock mixture, with the herb bundle, and stir in the tomato paste. Lower the heat, then simmer gently, stirring frequently, for about 20 minutes. Taste and adjust the seasoning, if necessary.

8 Place the pork skin, if using, rind-side down in a flameproof casserole, then add the chicken pieces and bacon or pancetta. Pour in the sauce (with the bundle of herbs). Cover and place in the oven. Reduce the temperature to 325°F immediately and cook for 1½ hours. Add the whole browned onions and cook for another 30 minutes.

9 Meanwhile, fry the mushrooms in another 1 tablespoon butter and the remaining oil until browned. Set them aside. Mix the remaining butter and flour to make a paste (known in French as beurre manié).

10 Using a slotted spoon, transfer the chicken and onions to a serving plate. Discard the pork skin from the casserole and heat the cooking juices on the stove until simmering. Add the beurre manié in small lumps, whisking to blend the paste into the sauce as it melts. Continue adding small pieces of paste, allowing each to melt completely before adding the next, until the simmering sauce is thickened to taste. (You may not need to use all the beurre manié.)

11 Add the mushrooms and cook for a few minutes. Pour the sauce on the chicken and sprinkle with chopped parsley. Garnish with croutons, if using, and serve immediately.

GUINEA FOWL AND SPRING VEGETABLE STEW

*MILD, SWEET LEEKS ARE EXCELLENT IN THIS LIGHT STEW OF GUINEA FOWL AND SPRING VEGETABLES.
CHICKEN OR RABBIT CAN BE USED INSTEAD OF GUINEA FOWL.*

SERVES FOUR

INGREDIENTS

3 tablespoons olive oil
4 ounces pancetta, cut into lardons
2 tablespoons all-purpose flour
2 2½–3½-pound guinea fowl, each
  jointed in 4 portions
1 onion, chopped
1 head of garlic, separated into
  cloves and peeled
1 bottle dry white wine
fresh thyme sprig
1 fresh bay leaf
a few parsley stems
9 ounces baby carrots
9 ounces baby turnips
6 slender leeks, cut into
  3-inch lengths
9 ounces shelled peas
1 tablespoon French herb mustard
½ ounce flat-leaf parsley, chopped
1 tablespoon chopped fresh mint
salt and ground black pepper

1 Heat 2 tablespoons of the oil in a large frying pan and cook the pancetta over medium heat until lightly browned, stirring occasionally. Remove the pancetta from the pan and set aside.

2 Season the flour with salt and pepper and toss the guinea fowl portions in it. Fry in the oil remaining in the pan until browned on all sides. Transfer to a flameproof casserole. Preheat the oven to 350°F.

3 Add the remaining oil to the pan and cook the onion gently until soft. Add the garlic and fry for 3–4 minutes, then stir in the pancetta and wine.

4 Tie the thyme, bay leaf and parsley into a bundle and add to the pan. Bring to a boil, then simmer gently for 3–4 minutes. Pour onto the guinea fowl and add seasoning. Cover and cook for 40 minutes.

5 Add the baby carrots and turnips to the casserole and cook, covered, for another 30 minutes or until the vegetables are just tender.

6 Stir in the leeks and cook for another 15–20 minutes or until all the vegetables are fully cooked.

7 Meanwhile, blanch the peas in boiling water for 2 minutes, then drain. Transfer the guinea fowl and vegetables to a warmed serving dish. Place the casserole on the stove and boil the juices vigorously over high heat until they are reduced by about half.

8 Stir in the peas and cook gently for 2–3 minutes, then stir in the mustard and adjust the seasoning. Stir in most of the parsley and the mint. Pour this sauce on the guinea fowl or return the meat and vegetables to the casserole. Sprinkle the remaining parsley on top and serve immediately.

CHICKEN FAJITAS <u>WITH</u> BROILED ONIONS

BROILED MARINATED CHICKEN AND ONIONS, SERVED WITH SOFT TORTILLAS, SALSA, GUACAMOLE AND SOUR CREAM MAKES A CLASSIC TEX-MEX MEAL AND IS A GOOD CHOICE FOR AN INFORMAL SUPPER.

<u>SERVES SIX</u>

INGREDIENTS
finely grated zest of 1 lime and the
juice of 2 limes
½ cup olive oil
1 garlic clove, finely chopped
½ teaspoon dried oregano
good pinch of dried red chile flakes
1 teaspoon coriander seeds, crushed
6 boneless chicken breasts
3 Spanish onions, thickly sliced
2 large red, yellow or orange bell
peppers, seeded and cut into strips
2 tablespoons chopped cilantro
salt and ground black pepper
For the salsa
1 pound tomatoes, peeled, seeded
and chopped
2 garlic cloves, finely chopped
1 small red onion, finely chopped
1–2 green chiles, seeded and
finely chopped
finely grated zest of ½ lime
2 tablespoons chopped cilantro
pinch of sugar
½–1 teaspoon ground roasted
cumin seeds
To serve
12–18 soft flour tortillas
guacamole
½ cup sour cream
crisp lettuce leaves
cilantro sprigs
lime wedges

1 In an ovenproof dish, combine the lime zest and juice, 5 tablespoons of the oil, the garlic, oregano, chile flakes and coriander seeds and season with salt and pepper. Slash the skin on the chicken breasts several times and turn them in the mixture, then cover and set aside to marinate for several hours.

2 To make the salsa, combine the tomatoes, garlic, onion, chiles, lime zest and crushed coriander. Season to taste with salt, pepper, sugar and cumin. Set aside for 30 minutes, then taste and adjust the seasoning, adding more cumin and sugar, if necessary.

3 Heat the broiler. Thread the onion slices onto a skewer or place them on a broiler pan. Brush with 1 tablespoon of the remaining oil and season. Broil until softened and slightly charred in places. Preheat the oven to 400°F.

4 Cook the chicken breasts in their marinade, covered, for 20 minutes. Remove, then broil the chicken for 8–10 minutes, until browned and fully cooked.

5 Meanwhile, heat the remaining oil in a large frying pan and cook the peppers for about 10 minutes, until softened and browned in places. Add the broiled onions and fry briskly for 2–3 minutes.

6 Add the chicken cooking juices and fry over high heat, stirring frequently, until the liquid evaporates. Stir in the chopped cilantro.

7 Reheat the tortillas following the instructions on the package. Using a sharp knife, cut the chicken into strips and transfer to a serving dish. Place the onion and pepper mixture and the salsa in separate dishes.

8 Serve the dishes of chicken, onions and peppers and salsa with the tortillas, guacamole, sour cream, lettuce and cilantro for people to help themselves. Serve lime wedges so that the juice can be squeezed on to taste.

For countless vegetarians around the world

onions are an essential and delicious ingredient.

From the strongest garlic to the mildest chives,

all members of the onion family are delicious in

vegetarian dishes of all kinds. Classic dishes

such as French onion tart, Spanish tortilla and

Italian risotto would be unimaginable without onions.

Here is a selection of meat-free dishes that shows

just how versatile onions really are.

Vegetarian
Main Courses

ONION TART

No book on onion recipes would be complete without a recipe for this classic tart from Alsace in eastern France. Traditionally served in small slices as a first course, it also makes a delicious main course when served warm and accompanied by a green salad.

SERVES FOUR TO SIX

INGREDIENTS

   1½ cups all-purpose flour
   6 tablespoons butter, chilled
   2–3 tablespoons ice water
For the filling
   ¼ cup butter
   2 pounds Spanish onions,
    thinly sliced
   1 egg plus 2 egg yolks
   1 cup heavy cream
   ¼ teaspoon freshly grated nutmeg
   salt and ground black pepper

VARIATIONS

There are endless variations on this classic tart: try adding chopped fresh herbs such as thyme. The tart is also delicious made with cheese pastry; add ⅔ cup grated Parmesan to the flour.

1 Process the flour, a pinch of salt and the chilled butter or butter and lard in a food processor until reduced to fine crumbs. Add the ice water and process briefly to form a dough. Wrap in plastic wrap and chill for 40 minutes.

2 Melt the butter in a large saucepan and add the onions and a pinch of salt. Turn them in the butter. Cover and cook very gently, stirring frequently, for 30–40 minutes. Cool slightly.

3 Preheat the oven to 375°F. Roll out the dough thinly and use to line a 9–10-inch loose-bottomed tart pan. Line with aluminum foil or baking parchment and baking beans, then bake blind for 10 minutes.

4 Remove the foil or parchment and baking beans, and bake for another 4–5 minutes, until the pastry is lightly cooked to a pale brown color (blonde is a good description). Reduce the oven temperature to 350°F.

5 Beat the egg, egg yolks and cream together. Season with salt, lots of black pepper and the grated nutmeg. Place half the onions in the pastry shell and add half the egg mixture. Add the remaining onions, then pour in as much of the remaining custard as you can.

6 Place on a baking sheet and bake on the middle shelf for 40–50 minutes or until the custard is risen, browned and set in the center. Serve warm rather than piping hot.

RED ONION TART WITH A CORNMEAL CRUST

RED ONIONS ARE WONDERFULLY MILD AND SWEET WHEN COOKED, AND THEY GO WELL WITH FONTINA CHEESE AND THYME IN THIS TART. CORNMEAL GIVES THE PASTRY A CRUMBLY TEXTURE TO CONTRAST WITH THE JUICINESS OF THE ONION FILLING. A TOMATO AND BASIL SALAD IS GOOD WITH THE TART.

SERVES FIVE TO SIX

INGREDIENTS
    4 tablespoons olive oil
    2¼ pounds red onions, thinly sliced
    2–3 garlic cloves, thinly sliced
    1 teaspoon chopped fresh thyme,
        plus a few whole sprigs
    1 teaspoon dark brown sugar
    2 teaspoons sherry vinegar
    8 ounces fontina cheese,
        thinly sliced
    salt and ground black pepper
For the pastry
    1 cup all-purpose flour
    ¾ cup fine yellow cornmeal
    1 teaspoon dark brown sugar
    1 teaspoon chopped fresh thyme
    7 tablespoons butter
    1 egg yolk
    2–3 tablespoons ice water

1 To make the pastry, sift the flour and cornmeal into a bowl with 1 teaspoon salt. Add plenty of black pepper and stir in the sugar and thyme. Rub in the butter until the mixture looks like bread crumbs. Beat the egg yolk with 2 tablespoons ice water and use to bind the pastry, adding another 1 tablespoon ice water, if necessary. Gather the dough into a ball with your fingertips, wrap in plastic wrap and chill it for 30–40 minutes.

2 Heat 3 tablespoons of the oil in a large, deep frying pan and add the onions. Cover and cook slowly, stirring occasionally, for 20–30 minutes. They should collapse but not brown.

3 Add the garlic and chopped thyme, then cook, stirring occasionally, for another 10 minutes. Increase the heat slightly, then add the sugar and sherry vinegar. Cook, uncovered, for another 5–6 minutes, until the onions start to caramelize slightly. Season to taste with salt and pepper. Cool.

4 Preheat the oven to 375°F. Roll out the pastry thinly and use to line a 10-inch loose-bottomed metal tart pan.

5 Prick the pastry all over with a fork and support the sides with aluminum foil. Bake for 12–15 minutes, until lightly colored.

6 Remove the foil and spread the caramelized onions evenly on the pastry shell. Add the slices of fontina and sprigs of thyme and season with pepper. Drizzle on the remaining oil, then bake for 15–20 minutes, until the filling is piping hot and the cheese is beginning to bubble. Garnish the tart with thyme and serve immediately.

LEEK AND ROQUEFORT TART WITH WALNUT PASTRY

MILD LEEKS GO EXCEPTIONALLY WELL WITH THE SALTY FLAVOR OF THE ROQUEFORT CHEESE, AND THE NUTTINESS OF THE PASTRY MARRIES THE INGREDIENTS PERFECTLY IN THIS TART. SERVE THE TART WARM WITH A PEPPERY GREEN SALAD OF ARUGULA, MIZUNA OR WATERCRESS.

SERVES FOUR TO SIX

INGREDIENTS
    2 tablespoons butter
    1 pound leeks (trimmed
        weight), sliced
    6 ounces Roquefort cheese, sliced
    2 large eggs
    1 cup heavy cream
    2 teaspoons chopped fresh tarragon
    salt and ground black pepper
For the pastry
    1½ cups all-purpose flour
    1 teaspoon dark brown sugar
    ¼ cup butter
    3 ounces walnuts, ground
    1 tablespoon lemon juice
    2 tablespoons ice water

1 First, make the pastry. Sift the flour and ½ teaspoon salt into a bowl. Add some black pepper and the sugar. Rub in the butter until the mixture looks like bread crumbs, then stir in the ground walnuts. Bind with the lemon juice and ice water. Gather into a ball, wrap in plastic wrap and chill for 30–40 minutes.

2 Preheat the oven to 375°F. Roll out the pastry and use to line an 8½–9-inch loose-bottomed metal tart pan.

COOK'S TIP
Grind walnuts in a small food processor or clean coffee mill with a little of the pastry flour.

3 Protect the sides of the pastry with foil, prick with a fork and bake for 15 minutes. Remove the foil and bake for another 5–10 minutes, until just firm to the touch. Reduce the oven temperature to 350°F.

4 Meanwhile, to make the filling, melt the butter in a pan, add the leeks, cover and cook for 10 minutes. Season and cook for another 10 minutes. Cool.

5 Spoon the leeks into the pastry and arrange the slices of Roquefort on top. Beat the eggs with the cream and season with pepper (the cheese will probably be sufficiently salty). Beat in the tarragon and carefully pour the mixture into the tart.

6 Bake the tart on the center shelf of the oven for 30–40 minutes, until the filling has risen and browned and become firm to a gentle touch. Let cool for 10 minutes before serving.

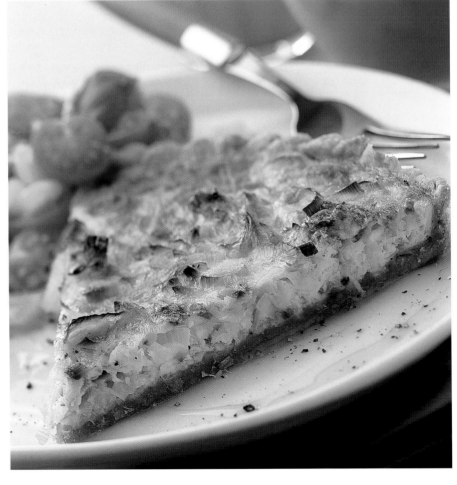

SHALLOT AND GARLIC TARTE TATIN WITH PARMESAN PASTRY

SAVORY VERSIONS OF THE FAMOUS APPLE TARTE TATIN HAVE BEEN POPULAR FOR SOME YEARS. HERE, SHALLOTS ARE CARAMELIZED IN BUTTER, SUGAR AND VINEGAR BEFORE BEING BAKED BENEATH A LAYER OF PARMESAN PASTRY. THIS IS DELICIOUS SERVED WITH A PEAR, CHEESE AND WATERCRESS SALAD.

2 Melt the butter in a 9–10-inch round heavy pan or skillet that will go in the oven. Add the shallots and garlic, and cook until lightly browned all over.

3 Sprinkle the sugar on top and increase the heat a little. Cook until the sugar begins to caramelize, then turn the shallots and garlic in the buttery juices. Add the vinegar, water, thyme and seasoning. Cook, part-covered, for 5–8 minutes, until the garlic cloves are just tender. Cool.

4 Preheat the oven to 375°F. Roll out the pastry to the diameter of the pan or skillet and lay it on the shallots and garlic. Prick the pastry with a sharp knife, then bake for 25–35 minutes or until the pastry is risen and golden. Set aside to cool for 5–10 minutes, then invert the tart onto a serving platter. Sprinkle on a few thyme sprigs, if desired, and serve.

SERVES FOUR TO SIX

INGREDIENTS
   11 ounces puff pastry, thawed
      if frozen
   ¼ cup butter
   1 cup freshly grated Parmesan
      cheese
For the topping
   3 tablespoons butter
   1¼ pounds shallots
   12–16 large garlic cloves, peeled but
      left whole
   1 tablespoon sugar
   1 tablespoon balsamic or
      sherry vinegar
   3 tablespoons water
   1 teaspoon chopped fresh thyme,
      plus a few extra sprigs (optional)
   salt and ground black pepper

1 Roll out the pastry into a rectangle. Spread the butter on it, leaving a 1-inch border. Scatter the Parmesan on top. Fold the bottom third of the pastry up to cover the middle and the top third down. Seal the edges, give a quarter turn and roll out into a rectangle, then fold as before. Chill for 30 minutes.

POTATO AND LEEK PHYLLO PIE

THIS PIE MAKES AN ATTRACTIVE AND UNUSUAL CENTERPIECE FOR A VEGETARIAN BUFFET. SERVE IT COOL, WITH A CHOICE OF SALADS.

SERVES EIGHT

INGREDIENTS
  1¾ pounds new potatoes, sliced
  14 ounces leeks (trimmed weight)
  6 tablespoons butter
  ½ ounce parsley, finely chopped
  4 tablespoons chopped mixed fresh
    herbs (such as chervil, chives, a
    little tarragon and basil)
  12 sheets phyllo pastry
  5 ounces white Cheshire,
    Lancashire or Cantal
    cheese, sliced
  2 garlic cloves, finely chopped
  1 cup heavy cream
  2 large egg yolks
  salt and ground black pepper

1 Preheat the oven to 375°F. Cook the potatoes in boiling, lightly salted water for 3–4 minutes, then drain and set aside.

2 Thinly slice the leeks. Melt 2 tablespoons of the butter in a frying pan and fry the leeks gently, stirring occasionally, until softened. Remove from heat, season with pepper and stir in half the parsley and half the mixed herbs.

3 Melt the remaining butter. Line a 9-inch loose-bottomed metal cake pan with 6–7 sheets of phyllo pastry, brushing each layer with butter. Let the edges of the pastry overhang the pan.

4 Layer the potatoes, leeks and cheese in the pan, sprinkling a few herbs and the garlic between the layers. Season.

5 Flip the overhanging pastry over the filling and cover with 2 sheets of phyllo, tucking in the sides to fit and brushing with melted butter as before. Cover the pie loosely with aluminum foil and bake for 35 minutes. (Keep the remaining pastry covered with a plastic bag and a damp cloth.)

6 Meanwhile, beat the cream, egg yolks and remaining herbs together. Make a hole in the center of the pie and gradually pour in the eggs and cream.

7 Arrange the remaining pastry on top, teasing it into swirls and folds, then brush with melted butter. Reduce the oven temperature to 350°F and bake the pie for another 25–30 minutes, until the top is golden and crisp. Let cool before serving.

POTATO AND ONION TORTILLA WITH FAVA BEANS

THE CLASSIC TORTILLA OR SPANISH OMELET INCLUDES NOTHING MORE THAN ONIONS, POTATO, EGGS AND OLIVE OIL. ADDING CHOPPED HERBS AND A FEW SKINNED FAVA BEANS MAKES THIS A VERY SUMMERY DISH TO ENJOY AT LUNCH, OR CUT IT INTO SMALL PIECES AND SERVE AS A SPANISH TAPAS.

SERVES TWO

INGREDIENTS

- 3 tablespoons olive oil
- 2 Spanish onions, thinly sliced
- 11 ounces waxy potatoes, cut into ½-inch dice
- 1¾ cups shelled fava beans
- 1 teaspoon chopped fresh thyme or summer savory
- 6 large eggs
- 3 tablespoons mixed snipped chives and chopped flat-leaf parsley
- salt and ground black pepper

1 Heat 2 tablespoons of the oil in a 9-inch deep nonstick frying pan. Add the onions and potatoes and stir to coat. Cover and cook gently, stirring frequently, for 20–25 minutes, until the potatoes are cooked and the onions collapsed. Do not let the mixture brown.

2 Meanwhile, cook the beans in boiling salted water for 5 minutes. Drain well and set aside to cool.

3 When the beans are cool enough to handle, peel off the gray outer skins. Add the beans to the frying pan, together with the thyme or summer savory and season with salt and pepper to taste. Stir well to mix and cook for another 2–3 minutes.

4 Beat the eggs with salt and pepper to taste and the mixed herbs, then pour onto the potatoes and onions and increase the heat slightly. Cook gently until the egg on the bottom sets and browns, gently pulling the omelet away from the sides of the pan and tilting it to let the uncooked egg run underneath.

5 Invert the tortilla onto a plate. Add the remaining oil to the pan and heat until hot. Slip the tortilla back into the pan, uncooked side down, and cook for another 3–5 minutes to let the underneath brown. Slide the tortilla out onto a plate. Divide as desired, and serve warm rather than piping hot.

FRITTATA WITH LEEK, RED BELL PEPPER AND SPINACH

APART FROM THE FACT THAT ITALIAN FRITTATA DOES NOT USUALLY CONTAIN POTATO AND IS GENERALLY SLIGHTLY SOFTER IN TEXTURE, IT IS NOT VERY DIFFERENT FROM SPANISH TORTILLA. THIS COMBINATION OF SWEET LEEKS, RED PEPPER AND SPINACH IS DELICIOUS WITH THE EGG.

SERVES THREE TO FOUR

INGREDIENTS
2 tablespoons olive oil
1 large red bell pepper, seeded
  and diced
½–1 teaspoon ground toasted cumin
3 leeks (about 1 pound),
  thinly sliced
5 ounces small spinach leaves
3 tablespoons pine nuts, toasted
5 large eggs
1 tablespoon chopped fresh basil
1 tablespoon chopped fresh
  flat-leaf parsley
salt and ground black pepper
watercress, to garnish
2 ounces Parmesan cheese, grated,
  to serve (optional)

1 Heat a frying pan and add the oil. Add the red pepper and cook over medium heat, stirring occasionally, for 6–8 minutes, until soft and beginning to brown. Add ½ teaspoon of the cumin and cook for another 1–2 minutes.

2 Stir in the leeks, then part-cover the pan and cook gently for about 5 minutes, until the leeks have softened and collapsed. Season with salt and ground black pepper.

3 Add the spinach and cover. Let the spinach wilt in the steam for 3–4 minutes, then stir to mix it into the vegetables, adding the pine nuts.

4 Beat the eggs with salt, pepper, the remaining cumin, basil and parsley. Add to the pan and cook over low heat until the bottom of the omelet sets and turns golden brown. Pull the edges of the omelet away from the sides of the pan as it cooks, and tilt the pan so that the uncooked egg runs underneath.

5 Preheat the broiler. Flash the frittata under the hot broiler to set the egg on top, but do not let it become too brown. Cut the frittata into wedges and serve warm, garnished with watercress and sprinkled with Parmesan, if using.

VARIATION
A delicious way to serve frittata is to pack it into a slightly hollowed-out loaf and then drizzle it with a little extra virgin olive oil. Wrap tightly in plastic wrap and let stand for 1–2 hours before cutting into thick slices. A frittata-filled loaf is ideal picnic fare.

BELL PEPPERS FILLED WITH SPICED VEGETABLES

INDIAN SPICES SEASON THE POTATO AND EGGPLANT STUFFING IN THESE COLORFUL BAKED PEPPERS. THEY ARE GOOD WITH PLAIN RICE AND A LENTIL DHAL. ALTERNATIVELY, SERVE THEM WITH A SALAD, INDIAN BREADS AND A CUCUMBER OR MINT AND YOGURT RAITA.

SERVES SIX

INGREDIENTS

6 large evenly shaped red or
  yellow bell peppers
1¼ pounds waxy potatoes
1 small onion, chopped
4–5 garlic cloves, chopped
2-inch piece fresh ginger root,
  chopped
1–2 fresh green chiles, seeded
  and chopped
7 tablespoons water
6–7 tablespoons peanut oil
1 eggplant, cut into
  ½-inch dice
2 teaspoons cumin seeds
1 teaspoon kalonji seeds
½ teaspoon ground turmeric
1 teaspoon ground coriander
1 teaspoon ground toasted
  cumin seeds
pinch of cayenne pepper
about 2 tablespoons lemon juice
salt and ground black pepper
2 tablespoons chopped cilantro,
  to garnish

1 Cut the tops off the red or yellow peppers, then remove and discard the seeds. Cut a thin slice off the bottom of the peppers, if necessary, to make them stand upright.

2 Bring a large saucepan of lightly salted water to a boil. Add the peppers and cook for 5–6 minutes. Drain and leave the peppers upside down in a colander.

3 Cook the potatoes in boiling, salted water for 10–12 minutes, until just tender. Drain, cool and peel, then cut into ½-inch dice.

4 Put the onion, garlic, ginger and green chiles in a food processor or blender with 4 tablespoons of the water and process into a purée.

5 Heat 3 tablespoons of the oil in a large, deep frying pan and cook the eggplant, stirring occasionally, until browned on all sides. Remove from the pan and set aside. Add another 2 tablespoons of the oil to the pan and cook the potatoes until lightly browned. Remove from the pan and set aside.

6 If necessary, add another 1 tablespoon oil to the pan, then add the cumin and kalonji seeds. Fry briefly until the seeds darken, then add the turmeric, coriander and ground cumin. Cook for 15 seconds. Stir in the onion and garlic purée and fry, scraping the pan with a spatula, until it begins to brown.

7 Return the potatoes and eggplant to the pan, season with salt, pepper and 1–2 pinches of cayenne. Add the remaining water and 1 tablespoon lemon juice and then cook, stirring, until the liquid evaporates. Preheat the oven to 375°F.

8 Fill the peppers with the potato mixture and place on a lightly greased baking tray. Brush the peppers with a little oil and bake for 30–35 minutes, until the peppers are cooked. Let cool a little, then sprinkle with a little more lemon juice, garnish with the cilantro and serve.

COOK'S TIP
Kalonji, or nigella as it is sometimes known, is a tiny black seed. It is widely used in Indian cookery, especially sprinkled over breads or in potato dishes. It has a mild, slightly nutty flavor and is best toasted for a few seconds in a dry frying pan over a medium heat. This helps to bring out its flavor.

POTATO AND ONION CAKES WITH BEET RELISH

THESE IRRESISTIBLE PANCAKES ARE BASED ON TRADITIONAL LATKE, GRATED POTATO CAKES. THEY ARE ESPECIALLY DELICIOUS WITH A SWEET-SHARP BEET RELISH AND SOUR CREAM.

SERVES FOUR

INGREDIENTS

1¼ pounds potatoes (such as King
   Edward, Estima or Desirée)
1 small Bramley apple, peeled, cored
   and coarsely grated
1 small onion, finely chopped
½ cup all-purpose flour
2 large eggs, beaten
2 tablespoons snipped chives
vegetable oil, for shallow-frying
salt and ground black pepper
1 cup sour cream
   or crème fraîche
fresh dill sprigs and fresh chives
   or chive flowers, to garnish
For the beet relish
9 ounces beets, cooked and peeled
1 large apple, cored and finely diced
1 tablespoon finely chopped
   red onion
1–2 tablespoons tarragon vinegar
1 tablespoon chopped fresh dill
1–2 tablespoons light olive oil
pinch of sugar (optional)

1 To make the relish, finely dice the beets, then mix it with the apple and onion. Add 1 tablespoon of the vinegar, the dill and 1 tablespoon of the oil. Season, adding more vinegar and oil, and a pinch of sugar to taste.

2 Coarsely grate the potatoes, then rinse, drain and dry them on a clean dish towel.

3 Mix the potatoes, apple and onion in a bowl. Stir in the flour, eggs and chives. Season and mix again.

4 Heat about ¼-inch depth of oil in a frying pan and fry spoonfuls of the mixture. Flatten them to make pancakes 3–4 inches across and cook for 3–4 minutes on each side, until browned. Drain on paper towels and keep warm until the mixture is used up.

5 Serve a stack of pancakes—there should be about 16–20 in total—with spoonfuls of sour cream or crème fraîche, and beet relish. Garnish with dill sprigs and chives or chive flowers and grind black pepper on top just before serving.

VARIATION
To make a leek and potato cake, melt 2 tablespoons butter in a saucepan, add 14oz thinly sliced leeks and cook until tender. Season well. Coarsely grate 1¼lb peeled potatoes, then season. Melt another 2 tablespoons butter in a medium frying pan and add a layer of half the potatoes. Cover with the leeks, then add the remaining potatoes, pressing down with a spatula to form a cake. Cook for 20–25 minutes over a low heat, then turn over and cook the other side for a further 15–20 minutes until the potatoes are browned and cooked.

BROILED POLENTA WITH CARAMELIZED ONIONS, RADICCHIO AND TALEGGIO CHEESE

SLICES OF BROILED POLENTA, ONE OF THE STAPLES OF NORTH ITALIAN COOKING, ARE TASTY TOPPED WITH SLOWLY CARAMELIZED ONIONS AND BUBBLING TALEGGIO CHEESE, ALSO FROM NORTH ITALY.

SERVES FOUR

INGREDIENTS

3¾ cups water
1 teaspoon salt
generous 1 cup polenta
   or cornmeal
⅓ cup freshly grated Parmesan
   cheese
1 teaspoon chopped fresh thyme
6 tablespoons olive oil
1½ pounds onions, halved and sliced
2 garlic cloves, chopped
a few fresh thyme sprigs
1 teaspoon brown sugar
1–2 tablespoons balsamic vinegar
2 heads radicchio, cut into thick
   slices or wedges
8 ounces Taleggio cheese, sliced
salt and ground black pepper

1 In a large saucepan, bring the water to a boil and add the salt. Adjust the heat so that it simmers. Stirring constantly, add the polenta in a steady stream, then bring to a boil. Cook over very low heat, stirring frequently, for 30–40 minutes, until thick and smooth.

2 Beat in the Parmesan and chopped thyme, then turn onto a work surface or tray. Spread evenly, then let cool.

3 Heat 2 tablespoons of the oil in a frying pan over medium heat. Add the onions and stir to coat in the oil, then cover and cook over very low heat for 15 minutes, stirring occasionally.

4 Add the garlic and most of the thyme sprigs and cook, uncovered, for another 10 minutes or until light brown.

5 Add the sugar, 1 tablespoon of the vinegar and salt and pepper. Cook for another 5–10 minutes, until soft and well-browned. Taste and add more vinegar and seasoning as necessary.

6 Preheat the broiler. Cut the polenta into thick slices and brush with a little of the remaining oil, then broil until crusty and lightly browned.

7 Turn over the polenta and add the radicchio to the broiler pan. Season the radicchio and brush with a little oil. Broil for about 5 minutes, until the polenta and radicchio are browned. Drizzle a little vinegar on the radicchio.

8 Heap the onions onto the polenta. Sprinkle the cheese and a few sprigs of thyme on both polenta and radicchio. Broil until the cheese is bubbling. Season with pepper and serve immediately.

PANCAKES WITH LEEK, ENDIVE AND SQUASH STUFFING

SERVE A CHUNKY HOMEMADE TOMATO SAUCE AND A CRISP GREEN SALAD WITH THESE DELICIOUS, MELT-IN-YOUR-MOUTH STUFFED PANCAKES.

SERVES FOUR

INGREDIENTS

1 cup all-purpose flour
½ cup yellow cornmeal
½ teaspoon salt
½ teaspoon chili powder
2 large eggs
scant 2 cups milk
2 tablespoons butter, melted
vegetable oil, for greasing

For the filling

2 tablespoons olive oil
1 pound butternut squash (peeled
  weight), seeded and diced
large pinch of dried red chile flakes
2 large leeks, thickly sliced
½ teaspoon chopped fresh thyme
3 heads endive, thickly sliced
4 ounces full-flavored goat cheese,
  cut into cubes
3½ ounces walnuts, roughly chopped
2 tablespoons chopped fresh
  flat-leaf parsley
1 ounce Parmesan cheese, grated
3 tablespoons melted butter or olive oil
salt and ground black pepper

2 When ready to cook the pancakes, whisk the melted butter into the batter. Heat a lightly greased or oiled 7-inch heavy frying pan or crêpe pan. Pour about 4 tablespoons batter into the pan and cook for 2–3 minutes, until set and lightly browned underneath. Turn and cook the pancake on the second side for 2–3 minutes. Lightly grease the pan after every second pancake.

3 To make the filling, heat the oil in a large frying pan. Add the squash and cook, stirring frequently, for 10 minutes, until almost tender. Add the chile flakes and cook, stirring, for 1–2 minutes. Stir in the leeks and thyme and cook for another 4–5 minutes.

5 Preheat the oven to 400°F. Lightly grease an ovenproof dish. Spoon 2–3 tablespoons filling onto each pancake. Roll or fold each pancake to enclose the filling, then place in the prepared dish.

6 Sprinkle the Parmesan on the pancakes and drizzle on about 3 tablespoons melted butter or olive oil. Bake for 10–15 minutes, until the cheese is bubbling and the pancakes are piping hot. Serve immediately.

1 Sift the flour, cornmeal, salt and chili powder into a bowl and make a well in the center. Add the eggs and a little milk. Whisk the eggs and milk, gradually incorporating the dry ingredients and adding more milk as the mixture comes together. You may not need all the milk—add enough to make a batter similar to thick cream.

4 Add the endive and cook, stirring frequently, for another 4–5 minutes, until the leeks are cooked and the endive is hot, but still has some bite to its texture. Cool slightly, then stir in the cheese, walnuts and parsley. Season the mixture well.

ONIONS STUFFED WITH GOAT CHEESE AND SUN-DRIED TOMATOES

ROASTED ONIONS AND GOAT CHEESE ARE A WINNING COMBINATION. THESE STUFFED ONIONS MAKE AN EXCELLENT MAIN COURSE WHEN SERVED WITH A RICE OR CRACKED WHEAT PILAF.

SERVES FOUR

INGREDIENTS
4 large onions
5 ounces goat cheese, crumbled
  or cubed
2 ounces fresh bread crumbs
8 sun-dried tomatoes in olive oil,
  drained and chopped
1–2 garlic cloves, finely chopped
½ teaspoon chopped fresh thyme
2 tablespoons chopped fresh parsley
1 small egg, beaten
3 tablespoons pine nuts, toasted
2 tablespoons olive oil (use oil from
  the tomatoes)
salt and ground black pepper

1 Bring a large pan of lightly salted water to a boil. Add the whole onions in their skins and boil for 10 minutes. Drain and cool, then cut each onion in half horizontally and peel.

2 Using a teaspoon, remove the center of each onion, leaving a thick shell. Reserve the flesh and place the shells in an oiled baking dish. Preheat the oven to 375°F.

3 Chop the scooped-out onion flesh and place in a bowl. Add the goat cheese, bread crumbs, sun-dried tomatoes, garlic, thyme, parsley and egg. Mix well, then season with salt and pepper and add the toasted pine nuts.

4 Divide the stuffing among the onions and cover with aluminum foil. Bake for about 25 minutes. Uncover, drizzle with the oil and cook for another 30–40 minutes, until bubbling and well cooked. Baste occasionally during cooking.

VARIATIONS
• Use feta in place of the goat cheese and substitute chopped mint, currants and black olives for the other flavourings.
• Stuff the onions with spinach and rice mixed with some smoked mozzarella and toasted almonds instead of the goat cheese and sun-dried tomato mixture.
• Use red and yellow peppers preserved in olive oil instead of sun-dried tomatoes.
• Substitute 6 ounces Roquefort or Gorgonzola for the goat cheese, omit the sun-dried tomatoes and pine nuts, and add 3 ounces chopped walnuts and 4 ounces chopped celery, cooked until soft with the chopped onion in 1½ tablespoons olive oil.

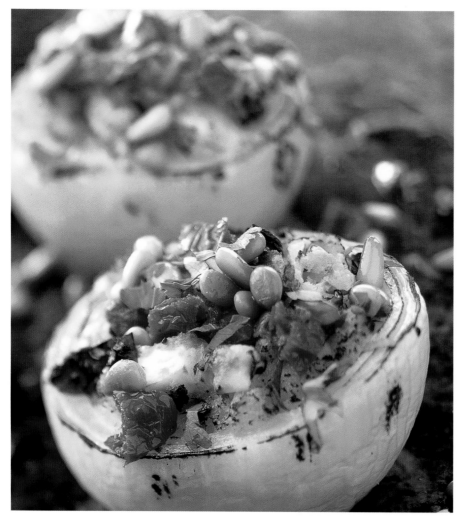

ROASTED GARLIC AND GOAT CHEESE SOUFFLÉ

THE MELLOW FLAVOR OF ROASTED GARLIC PERVADES THIS SIMPLE SOUFFLÉ. BALANCE THE RICH SOUFFLÉ WITH A CRISP GREEN SALAD, INCLUDING PEPPERY LEAVES, SUCH AS WATERCRESS.

5 Cook the sauce very gently for 10 minutes, stirring frequently. Season with salt, pepper and a pinch of cayenne. Cool slightly. Preheat the oven to 400°F.

6 Beat in the egg yolks one at a time. Then beat in the goat cheese, all but 1 tablespoon of the Parmesan and the chopped thyme. Use the remaining butter to grease 1 large soufflé dish (4 cups) or 4 large ramekins (about 1 cup).

7 Whisk the egg whites and cream of tartar in a scrupulously clean bowl until firm, but not dry. Stir 3 tablespoons of the whites into the sauce, then gently, but thoroughly, fold in the remainder.

8 Pour the mixture into the prepared dish or dishes. Run a knife around the edge of each dish, pushing the mixture away from the rim. Sprinkle on the reserved Parmesan.

9 Place the dish or dishes on a baking sheet and cook for 25–30 minutes for a large soufflé or 20 minutes for small soufflés. The mixture should be risen and firm to a light touch in the center; it should not wobble excessively when given a light push. Serve immediately.

SERVES THREE TO FOUR

INGREDIENTS
2 large heads of garlic (choose heads with plump cloves)
3 fresh thyme sprigs
1 tablespoon olive oil
1 cup milk
1 fresh bay leaf
2 ½-inch thick onion slices
2 cloves
¼ cup butter
⅓ cup all-purpose flour, sifted
cayenne pepper
3 eggs, separated, plus 1 egg white
5 ounces goat cheese, crumbled
⅔ cup freshly grated Parmesan cheese
½–1 teaspoon chopped fresh thyme
½ teaspoon cream of tartar
salt and ground black pepper

1 Preheat the oven to 350°F. Place the garlic and thyme sprigs on a piece of aluminum foil. Sprinkle with the oil and close the foil around the garlic, then bake for about 1 hour, until the garlic is soft. Let cool.

2 Squeeze the garlic out of its skin. Discard the thyme and garlic skins, then purée the garlic flesh with the oil.

3 Meanwhile, place the milk, bay leaf, onion slices and cloves in a small saucepan. Bring to a boil, then remove from heat. Cover and let stand for 30 minutes.

4 Melt 3 tablespoons of the butter in another saucepan. Stir in the flour and cook gently for 2 minutes, stirring. Reheat and strain the milk, then gradually stir it into the flour and butter.

ROASTED GARLIC AND EGGPLANT CUSTARDS WITH RED BELL PEPPER DRESSING

THESE ELEGANT LITTLE MOLDS MAKE A GREAT MAIN COURSE FOR A SPECIAL DINNER. SERVE GOOD BREAD AND STEAMED BROCCOLI AS ACCOMPANIMENTS.

SERVES SIX

INGREDIENTS

  2 large heads of garlic
  6–7 fresh thyme sprigs
  4 tablespoons extra virgin olive oil,
    plus extra for greasing
  12 ounces eggplant, cut into
    ½-inch dice
  2 large red bell peppers, halved
    and seeded
  pinch of saffron threads
  1¼ cups whipping cream
  2 large eggs
  pinch of sugar
  2 tablespoons shredded fresh
    basil leaves
  salt and ground black pepper
For the dressing
  6 tablespoons extra virgin oil
  1–1½ tablespoons balsamic vinegar
  pinch of sugar
  4 ounces tomatoes, peeled, seeded
    and finely diced
  ½ small red onion, finely chopped
  generous pinch of ground toasted
    cumin seeds
  handful of fresh basil leaves

1 Preheat the oven to 375°F. Place the garlic on a piece of aluminum foil with the thyme and sprinkle with 1 tablespoon of the oil. Wrap the foil around the garlic and cook for 35–45 minutes or until the garlic is soft. Cool slightly. Reduce the oven temperature to 350°F.

2 Meanwhile, heat the remaining olive oil in a heavy saucepan. Add the diced eggplant and fry over medium heat, stirring frequently, for 5–8 minutes, until they are browned and cooked.

3 Grill the peppers, skin-sides facing up, until they are black. Place the peppers in a bowl, cover and leave for 10 minutes.

4 When the peppers are cool enough to handle, peel and dice them. Soak the saffron in 1 tablespoon hot water for 10 minutes.

5 Unwrap the roasted garlic and pop it out of its skin into a blender or food processor. Discard the thyme sprigs. Add the oil from cooking, the cream and eggs to the garlic. Process until smooth. Add the soaked saffron with its liquid and season well with salt, pepper and a pinch of sugar. Stir in half the diced red pepper and the basil.

6 Lightly grease 6 large ovenproof ramekins (about 1 cup capacity) and line the bottom of each with a circle of nonstick baking parchment. Grease the parchment.

COOK'S TIP
It is important that the custards cook at an even temperature throughout and are surrounded by a water bath or they may crack, spoiling their appearance.

7 Divide the eggplant among the dishes. Pour the egg mixture into the ramekins, then place them in a roasting pan. Cover each dish with aluminum foil and make a little hole in the center of the foil to let steam escape. Pour hot water into the pan to come halfway up the outsides of the ramekins. Bake for 25–30 minutes, until the custards are just set in the center.

8 Make the dressing while the custards are cooking. Whisk the oil and vinegar with salt, pepper and a pinch of sugar. Stir in the tomatoes, red onion, remaining red pepper and cumin. Set aside some basil leaves for garnishing, then chop the rest and add to the dressing.

9 Let the custards cool for about 5 minutes, then turn them out onto warmed serving plates. Spoon the dressing around the custards and garnish each with the reserved fresh basil leaves.

LEEK ROULADE <u>WITH</u> CHEESE, WALNUT <u>AND</u> SWEET BELL PEPPER FILLING

THIS ROULADE IS SURPRISINGLY EASY TO PREPARE AND IT MAKES A GOOD MAIN COURSE, SERVED WITH HOMEMADE TOMATO SAUCE. IT IS ALSO EXCELLENT AS PART OF A BUFFET.

SERVES FOUR TO SIX

INGREDIENTS
    butter or oil, for greasing
    2 tablespoons fine dry
      white bread crumbs
    1 cup finely grated Parmesan cheese
    ¼ cup butter
    2 leeks, thinly sliced
    ⅓ cup all-purpose flour
    1 cup milk
    1 teaspoon Dijon mustard
    ¼ teaspoon freshly grated nutmeg
    2 large eggs, separated, plus
      1 egg white
    ½ teaspoon cream of tartar
    salt and ground black pepper
    arugula and balsamic dressing,
      to serve
For the filling
    2 large red bell peppers
    1½ cups ricotta cheese, cottage
      cheese or soft goat cheese (or a
      mixture)
    3½ ounces chopped walnuts
    4 scallions, finely chopped
    ½ ounce fresh basil leaves

1 Grease and line a 12 × 9-inch jelly roll pan with baking parchment, then sprinkle with the bread crumbs and 2 tablespoons of the grated Parmesan. Preheat the oven to 375°F.

2 Melt the butter in a saucepan and fry the leeks for 5 minutes, until softened.

3 Stir in the flour and cook over low heat, stirring constantly, for 2 minutes, then gradually stir in the milk. Cook for 3–4 minutes, stirring constantly to make a thick sauce.

4 Stir in the mustard and nutmeg and season with salt and plenty of pepper. Reserve 2–3 tablespoons of the remaining Parmesan, then stir the rest into the sauce. Cool slightly.

5 Beat the egg yolks into the sauce. In a scrupulously clean bowl, whisk the egg whites and cream of tartar until stiff. Stir 2–3 spoonfuls of the egg white into the leek mixture, then carefully fold in the remaining egg white.

6 Pour the mixture into the pan and gently level it out using a spatula. Bake for 15–18 minutes, until risen and just firm to a light touch in the center. If the roulade is to be served hot, increase the oven temperature to 400°F after removing the roulade.

7 Meanwhile, heat the broiler. Halve and seed the peppers, then broil them, skin-sides facing up, until black. Place in a bowl, cover and let sit for 10 minutes. Peel off the skin and cut into strips.

8 Beat the cheese with the walnuts and scallions. Chop half the basil and beat it into the mixture. Season to taste.

9 Place a large sheet of baking parchment on the work surface and sprinkle on the remaining Parmesan. Turn the roulade out onto it. Strip off the lining paper and let the roulade cool slightly. Spread the cheese mixture on it and top with the red pepper strips. Tear the remaining basil leaves and sprinkle them on top.

10 Using the paper as a guide, roll up the roulade and roll it onto a serving platter. If serving hot, roll the roulade on to a baking sheet, cover with a tent of aluminum foil and bake for 15–20 minutes. Serve with arugula and drizzle on dressing.

THREE ALLIUM RISOTTO WITH FRIZZLED ONIONS AND PARMESAN

GENTLY COOKING CHOPPED ONIONS IN BUTTER IS THE FIRST STEP IN MAKING ALL CLASSIC RISOTTOS. IN THIS RECIPE, GARLIC AND CHIVES ARE ALSO ADDED, AND A FINAL SPRINKLING OF CRISP FRIED ONIONS BRING A DELICIOUS CHANGE OF TEXTURE TO THE COOKED DISH.

SERVES FOUR

INGREDIENTS

6 tablespoons butter
1 tablespoon olive oil, plus extra
1 onion, finely chopped
4 garlic cloves, finely chopped
1¾ cups risotto rice
⅔ cup dry white wine
pinch of saffron threads (12 threads)
about 5 cups hot vegetable stock
1 large yellow onion, thinly sliced
½ ounce chives, snipped, plus extra
  to garnish
1 cup grated Parmesan cheese, plus
  more to taste
salt and ground black pepper

1 Melt half the butter with the oil in a large deep frying pan or heavy saucepan. Add the onion with a pinch of salt and cook over very low heat, stirring frequently, for 10–15 minutes, until softened and just turning golden. Do not let the onions brown.

2 Add the garlic and rice and cook, stirring constantly, for 3–4 minutes, until the rice is coated and looks translucent. Season with a little salt and black pepper.

3 Pour in the wine and stir in the saffron with a ladleful of hot stock. Cook slowly, stirring frequently, until the liquid is absorbed.

4 Continue cooking for 18–20 minutes, adding 1–2 ladlefuls of stock at a time, until the rice is swollen and tender outside, but still *al dente* on the inside. Keep the heat low and stir frequently. The finished risotto should be moist, but not like soup.

5 Separate the slices of yellow onion into rings while the risotto is cooking. Heat a shallow layer of oil in a frying pan. Cook the onion rings slowly at first until soft, then increase the heat and fry briskly until they are brown and crisp. Drain on paper towels.

6 Beat the chives, the remaining butter and half the Parmesan into the risotto until it looks creamy. Taste and add seasoning, if necessary.

7 Serve the risotto in warm serving bowls, topped with the crisp onions and chives. Add more grated Parmesan to taste at the table.

BARLEY RISOTTO <u>WITH</u> ROASTED SQUASH <u>AND</u> LEEKS

THIS IS MORE LIKE A PILAF, MADE WITH SLIGHTLY CHEWY, NUTTY-FLAVORED PEARL BARLEY, THAN A CLASSIC RISOTTO. SWEET LEEKS AND ROASTED SQUASH ARE SUPERB WITH THIS EARTHY GRAIN.

3 Heat half the butter with the remaining oil in a large frying pan. Cook the leeks and garlic gently for 5 minutes. Add the mushrooms and remaining thyme, then cook until the liquid from the mushrooms evaporates and they begin to fry.

4 Stir in the carrots and cook for 2 minutes, then add the barley and most of the stock. Season well and part-cover the pan. Cook for another 5 minutes. Pour in the remaining stock if the mixture seems dry.

5 Stir in the parsley, the remaining butter and half the Pecorino. Then stir in the squash. Add seasoning to taste and serve immediately, sprinkled with the toasted pumpkin seeds or walnuts and the remaining Pecorino.

SERVES FOUR TO FIVE

INGREDIENTS
1 cup pearl barley
1 butternut squash, peeled, seeded and cut into chunks
2 teaspoons chopped fresh thyme
4 tablespoons olive oil
2 tablespoons butter
4 leeks, cut into fairly thick diagonal slices
2 garlic cloves, finely chopped
6 ounces chestnut mushrooms, sliced
2 carrots, coarsely grated
about ½ cup vegetable stock
2 tablespoons chopped fresh flat-leaf parsley
2 ounces Pecorino cheese, grated or shaved
3 tablespoons pumpkin seeds, toasted, or chopped walnuts
salt and ground black pepper

1 Rinse the barley, then cook it in simmering water, keeping the saucepan part-covered, for 35–45 minutes or until tender. Drain. Preheat the oven to 400°F.

2 Place the squash in a roasting pan with half the thyme. Season with pepper and toss with half the oil. Roast, stirring once, for 30–35 minutes, until tender and beginning to brown.

PASTA WITH GARLIC AND CHILI

THIS IS THE SIMPLEST OF PASTA DISHES AND ONE OF THE BEST. MINT AND OREGANO GIVE VERY DIFFERENT RESULTS, BOTH GOOD. THERE IS NO NEED TO SERVE GRATED PARMESAN WITH THIS DISH— INSTEAD, LET THE CLEAR FLAVORS OF THE GARLIC AND OLIVE OIL SING OUT.

SERVES THREE TO FOUR

INGREDIENTS

14 ounces dried spaghetti
7 tablespoons extra virgin olive oil, plus more to taste
¼ teaspoon dried red chile flakes or 2 small whole dried red chiles
6 large garlic cloves, finely chopped
1 tablespoon chopped fresh mint or oregano
½ ounce chopped fresh flat-leaf parsley
salt and ground black pepper

1 Cook the spaghetti in boiling lightly salted water for 9–11 minutes or according to the package instructions, until just tender.

2 Meanwhile, warm the oil in a large frying pan or saucepan over very low heat. Add the chile flakes or whole chiles and cook very gently for 2–3 minutes.

COOK'S TIP
If you use fresh spaghetti, cook for only 2–3 minutes in boiling salted water.

3 Add the garlic to the pan. Keep the heat very low, so that the garlic barely bubbles and does not brown, then cook, shaking the pan occasionally, for about 2 minutes. Remove the pan from heat and cool a little, then add the fresh mint or oregano.

4 Drain the pasta, then immediately add it to the oil and garlic mixture, with the parsley. Toss thoroughly. Season with freshly ground black pepper and transfer to warmed serving bowls. Serve immediately, offering more olive oil at the table.

VARIATION
Cook 9 ounces broccoli florets in boiling salted water for 4 minutes. Add to the chili oil and gently fry for 5–8 minutes.

PASTA WITH SLOWLY COOKED ONIONS, CABBAGE, PARMESAN AND PINE NUTS

THIS IS AN UNUSUAL, BUT QUITE DELICIOUS, WAY OF SERVING PASTA. CAVOLO NERO, TUSCAN BLACK CABBAGE, IS A CLOSE RELATIVE OF CURLY KALE, WITH LONG LEAVES AND A SPICY FLAVOR.

SERVES FOUR

INGREDIENTS
  2 tablespoons butter
  1 tablespoon extra virgin olive oil,
    plus more for drizzling (optional)
  1¼ pounds Spanish onions, halved
    and thinly sliced
  1–2 teaspoons balsamic vinegar
  14 ounces–1¼ pounds cavolo nero,
    spring greens, kale or Brussels
    sprout tops, shredded
  14–20 ounces dried pasta (such as
    penne or fusilli)
  1 cup freshly grated Parmesan cheese
  ½ cup pine nuts, toasted
  salt and ground black pepper

VARIATION
To make a delicious pilaf, cook 1¼ cups
brown basmati rice and use instead of
the pasta.

1 Heat the butter and olive oil together
in a large saucepan. Stir in the onions,
cover and cook very gently, stirring
occasionally, for about 20 minutes,
until very soft.

2 Uncover, and continue to cook
gently, until the onions have turned
golden yellow. Add the balsamic vinegar
and season well, then cook for another
1–2 minutes. Set aside.

3 Blanch the cavolo nero, spring
greens, kale or Brussels sprout tops in
boiling, lightly salted water for about
3 minutes. Drain well and add to the
onions, then cook over low heat for
3–4 minutes.

4 Cook the pasta in boiling, lightly
salted water for 8–12 minutes or
according to the package instructions,
until just tender. Drain, then add to the
pan of onions and greens and toss
thoroughly to mix.

5 Season well with salt and pepper and
stir in half the Parmesan. Transfer the
pasta to warmed plates. Sprinkle the
pine nuts and more Parmesan on top
and serve immediately, offering more
olive oil for drizzling on to taste.

PASTA WITH PESTO, POTATOES AND GREEN BEANS

THIS IS ONE OF THE TRADITIONAL WAYS TO SERVE PESTO IN LIGURIA. ALTHOUGH THE COMBINATION OF PASTA AND POTATOES MAY SEEM ODD, IT IS DELICIOUS WITH THE RICH PESTO SAUCE.

SERVES FOUR

INGREDIENTS
½ cup pine nuts
2 large garlic cloves, chopped
3½ ounces fresh basil leaves, plus a few extra leaves
6 tablespoons extra virgin olive oil (use a mild Ligurian or French oil)
⅔ cup freshly grated Parmesan cheese
½ cup freshly grated Pecorino cheese
For the pasta mixture
10 ounces waxy potatoes, thickly sliced or cut into ½-inch cubes
7 ounces fine green beans
12 ounces dried trenette, linguine, tagliatelle or tagliarini
salt and ground black pepper
To serve
extra virgin olive oil
pine nuts, toasted
Parmesan cheese, grated

1 Toast the pine nuts in a dry frying pan until golden. (Watch them carefully or they will burn.) Place in a mortar with the garlic and a pinch of salt, and crush with a pestle. Add the basil and continue pounding the mixture. Gradually add a little oil as you work the mixture to form a paste. Then work the Parmesan and Pecorino with the remaining oil. (Alternatively, blend the pine nuts, garlic, basil and oil in a food processor, then stir in the cheeses.)

2 Bring a pan of lightly salted water to a boil and add the potatoes. Cook for 10–12 minutes, until tender. Add the green beans to the pan for the last 5–6 minutes of cooking.

3 Meanwhile, cook the pasta in boiling salted water for 8–12 minutes or according to the package instructions, until just tender. Times vary according to the pasta shapes. Try to time the cooking so that both pasta and potatoes are ready at the same time.

4 Drain the pasta and potatoes and beans. Place in a large, warmed bowl and toss with two-thirds of the pesto. Season with black pepper and sprinkle extra basil leaves on top.

5 Serve immediately with the rest of the pesto, extra olive oil, pine nuts and grated Parmesan.

COOK'S TIP
To freeze pesto, make it without the cheeses, then freeze. To use, remove from the freezer and leave to thaw, then simply stir in the grated cheeses. If you plan to freeze pesto for more than a few weeks, omit the garlic as well and stir it in with the cheeses on thawing as the flavor of garlic can change during prolonged freezing.

CHEESE AND LEEK SAUSAGES WITH TOMATO, GARLIC AND CHILI SAUCE

THESE ARE BASED ON THE WELSH SPECIALTY OF GLAMORGAN SAUSAGES, WHICH ARE TRADITIONALLY MADE USING WHITE OR WHOLE-WHEAT BREAD CRUMBS ALONE. HOWEVER, ADDING MASHED POTATOES LIGHTENS THE SAUSAGES AND MAKES THEM MUCH EASIER TO HANDLE.

SERVES FOUR

INGREDIENTS

2 tablespoons butter
6 ounces leeks, finely chopped
6 tablespoons cold mashed potatoes
2 cups fresh white or whole-wheat
   bread crumbs
1¼ cups grated Caerphilly,
   Lancashire or Cantal cheese
2 tablespoons chopped fresh parsley
1 teaspoon chopped fresh sage
   or marjoram
2 large eggs, beaten
cayenne pepper
1 cup dry white bread crumbs
oil for shallow-frying

For the sauce

2 tablespoons olive oil
2 garlic cloves, thinly sliced
1 fresh red chile, seeded and finely
   chopped, or a good pinch of dried
   red chile flakes
1 small onion, finely chopped
1¼ pounds tomatoes, peeled, seeded
   and chopped
few fresh thyme sprigs
2 teaspoons balsamic vinegar or red
   wine vinegar
pinch of light brown sugar
1–2 tablespoons chopped fresh
   marjoram or oregano
salt and ground black pepper

1 Melt the butter and fry the leeks for 4–5 minutes, until softened but not browned. Mix with the mashed potatoes, fresh bread crumbs, cheese, parsley and sage or marjoram. Add beaten egg to bind the mixture. Season well and add a good pinch of cayenne.

2 Shape the mixture into 12 sausage shapes. Dip in the remaining egg, then coat with the dry bread crumbs. Chill the coated sausages.

3 To make the sauce, heat the oil over low heat in a pan, add the garlic, chile and onion and cook for 3–4 minutes. Add the tomatoes, thyme and vinegar. Season with salt, pepper and sugar.

4 Cook the sauce for 40–50 minutes, until much reduced. Remove the thyme and purée the sauce in a blender. Reheat with the marjoram or oregano, then adjust the seasoning, adding more sugar, if necessary.

5 Fry the sausages in shallow oil until golden brown on all sides. Drain on paper towels and serve with the sauce.

COOK'S TIP
These sausages are also delicious served with garlic mayonnaise or a confit of slow-cooked onions.

Vegetable Stew with Roasted Tomatoes and Garlic Sauce

This lightly spiced stew makes a perfect match for couscous, enriched with a little butter or olive oil. Add some chopped cilantro and a handful each of raisins and toasted pine nuts to the couscous to make it extra special.

SERVES SIX

INGREDIENTS

3 tablespoons olive oil
9 ounces small pickling onions
  or shallots
1 large onion, chopped
2 garlic cloves, chopped
1 teaspoon cumin seeds
1 teaspoon ground coriander seeds
1 teaspoon paprika
2-inch piece cinnamon stick
2 fresh bay leaves
1¼–scant 2 cups good
  vegetable stock
good pinch of saffron threads
1 pound carrots, thickly sliced
2 green bell peppers, seeded and
  thickly sliced
4 ounces dried apricots, halved
  if large
1–1½ teaspoons ground toasted
  cumin seeds
1 pound squash, peeled, seeded
  and cut into chunks
pinch of sugar, to taste
2 tablespoons butter (optional)
salt and ground black pepper
3 tablespoons cilantro leaves, to
  garnish
For the roasted tomato and garlic sauce
2¼ pounds tomatoes, halved
1 teaspoon sugar
3 tablespoons olive oil
1–2 fresh red chiles, seeded
  and chopped
2–3 garlic cloves, chopped
1 teaspoon fresh thyme leaves

VARIATION
Other vegetables could be used. A mixture of eggplant and potato is good. Fry the cubed eggplant with the shallots until brown, and cook the potatoes as you would the squash. Allow 2 medium eggplant and about 1¼ pounds small potatoes. Omit the carrots and apricots.

1 Preheat the oven to 350°F. First make the sauce. Place the tomatoes, cut sides facing up, in a roasting pan. Season well with salt and pepper and sprinkle the sugar on the top, then drizzle with the olive oil. Roast for 30 minutes.

2 Sprinkle the chiles, garlic and thyme on the tomatoes, stir to mix and roast for another 30–45 minutes, until the tomatoes are collapsed but still a little juicy. Cool, then process in a food processor or blender to make a thick sauce. Sieve to remove the seeds.

3 Heat 2 tablespoons of the oil in a large, wide saucepan or deep frying pan and cook the pickling onions or shallots until browned all over. Remove from the pan and set aside. Add the chopped onion to the pan and cook over low heat for 5–7 minutes, until softened. Stir in the garlic and cumin seeds and cook for another 3–4 minutes.

4 Add the ground coriander seeds, paprika, cinnamon stick and bay leaves. Cook, stirring constantly, for another 2 minutes, then mix in the vegetable stock, saffron, carrots and green peppers. Season well, cover and simmer gently for 10 minutes.

5 Stir in the apricots, 1 teaspoon of the ground toasted cumin, the browned onions or shallots and the squash. Stir in the tomato sauce.

6 Cover the pan and cook for another 5 minutes. Uncover the pan and continue to cook, stirring occasionally, for 10–15 minutes, until the vegetables are all fully cooked.

7 Adjust the seasoning, adding a little more cumin and a pinch of sugar to taste. Remove and discard the cinnamon stick. Stir in the butter, if using, and serve scattered with the cilantro leaves.

EGGPLANT <u>AND</u> SWEET POTATO STEW <u>WITH</u> GARLIC <u>AND</u> COCONUT MILK

INSPIRED BY THAI COOKING, THIS EGGPLANT AND SWEET POTATO STEW COOKED IN COCONUT SAUCE IS SCENTED WITH FRAGRANT LEMONGRASS, GINGER AND LOTS OF GARLIC.

SERVES SIX

INGREDIENTS

  4 tablespoons peanut oil
  14 ounces baby eggplant, halved, or
    2 standard eggplant, cut
    into chunks
  8 ounces Thai red shallots or other
    small shallots or pickling onions
  1 teaspoon fennel seeds,
    lightly crushed
  4–5 garlic cloves, thinly sliced
  1½ tablespoons finely chopped fresh
    ginger root
  2 cups vegetable stock
  2 stems lemongrass, outer layers
    discarded, finely chopped or minced
  ½ ounce cilantro, stems and leaves
    chopped separately
  3 kaffir lime leaves, lightly bruised
  2–3 small red chiles
  3–4 tablespoons Thai green
    curry paste
  1½ pounds sweet potatoes, peeled
    and cut into thick chunks
  1⅔ cups coconut milk
  ½–1 teaspoon light brown sugar
  9 ounces mushrooms,
    thickly sliced
  juice of 1 lime, to taste
  salt and ground black pepper
  18 fresh Thai basil leaves or ordinary
    basil, to serve

1 Heat half the oil in a wide saucepan or deep, lidded frying pan. Add the eggplant and cook over medium heat, stirring occasionally, until lightly browned on all sides. Remove from the pan and set aside.

2 Slice 4–5 of the shallots and set aside. Fry the remaining whole shallots in the oil remaining in the pan, adding a little more oil if necessary, until lightly browned. Set aside with the eggplant. Add the remaining oil to the pan and cook the sliced shallots, fennel seeds, garlic and ginger very gently until soft but not browned.

3 Add the vegetable stock, lemongrass, chopped cilantro stems and any roots, lime leaves and whole chiles. Cover and simmer over a low heat for 5 minutes.

4 Stir in 2 tablespoons of the curry paste and the sweet potatoes. Simmer gently for about 10 minutes, then return the eggplant and browned shallots to the pan and cook for another 5 minutes.

5 Stir in the coconut milk and the sugar. Season to taste, then stir in the mushrooms and simmer for 5 minutes or until all the vegetables are cooked.

6 Stir in more curry paste and lime juice to taste, followed by the chopped cilantro leaves. Adjust the seasoning and ladle the vegetables into warmed bowls. Sprinkle basil leaves on the vegetables and serve.

PARSNIPS AND CHICKPEAS IN GARLIC, ONION, CHILI AND GINGER PASTE

THE SWEET FLAVOR OF PARSNIPS GOES VERY WELL WITH THE SPICES IN THIS INDIAN-STYLE VEGETABLE STEW. OFFER INDIAN BREADS TO MOP UP THE DELICIOUS SAUCE.

SERVES FOUR

INGREDIENTS
7 ounces dried chickpeas,
   soaked overnight in cold water,
   then drained
7 garlic cloves, finely chopped
1 small onion, chopped
2-inch piece fresh ginger root,
   chopped
2 green chiles, seeded and
   finely chopped
scant 2 cups plus 5 tablespoons water
4 tablespoons peanut oil
1 teaspoon cumin seeds
2 teaspoons ground coriander seeds
1 teaspoon ground turmeric
½–1 teaspoon chili powder or mild
   paprika
2 ounces cashews, toasted
   and ground
9 ounces tomatoes, peeled
   and chopped
2 pounds parsnips, cut
   into chunks
1 teaspoon ground roasted
   cumin seeds
juice of 1 lime, to taste
salt and ground black pepper
To serve
   cilantro leaves
   a few cashews, toasted

1 Put the soaked chickpeas in a saucepan, cover with cold water and bring to a boil. Boil vigorously for 10 minutes, then reduce the heat so that the water boils steadily and cook for 1–1½ hours or until the chickpeas are tender. (The cooking time depends on how long the chickpeas have been stored.) Drain.

2 Set 2 teaspoons of the garlic aside, then place the remainder in a food processor or blender with the onion, ginger and half the chiles. Add the 5 tablespoons water and process to make a smooth paste.

3 Heat the oil in a large, deep, frying pan and cook the cumin seeds for 30 seconds. Stir in the coriander seeds, turmeric, chili powder or paprika and the ground cashews. Add the ginger and chili paste and cook, stirring frequently, until the water begins to evaporate. Add the tomatoes and stir-fry until the mixture begins to turn red-brown in color.

4 Mix in the chickpeas and parsnips with the main batch of water, 1 teaspoon salt and plenty of black pepper. Bring to a boil, stir, then simmer, uncovered, for 15–20 minutes, until the parsnips are completely tender.

5 Reduce the liquid, if necessary, by boiling fiercely until the sauce is thick. Add the ground roasted cumin with more salt and/or lime juice to taste. Stir in the reserved garlic and green chile, and cook for another 1–2 minutes. Sprinkle on the cilantro leaves and toasted cashews and serve immediately.

COOK'S TIP
Do not add salt to the water when cooking dried chickpeas, as this will toughen them.

We often forget that onions are vegetables in their own right, but the recipes in this section show how essential they really are. Foods such as bread and rice are particularly good with onions, garlic, leeks and chives. Onions roast beautifully and are wonderful cooked with other vegetables, adding a delicious caramelized sweetness. Whether it's a pan of caramelized shallots, a pile of onion rings or a heap of chive-flavored rice, alliums are essential for adding savor to a whole host of meals.

Side Dishes

CARAMELIZED SHALLOTS

THESE SHALLOTS ARE GOOD WITH GRILLED OR BRAISED POULTRY OR MEAT, ESPECIALLY TURKEY, PORK, VEAL AND BEEF. THEY ARE ALSO EXCELLENT MIXED WITH OTHER BRAISED OR ROASTED VEGETABLES, SUCH AS CHESTNUTS, CARROTS OR CHUNKS OF BUTTERNUT SQUASH.

SERVES FOUR TO SIX

INGREDIENTS

¼ cup butter or 4 tablespoons olive oil
1¼ pounds shallots or small onions,
  peeled with root ends intact
1 tablespoon brown sugar
2 tablespoons red or white wine
  or port
⅔ cup rich veal, chicken or beef
  stock or water
2–3 fresh bay leaves and/or
  2–3 fresh thyme sprigs
salt and ground black pepper
chopped fresh parsley,
  to garnish (optional)

1 Heat the butter or oil in a large frying pan and add the shallots or onions in a single layer. Fry gently, turning occasionally, until lightly browned.

2 Sprinkle the sugar on the shallots and cook gently, turning the shallots in the juices, until the sugar begins to caramelize. Add the wine or port and let the mixture bubble for 4–5 minutes.

3 Add the stock, seasoning and herbs. Cover and cook for 5 minutes, then remove the lid and cook until the liquid evaporates and the shallots are tender and glazed. Adjust the seasoning and sprinkle with the parsley, if desired.

VARIATION
Shallots with chestnuts and pancetta
Cook the shallots in butter or bacon fat with 3½ ounces pancetta, cut into thick strips. Use water or ham stock instead of the wine or port. Toss in 9–12 ounces part-cooked chestnuts in step 3. Cook for 5–10 minutes, then serve sprinkled with chopped flat-leaf parsley.

JERUSALEM ARTICHOKES WITH GARLIC, SHALLOTS AND BACON

THE SLIGHTLY SMOKY AND EARTHY FLAVOR OF JERUSALEM ARTICHOKES IS EXCELLENT WITH SHALLOTS AND SMOKED BACON. THESE ARE GOOD WITH CHICKEN, ROAST COD OR MONKFISH, OR PORK.

3 Season with salt and black pepper to taste and stir in the water. Cover and cook for another 8–10 minutes, shaking the pan occasionally.

4 Uncover the pan, increase the heat and cook for 5–6 minutes, until all the moisture has evaporated and the artichokes are tender.

SERVES FOUR

INGREDIENTS
¼ cup butter
4 ounces smoked bacon or pancetta, chopped
1¾ pounds Jerusalem artichokes, peeled
8–12 garlic cloves, peeled
4 ounces shallots, chopped
5 tablespoons water
2 tablespoons olive oil
½ cup fresh white bread crumbs
2–3 tablespoons chopped fresh parsley
salt and ground black pepper

1 Melt half the butter in a heavy frying pan and cook the chopped bacon or pancetta until brown and beginning to crisp. Remove half the bacon or pancetta from the pan and set aside.

2 Add the artichokes, garlic and shallots, and cook, stirring frequently, until the artichokes and garlic begin to brown slightly.

COOK'S TIP
Do not peel the artichokes too much in advance, as they discolor quickly on exposure to air. If necessary, drop them into a bowl of acidulated water.

5 In another frying pan, melt the remaining butter in the olive oil. Add the white bread crumbs and fry over medium heat, stirring frequently, until crisp and golden. Stir in the chopped parsley and the reserved cooked bacon or pancetta.

6 Combine the artichokes with the bread crumb mixture, mixing well. Adjust the seasoning, if necessary, then turn into a warmed serving dish. Serve immediately.

CHAMP

THIS TRADITIONAL IRISH DISH OF POTATOES, SCALLIONS, AND BUTTERMILK OR CREAMY MILK, IS ENRICHED WITH A WICKEDLY INDULGENT AMOUNT OF GOOD BUTTER.

SERVES FOUR

INGREDIENTS

    2¼ pounds boiling potatoes,
      cut into chunks
    1 cup milk
    1 bunch scallions,
      thinly sliced, plus extra
      to garnish
    ½ cup slightly salted butter
    4 tablespoons buttermilk or
      crème fraîche
    salt and ground black pepper

1 Boil the potatoes in lightly salted water for 20–25 minutes, until tender. Drain and mash with a fork until smooth.

2 Place the milk, scallions and half the butter in a small saucepan and set over low heat until just simmering. Cook for 2–3 minutes, until the butter has melted and the scallions have softened.

3 Beat the milk mixture into the mashed potatoes using a wooden spoon. Beat in the buttermilk or crème fraîche until the mixture is light and fluffy. Reheat gently, adding salt and pepper to taste.

4 Turn the potato into a warmed serving dish and make a well in the center with a spoon. Place the remaining butter in the well and let it melt. Serve immediately, sprinkled with extra scallions.

VARIATIONS
• **Colcannon** This is another Irish specialty. Follow the main recipe, using half the butter. Cook about 1¼ pounds finely shredded green cabbage or kale in a little water until just tender, drain thoroughly and then beat into the creamed potatoes. This is delicious with sausages and grilled ham or bacon. It may also be fried in butter and then browned lightly under the broiler.
• **Clapshot** To make this Scottish dish, halve the amount of potato and replace with an equal weight (or slightly more) of rutabaga. Use less butter and omit the cream, then season with black pepper and plenty of freshly grated nutmeg. Traditionally, a chopped onion would be cooked with the potatoes and rutabaga.

FENNEL AND GARLIC MASHED POTATOES

THIS FLAVORSFUL DISH OF MASHED POTATOES WITH FENNEL AND GARLIC GOES PARTICULARLY WELL WITH FISH OR CHICKEN. IT IS ALSO EXTREMELY DELICIOUS WITH ROAST PORK.

SERVES FOUR

INGREDIENTS

1 head of garlic, separated
   into cloves
1¾ pounds boiling potatoes, cut
   into chunks
2 large fennel bulbs
5 tablespoons butter or
   6 tablespoons extra virgin olive oil
½–⅔ cup milk
   or light cream
freshly grated nutmeg
salt and ground black pepper

1 If using a food mill to mash the potatoes, leave the garlic unpeeled, otherwise peel it. Boil the garlic with the potatoes in salted water for 20 minutes.

2 Meanwhile, trim and roughly chop the fennel, reserving any feathery tops. Chop the tops and set them aside. Heat 2 tablespoons of the butter or 2 tablespoons of the oil in a heavy saucepan. Add the fennel, cover and cook over low heat for 20–30 minutes, until soft but not browned.

3 Drain and mash the potatoes. Purée the fennel in a food mill or blender and beat it into the potato with the remaining butter or olive oil.

COOK'S TIP
A food mill is good for mashing potatoes, as it ensures a smooth texture. Never mash potatoes in a food processor or blender, as this releases the starch, giving results that resembles wallpaper paste.

4 Warm the milk or cream and beat enough into the potatoes and fennel to make a creamy, light mixture. Season to taste and add a little grated nutmeg.

5 Reheat gently, then beat in any chopped fennel tops. Transfer to a warmed dish and serve immediately.

VARIATIONS
• For a stronger garlic flavor, use 2–3 tablespoons roasted garlic purée.
• To give a stronger fennel flavor, cook ½–1 teaspoons ground fennel seeds with the fennel.
• Substitute hot stock for some or all of the milk or cream; this is particularly good made with fish stock.
• Use 4–5 tablespoons orange juice instead of half the milk or cream and finely grated orange zest for the nutmeg.

SWEET-AND-SOUR ROASTED ONIONS

THESE ONIONS ARE DELICIOUS WITH ROAST PORK OR LAMB OR SERVED WITH A CRACKED WHEAT PILAF.

SERVES FOUR

INGREDIENTS
    4 large onions
    4 tablespoons olive oil
    2 teaspoons crushed coriander seeds
    1 tablespoon honey
    2 tablespoons pomegranate molasses
    1 tablespoon sherry vinegar
    salt and ground black pepper

COOK'S TIP
Pomegranate molasses is made by boiling down the juice of the fruit to produce a thick, sticky liquid with a wonderful sweet-and-sour taste. It is available at Middle Eastern food stores and some large supermarkets. There is no suitable substitute.

1 Cut the onions into wedges, leaving them attached at the root end. Preheat the oven to 400°F. Place the onion wedges, olive oil and crushed coriander in a roasting pan and mix thoroughly with your hands. Season to taste, then roast for 20 minutes.

2 Mix the honey, pomegranate molasses and vinegar with 1 tablespoon water. Drizzle this mixture on the onions and stir to mix. Reduce the oven temperature to 350°F and cook for another 20–30 minutes, until well browned. Serve immediately.

ROASTED RED ONIONS WITH CRUMBLY CHEESE AND SUN-DRIED TOMATO BUTTER

ONIONS ROAST TO A WONDERFUL SWEET CREAMINESS WHEN COOKED IN THEIR SKINS. THEY NEED BUTTER, LOTS OF BLACK PEPPER AND SALT TO SET OFF THEIR SWEETNESS.

SERVES SIX

INGREDIENTS
    6 even-sized red onions, unpeeled
    6–8 ounces crumbly cheese (such as Lancashire, Caerphilly or Cheshire), thinly sliced
    a few snipped chives
    salt and ground black pepper
For the sun-dried tomato butter
    4 ounces butter, softened
    2½ ounces sun-dried tomatoes in olive oil, drained and finely chopped
    2 tablespoons chopped fresh basil or parsley

VARIATIONS
• Use goat cheese instead of Lancashire, Caerphilly or Cheshire.
• Fry fresh white bread crumbs in butter with a little garlic until crisp and then mix with lots of chopped fresh parsley. Sprinkle the crisp crumb mixture onto the onions before serving.

1 Preheat the oven to 350°F. Put the unpeeled onions in a roasting pan and roast for 1¼–1½ hours, until they are tender and feel soft when lightly squeezed.

2 Meanwhile, prepare the sun-dried tomato butter. Cream the butter and then beat in the tomatoes and basil or parsley. Season to taste with salt and pepper and shape into a roll, then wrap in aluminum foil and chill.

3 Slit the tops of the onions and open them up. Season with plenty of black pepper and add chunks of the sun-dried tomato butter. Sprinkle the cheese and chives on top and eat immediately, mashing the butter and cheese into the soft, sweet onion.

COOK'S TIP
Sun-dried tomatoes are easiest to chop if you snip them into tiny pieces with a sharp pair of kitchen scissors.

POTATO, ONION AND GARLIC GRATIN

THIS IS A SIMPLE BUT DELICIOUS WAY OF COOKING POTATOES AND ONIONS TOGETHER. CHOOSE STOCK TO COMPLEMENT THE MAIN DISH THAT IT IS ACCOMPANYING. ALTERNATIVELY, USE WATER AND ADD SOME BACON TO GIVE FLAVOR. THE GRATIN ALSO MAKES A GOOD BASE ON WHICH TO BAKE FISH.

SERVES FOUR TO SIX

INGREDIENTS

3 tablespoons butter or bacon fat
  or 3 tablespoons olive oil
2–4 garlic cloves, finely chopped
2 pounds waxy potatoes, thinly sliced
1 pound onions, thinly sliced
scant 2 cups fish, chicken, beef or
  lamb stock
salt and ground black pepper

VARIATIONS
• Layer 6 ounces thinly sliced cheese with the potatoes. About 15–20 minutes before the end of cooking time, sprinkle the gratin with another ½ cup grated cheese, dot with more butter and finish baking. This version is also good made with leeks.
• For a simple topping, crumble 5½ ounces soft goat cheese on the gratin 15 minutes before the end of cooking.

1 Use half the butter, bacon fat or oil to grease a 6¼-cup gratin dish. Preheat the oven to 350°F.

2 Sprinkle a little of the chopped garlic in the dish and then layer the potatoes and onions, seasoning each layer with a little salt and pepper and adding the remaining garlic. Finish with a layer of overlapping potato slices on top.

3 Bring the stock to a boil in a saucepan and pour it onto the gratin. Dot the top with the remaining butter or bacon fat cut into small pieces, or drizzle the remaining olive oil on top. Cover tightly with aluminum foil and bake for 1½ hours.

4 Increase the oven temperature to 400°F. Uncover the gratin and then cook for another 35–50 minutes, until the potatoes are completely cooked and the top layer is browned and crusty. Serve immediately.

LEEK, SQUASH AND TOMATO GRATIN

THIS AUTUMNAL GRATIN COMPLEMENTS ROAST OR GRILLED LAMB OR CHICKEN. OR SERVE IT AS A SIMPLE SUPPER DISH ACCOMPANIED BY A GREEN SALAD AND GOOD BREAD.

4 Heat the cream in a small saucepan with the chile and garlic. Bring to a boil, then stir in the mint and pour onto the gratin, thoroughly scraping the contents out of the pan.

5 Bake for 50–55 minutes or until the gratin is bubbling and the vegetables are tender. Sprinkle the parsley and bread crumbs on top and drizzle on the remaining oil. Then bake for another 15–20 minutes, until the bread crumbs are browned and crisp. Serve immediately.

SERVES FOUR TO SIX

INGREDIENTS
  1 pound peeled and seeded squash, cut into ½-inch slices
  4 tablespoons olive oil
  1 pound leeks, cut into thick, diagonal slices
  1½ pounds tomatoes, peeled and thickly sliced
  ½ teaspoon ground toasted cumin seeds
  scant 2 cups light cream
  1 fresh red chile, seeded and thinly sliced
  1 garlic clove, finely chopped
  1 tablespoon chopped fresh mint
  2 tablespoons chopped fresh parsley
  4 tablespoons fine white bread crumbs
  salt and ground black pepper

1 Steam the squash over boiling salted water for 10 minutes.

2 Heat half the oil in a frying pan and cook the leeks gently for 5–6 minutes until lightly colored. Try to keep the slices intact. Preheat the oven to 375°F.

3 Layer the squash, leeks and tomatoes in an 8¾-cup gratin dish, arranging them in rows. Season with salt, pepper and cumin.

BRAISED LETTUCE AND PEAS WITH SCALLIONS AND MINT

THIS IS BASED ON THE TRADITIONAL FRENCH WAY OF BRAISING PEAS WITH LETTUCE AND SCALLIONS IN BUTTER. IT IS DELICIOUS WITH SIMPLY COOKED FISH OR ROAST OR GRILLED DUCK.

SERVES FOUR

INGREDIENTS

¼ cup butter
4 Little Gem lettuces,
   halved lengthwise
2 bunches scallions, trimmed
1 teaspoon sugar
14 ounces shelled peas (about
   2¼ pounds in pods)
4 fresh mint sprigs
½ cup chicken or vegetable stock or
   water
1 tablespoon chopped fresh mint
salt and ground black pepper

1 Melt half the butter in a wide, heavy saucepan over low heat. Add the lettuces and scallions.

2 Turn the vegetables in the butter, then sprinkle in the sugar, ½ teaspoon salt and plenty of black pepper. Cover, and cook very gently for 5 minutes, stirring once.

3 Add the peas and mint sprigs. Turn the peas in the buttery juices and pour in the stock or water, then cover and cook over low heat for another 5 minutes. Uncover and increase the heat to reduce the liquid to a few tablespoons.

4 Stir in the remaining butter and adjust the seasoning. Transfer to a warmed serving dish and sprinkle on the chopped mint. Serve immediately.

VARIATIONS
• Braise about 9 ounces baby carrots with the lettuce.
• Use 1 lettuce, shredding it coarsely, and omit the mint. Toward the end of cooking, stir in about 5 ounces arugula (preferably the stronger-flavored, wild rocket) and cook briefly until wilted.
• Fry 4 ounces chopped smoked bacon or pancetta with 1 small chopped onion in the butter. Use 1 bunch of scallions and omit the mint. Stir in some chopped parsley before serving. This version is also very good with small summer turnips, braised with the lettuce.

BRAISED LEEKS WITH CARROTS

SWEET CARROTS AND LEEKS GO WELL TOGETHER AND ARE GOOD FINISHED WITH A LITTLE CHOPPED MINT, CHERVIL OR PARSLEY. THIS IS A GOOD ACCOMPANIMENT TO ROAST BEEF, LAMB OR CHICKEN.

SERVES SIX

INGREDIENTS
 5 tablespoons butter
 1½ pounds carrots, thickly sliced
 2 fresh bay leaves
 sugar
 5 tablespoons water
 1½ pounds leeks, cut into
  2-inch lengths
 ½ cup white wine
 2 tablespoons chopped fresh mint,
  chervil or parsley
 salt and ground black pepper

1 Melt 2 tablespoons of the butter in a saucepan and cook the carrots gently, without allowing them to brown, for 4–5 minutes.

2 Add the bay leaves, seasoning, the sugar and water. Bring to a boil, cover and cook for 10–15 minutes, until the carrots are tender. Uncover, then boil until the juices have evaporated, leaving the carrots moist and glazed.

3 Meanwhile, melt another 2 tablespoons of the remaining butter in a wide saucepan or deep frying pan that will take the leeks in a single layer. Add the leeks and fry them in the butter over low heat for 4–5 minutes, without letting them brown.

4 Add seasoning, a good pinch of sugar, the wine and half the chopped herb. Heat until simmering, then cover and cook gently for 5–8 minutes, until the leeks are tender but not collapsed.

5 Uncover the leeks and turn them in the buttery juices. Increase the heat, then boil the liquid rapidly until reduced to a few tablespoons.

VARIATION
Braised leeks in tarragon cream
Cook 2 pounds leeks in 3 tablespoons butter as above. Season, add a pinch of sugar, 3 tablespoons tarragon vinegar, 6 fresh tarragon sprigs or 1 teaspoon dried tarragon and 4 tablespoons white wine. Cover and cook as above. Add ⅔ cup heavy cream and let bubble and thicken. Adjust the seasoning and serve sprinkled with chopped fresh tarragon. A spoonful of tarragon-flavored mustard is good stirred into these leeks.

6 Add the carrots to the leeks and reheat them gently, then swirl in the remaining butter. Adjust the seasoning, if necessary. Transfer to a warmed serving dish and serve sprinkled with the remaining chopped herbs.

CABBAGE WITH ONIONS, BACON AND GARLIC

SERVE THIS QUICK, EASY AND FLAVORFUL DISH WITH GOOSE, TURKEY OR PORK, OR TRY IT WITH
SAUSAGES OR CHOPS AND CREAMY MASHED POTATOES.

SERVES FOUR

INGREDIENTS
  2 tablespoons butter or bacon fat or
    pork fat, or 2 tablespoons olive oil
  4 ounces bacon or pancetta, chopped
  1 onion, halved and thinly sliced
  1 teaspoon caraway seeds or cumin
    seeds (optional)
  2 garlic cloves, finely chopped
  1 green cabbage (such as Savoy
    cabbage), thick stems removed and
    leaves shredded
  7 tablespoons water
  salt and ground black pepper

1 Melt the butter or fat or heat the oil
in a large frying pan over low heat. Cook
the bacon or pancetta and onion gently,
until the onion is soft.

2 Increase the heat slightly to medium-
low and sprinkle on the caraway seeds
or cumin seeds, if using, then cook,
stirring occasionally, until the onion
begins to brown.

3 Add the chopped garlic and stir-fry
for 2 minutes.

4 Add the cabbage and turn it in the
juices to coat, then stir in 1 teaspoon
salt and the water. Cover tightly and
cook over high heat for 5–6 minutes,
stirring once. The cabbage should be
tender, but still retain a little crispness.
Season to taste with black pepper and
serve immediately.

DEEP-FRIED ONION RINGS

THESE ARE A POPULAR ACCOMPANIMENT FOR GRILLED MEATS, ESPECIALLY STEAKS AND BURGERS. THEY
ALSO PROVIDE A CRISP CONTRAST WHEN SERVED WITH SLICED HARD-BOILED EGGS IN ONION SAUCE.

SERVES FOUR

INGREDIENTS
  2 Spanish onions, thickly sliced
  1 large egg white, lightly beaten
  4 tablespoons all-purpose flour
  peanut oil for deep-frying
  salt and ground black pepper

1 Separate the onion slices into rings.
Dip them into the egg white.

2 Season the flour with salt and
pepper, then dip the onion rings into it,
one at a time, until evenly coated,
shaking off any excess.

3 Heat the oil for deep-frying to 375°F
or until a cube of day-old bread browns
in 30–40 seconds. Fry the onion rings
for 3–4 minutes, until browned and
crisp. Drain on paper towels and
serve immediately.

VARIATIONS
• For corn-crusted onion rings, soak red
onion rings in milk for about 30 minutes.
Drain, then dip into coarse cornmeal
(polenta), mixed with a pinch each of
dried red chile flakes, paprika and
ground toasted cumin seeds. Deep-fry.
• For spicy onion rings, mix 6 tablespoons
chickpea flour (besan or gram flour) with
½ teaspoon each of ground cumin,
ground coriander, chili powder and garam
masala. Season and add 1 chopped
green chile and 2 tablespoons chopped
cilantro. Mix with 3–4 tablespoons cold
water to make a fairly thick batter. Dip
the onion rings into the batter, then
deep-fry until crisp.
• For onion tempura, beat 2 egg yolks
with ⅔ cup cold sparkling water. Lightly
mix in 4 ounces sifted self-rising flour
and a pinch of salt, leaving the batter
lumpy. Dip onion rings into the batter
and deep-fry.

POTATOES BAKED WITH FENNEL, ONIONS, GARLIC AND SAFFRON

POTATOES, FENNEL AND ONIONS INFUSED WITH GARLIC, SAFFRON AND SPICES MAKE A SOPHISTICATED AND ATTRACTIVE ACCOMPANIMENT FOR FISH OR CHICKEN OR AN EGG-BASED MAIN-COURSE DISH.

SERVES FOUR TO SIX

INGREDIENTS

1¼ pounds small waxy potatoes,
  cut into chunks or wedges
good pinch of saffron threads
  (12–15 threads)
1 head of garlic, separated
  into cloves
12 small red or yellow onions,
  peeled but left whole
3 fennel bulbs, cut into wedges,
  feathery tops reserved
4–6 fresh bay leaves
6–9 fresh thyme sprigs
¾ cup fish, chicken
  or vegetable stock
2 tablespoons sherry vinegar
½ teaspoon sugar
1 teaspoon fennel seeds,
  lightly crushed
½ teaspoon paprika
3 tablespoons olive oil
salt and ground black pepper

1 Boil the potatoes in salted water for 8–10 minutes. Drain. Preheat the oven to 375°F. Soak the saffron in 2 tablespoons warm water for 10 minutes.

2 Peel and finely chop 2 garlic cloves. Place the potatoes, onions, unpeeled garlic cloves, fennel wedges, bay leaves and thyme sprigs in a roasting dish.

3 Mix the stock, saffron and its soaking liquid, vinegar and sugar, then pour onto the vegetables. Stir in the fennel seeds, paprika, garlic and oil, and season with salt and pepper.

4 Cook for 1–1¼ hours, stirring occasionally, until the vegetables are tender. Chop the reserved fennel, sprinkle on the vegetables and serve.

ROASTED SWEET POTATOES, ONIONS AND BEETS IN COCONUT AND GINGER PASTE

SWEET POTATOES AND BEETS TAKE ON A WONDERFUL SWEETNESS WHEN ROASTED, AND THEY ARE DELICIOUS WITH THE SAVORY ONIONS AND AROMATIC COCONUT, GINGER AND GARLIC PASTE.

SERVES FOUR

INGREDIENTS

2 tablespoons peanut oil or
    mild olive oil
1 pound sweet potatoes, peeled and
    cut into thick strips or chunks
4 beets, cooked, peeled and cut into
    wedges
1 pound small red or yellow
    onions, halved
1 teaspoon coriander seeds,
    lightly crushed
3–4 small whole fresh red chiles
salt and ground black pepper
chopped cilantro, to garnish
For the paste
2 large garlic cloves, chopped
1–2 green chiles, seeded
    and chopped
1 tablespoon chopped fresh ginger root
3 tablespoons chopped cilantro
5 tablespoons coconut milk
2 tablespoons peanut oil or
    mild olive oil
grated zest of ½ lime
½ teaspoon light brown sugar

1 First, make the paste. Process the garlic, chiles, ginger, cilantro and coconut milk in a food processor, blender or coffee grinder.

2 Turn the paste into a small bowl and beat in the oil, lime zest and brown sugar. Preheat the oven to 400°F.

3 Heat the oil in a roasting pan in the oven for 5 minutes. Add the sweet potatoes, beets, onions and coriander seeds, tossing them in the hot oil. Roast for 10 minutes.

4 Stir in the paste and the whole red chiles. Season well with salt and pepper, and toss the vegetables to coat them thoroughly with the paste.

5 Roast the vegetables for another 25–35 minutes or until the sweet potatoes and onions are fully cooked and tender. Stir 2–3 times to prevent the paste from sticking to the pan. Serve immediately, sprinkled with a little chopped cilantro.

COOK'S TIP
Orange-fleshed sweet potatoes look more attractive than white-fleshed ones in this dish—and they are more nutritious.

GUACAMOLE

This dish has almost become a cliché of Tex-Mex cooking, usually served as a first course with bread or corn chips for dipping. Carefully seasoned, it is a great accompaniment for simple grilled fish, poultry or meat, especially steak.

SERVES FOUR

INGREDIENTS

2 large ripe avocados
1 small red onion, very
    finely chopped
1 red or green chile, seeded and very
    finely chopped
½–1 garlic clove, crushed with a
    little salt (optional)
finely shredded zest of ½ lime and
    juice of 1–1½ limes
pinch of sugar
8 ounces tomatoes, seeded
    and chopped
2 tablespoons roughly chopped
    cilantro
½–1 teaspoon ground toasted cumin
    seeds
1 tablespoon olive oil
1–2 tablespoons sour cream
    (optional)
salt and ground black pepper
lime wedges, dipped in sea salt, and
    cilantro sprigs, to garnish

1 Halve, pit and peel the avocados. Set one half aside and roughly mash the remainder in a bowl using a fork.

COOK'S TIP
Leaving some of the avocado in chunks adds a slightly different texture, but if you prefer, mash all the avocado together. Hard avocados will soften in a few seconds in a microwave. Check frequently until you get the softness you like.

2 Add the onion, chile, garlic (if using), lime zest, juice of 1 lime, sugar, tomatoes and cilantro. Add ground cumin, seasoning and more lime juice to taste. Stir in the olive oil.

3 Dice the remaining avocado and stir into the guacamole, then cover and let stand for 15 minutes so that the flavor develops. Stir in the sour cream, if using. Serve immediately with lime wedges, dipped in sea salt, and cilantro sprigs.

LENTIL DHAL <u>WITH</u> ROASTED GARLIC <u>AND</u> WHOLE SPICES

THIS SPICY LENTIL DHAL MAKES A SUSTAINING AND COMFORTING MEAL WHEN SERVED WITH RICE OR INDIAN BREADS AND ANY DRY-SPICED DISH, PARTICULARLY A CAULIFLOWER OR POTATO DISH.

<u>SERVES FOUR TO SIX</u>

INGREDIENTS
  3 tablespoons butter or ghee
  1 onion, chopped
  2 green chiles, seeded and chopped
  1 tablespoon chopped fresh
    ginger root
  1 cup yellow or red lentils
  3¾ cups water
  3 tablespoons roasted garlic purée
  1 teaspoon ground cumin
  1 teaspoon ground coriander
  7 ounces tomatoes, peeled and diced
  a little lemon juice
  salt and ground black pepper
  3–4 tablespoons cilantro sprigs and
    fried onion and garlic slices,
    to garnish
For the whole spice mix
  2 tablespoons peanut oil
  4–5 shallots, sliced
  2 garlic cloves, thinly sliced
  1 tablespoon butter or ghee
  1 teaspoon cumin seeds
  1 teaspoon mustard seeds
  3–4 small dried red chiles
  8–10 fresh curry leaves

1 Melt the butter or ghee in a large saucepan and cook the onion, chiles and ginger for 10 minutes, until golden.

2 Stir in the lentils and water, then bring to a boil, then reduce the heat and part-cover the pan. Simmer, stirring occasionally, for 50–60 minutes, until similar to a very thick soup.

3 Stir in the roasted garlic purée, cumin and ground coriander, then season with salt and pepper to taste. Cook for another 10–15 minutes, uncovered, stirring frequently.

4 Stir in the tomatoes and then adjust the seasoning, adding a little lemon juice to taste.

5 To make the whole spice mix, heat the oil in a small, heavy pan. Add the shallots and fry over medium heat, stirring occasionally, until crisp and browned. Add the garlic and cook, stirring frequently, until the garlic colors slightly. Use a draining spoon to remove the shallot mixture from the pan and set aside.

6 Melt the butter or ghee in the same pan. Add the cumin and mustard seeds and fry until the mustard seeds pop. Stir in the chiles, curry leaves and the shallot mixture, then immediately swirl the mixture into the cooked dhal. Garnish with cilantro, onions and garlic and serve.

SAFFRON RICE <u>WITH</u> ONION <u>AND</u> CARDAMOM

THIS DELIGHTFULLY FRAGRANT, BUTTERY PILAF IS WONDERFUL WITH BOTH INDIAN AND MIDDLE-EASTERN DISHES, ESPECIALLY ONES FEATURING SEAFOOD, CHICKEN OR LAMB.

SERVES FOUR

INGREDIENTS
    generous 1½ cups basmati rice
    good pinch of saffron threads
       (about 15 threads)
    2 tablespoons butter
    1 onion, finely chopped
    6 green cardamom pods,
       lightly crushed
    1 teaspoon salt
    2–3 fresh bay leaves
    2½ cups well-flavored chicken or
       vegetable stock or water

1 Put the rice into a sieve and rinse well under cold running water. Put it into a bowl, add cold water to cover and set aside to soak for 30–40 minutes. Drain in the sieve.

2 Toast the saffron threads in a dry pan over low heat for 1–2 minutes, then place in a small bowl and add 2 tablespoons warm water. Let soak for 10–15 minutes.

3 Melt the butter in a heavy saucepan, then cook the onion with the cardamoms very gently for 8–10 minutes, until soft and buttery yellow.

4 Add the drained rice and stir to coat the grains. Add the salt and bay leaves, followed by the stock and saffron with its liquid. Bring to a boil, stir, then reduce the heat to very low and cover tightly. Cook for 10–12 minutes, until the rice has absorbed all the liquid.

5 Lay a clean, folded dish towel over the pan under the lid and press on the lid to wedge it firmly in place. Let stand for 10–15 minutes.

6 Fluff up the grains of rice with a fork. Turn into a warmed serving dish and serve immediately.

COOK'S TIP
After boiling, when all the liquid has been absorbed, basmati rice is set aside to finish cooking in its own heat and become tender. Wedging a folded dish towel under the pan lid ensures that the heat is not lost and the steam is absorbed.

GARLIC CHIVE RICE <u>WITH</u> MUSHROOMS

RICE IS READILY INFUSED WITH THE PUNGENT AROMA AND FLAVOR OF GARLIC CHIVES, CREATING
A DISH WITH AN EXCELLENT FLAVOR. SERVE WITH VEGETARIAN DISHES, FISH OR CHICKEN.

3 Add the rice to the onions and fry over low heat, stirring frequently, for 4–5 minutes. Pour in the stock mixture, then stir in 1 teaspoon salt and a good grinding of black pepper. Bring to a boil, stir and reduce the heat to very low. Cover tightly and cook for 15–20 minutes, until the rice has absorbed all the liquid.

4 Lay a clean, folded dish towel over the pan under the lid and press on the lid to wedge it firmly in place. Let stand for 10 minutes, allowing the towel to absorb the steam while the rice becomes completely tender.

5 Meanwhile, heat the remaining oil in a frying pan and cook the mushrooms for 5–6 minutes, until tender and browned. Add the remaining chives and cook for another 1–2 minutes.

6 Stir the mushrooms and chopped cilantro leaves into the rice. Adjust the seasoning, transfer to a warmed serving dish and serve immediately, with the cashews.

SERVES FOUR

INGREDIENTS
generous 1½ cups long-grain rice
4 tablespoons peanut oil
1 small onion, finely chopped
2 green chiles, seeded and
  finely chopped
1 ounce garlic chives, chopped
½ ounce cilantro
2½ cups vegetable or mushroom
  stock
1 teaspoon salt
9 ounces mixed mushrooms,
  thickly sliced
2 ounces cashews,
  fried in 1 tablespoon oil
  until golden brown
ground black pepper

1 Wash and drain the rice. Heat half the oil in a saucepan and cook the onion and chiles over low heat, stirring occasionally, for 10–12 minutes, until soft but not browned.

2 Set half the garlic chives aside. Cut the stems off the cilantro and set the leaves aside. Purée the remaining chives and the cilantro stems with the stock in a blender or food processor.

COOK'S TIP
Wild mushrooms are often expensive, but they do have distinctive flavors. Mixing them with cultivated mushrooms is an economical way of using them. Look for oyster mushrooms, cèpes, chanterelles, morels and horse mushrooms.

ONION, PARMESAN AND OLIVE BREAD

THIS BREAD IS GOOD FOR SANDWICHES OR CUT INTO THICK SLICES AND DIPPED IN OLIVE OIL, THEN EATEN AS A SNACK. IT IS REALLY EXCELLENT WHEN TOASTED—FOR EXAMPLE, MAKING A WONDERFUL BASE FOR BRUSCHETTA OR DELICIOUS CROUTONS FOR TOSSING INTO SALAD.

MAKES ONE LARGE OR TWO SMALL LOAVES

INGREDIENTS
- 3 cups all-purpose flour, plus a little extra
- 1 cup yellow cornmeal, plus a little extra
- rounded 1 teaspoon salt
- ½ ounce fresh yeast or 2 teaspoons active dry yeast
- 1 teaspoon brown sugar
- generous 1 cup warm water
- 1 teaspoon chopped fresh thyme
- 2 tablespoons olive oil, plus a little extra for greasing
- 1 onion, finely chopped
- 1 cup freshly grated Parmesan cheese
- scant 1 cup pitted black olives, halved

1 Mix the flour, cornmeal and salt in a warmed bowl. If using fresh yeast, cream it with the sugar and gradually stir in ½ cup of the warm water. If using dried yeast, stir the sugar into the water and then sprinkle the dried yeast on the surface. Set in a warm place for 10 minutes, until frothy.

2 Make a well in the center of the dry ingredients and pour in the yeast liquid and another ⅔ cup of the remaining warm water.

3 Add the chopped fresh thyme and 1 tablespoon of the olive oil and mix thoroughly with a wooden spoon, gradually drawing in the dry ingredients until they are fully incorporated. Add a dash more warm water, if necessary, to make a soft, but not sticky, dough.

4 Knead the dough on a lightly floured work surface for 5 minutes, until smooth and elastic. Place in a clean, lightly oiled bowl and place in a plastic bag or cover with oiled plastic wrap. Set aside to rise in a warm, not hot place for 1–2 hours or until well risen.

5 Meanwhile, heat the remaining olive oil in a heavy frying pan. Add the onion and cook over fairly low heat, stirring occasionally, for 8 minutes, until softened but not at all browned. Set aside to cool.

6 Brush a baking sheet with olive oil. Turn out the dough onto a floured work surface. Gently knead in the onions, followed by the Parmesan and olives.

7 Shape the dough into one or two rough oval loaves. Sprinkle a little cornmeal on the work surface and roll the bread in it, then place on the prepared baking sheet. Make several slits across the top.

8 Slip the baking sheet into the plastic bag or cover with oiled plastic wrap and let rise in a warm place for about 1 hour or until well risen. Preheat the oven to 400°F. Bake for 30–35 minutes or until the bread sounds hollow when tapped on the bottom. Cool on a wire rack.

VARIATION
Alternatively, shape the dough into a loaf, roll in cornmeal and place in an oiled loaf pan. Let rise well above the rim of the pan, as in step 8. Bake for 35–40 minutes or until the loaf sounds hollow when tapped.

GARLIC AND HERB BREAD

EXCELLENT WITH SOUPS OR VEGETABLE FIRST COURSES, GARLIC BREAD IS ALSO IRRESISTIBLE JUST ON ITS OWN. THE BETTER THE BREAD, THE BETTER THE FINAL, GARLICKY VERSION WILL BE.

SERVES THREE TO FOUR

INGREDIENTS
1 baguette
For the garlic and herb butter
½ cup unsalted butter,
softened
5–6 large garlic cloves, finely
chopped or crushed
2–3 tablespoons chopped fresh herbs
(such as parsley, chervil and
a little tarragon)
1 tablespoon snipped fresh chives
sea salt and ground black pepper

1 Preheat the oven to 400°F. Make the garlic and herb butter by beating the butter with the garlic, herbs, chives and seasoning.

2 Cut the bread into ½-inch thick diagonal slices, but leave them attached at the bottom so that the loaf stays intact.

3 Spread the butter between the slices, being careful not to detach them, and spread any remaining butter on the top of the loaf.

4 Wrap the loaf in aluminum foil and bake for 20–25 minutes, until the garlic and herb butter is melted and the crust is crisp. Cut into slices to serve.

VARIATIONS
• Use 7 tablespoons extra virgin olive oil instead of butter.
• Flavor the butter with garlic, chopped fresh chile, grated lime zest and chopped cilantro.

• Add chopped, pitted black olives or sun-dried tomatoes to the butter with a little grated lemon zest.
• To make bruschetta, take thick slices of good country bread. Grill on a ridged cast-iron grill pan, then rub with garlic and drizzle on extra virgin olive oil. For a stronger garlic taste, grill one side of the bread, then spread some finely chopped garlic on the untoasted side, drizzle on oil, then toast until golden.

SCALLION, CHIVE AND RICOTTA BREAD

RICOTTA CHEESE AND CHIVES MAKE A MOIST, WELL-FLAVORED LOAF THAT IS EXCELLENT FOR SANDWICHES. SHAPE THE DOUGH INTO ROLLS, LOAVES OR EVEN A BRAID.

MAKES ONE LOAF OR SIXTEEN ROLLS

INGREDIENTS
½ ounce fresh yeast or 2 teaspoons
  active dry yeast
1 teaspoon sugar
generous 1 cup lukewarm water
1 pound all-purpose flour, plus a
  little extra
1½ teaspoons salt
1 large egg, beaten
½ cup ricotta cheese
1 bunch scallions, thinly sliced
2 tablespoons extra virgin olive oil
3 tablespoons snipped fresh chives
1 tablespoon milk
2 teaspoons poppy seeds (optional)
coarse sea salt

1 Cream the fresh yeast with the sugar and gradually stir in ½ cup of the water. If using dried yeast, stir the sugar into the water, then sprinkle it on the surface. Set in a warm place for 10 minutes.

2 Sift the flour and salt into a warmed bowl. Make a well in the center and pour in the yeast liquid and the remaining water. Save a little beaten egg, then put the rest in the bowl. Add the ricotta and mix to form a dough, adding a little more flour if the mixture is very sticky.

3 Knead the dough on a floured work surface until smooth and elastic. Set aside in a greased bowl, inside a plastic bag, in a warm place for 1–2 hours, until doubled in size.

4 Meanwhile, cook the scallions in the oil for 3–4 minutes, until soft but not browned. Set aside to cool.

5 Punch down the risen dough and knead in the onions, with their oil from cooking, and the chives. Shape the dough into rolls, a large or small loaf or a braid.

6 Grease a baking sheet or loaf pan and place the rolls or bread on it. Cover with greased plastic wrap and set in a warm place to rise for about 1 hour. Preheat the oven to 400°F.

7 Beat the milk into the reserved beaten egg and use to glaze the rolls or loaf. Sprinkle with poppy seeds, if using, and a little coarse sea salt, then bake rolls for about 15 minutes or a loaf for 30–40 minutes or until golden and well risen. When tapped firmly on the bottom, the bread should feel and sound firm. Cool on a wire rack.

COOK'S TIP
To make a braid, divide the dough into three equal sausage-shaped pieces about 16 inches long. Press them together at one end and then braid, pressing the ends together when completed.

RED ONION AND ROSEMARY FOCACCIA

THIS BREAD IS RICH IN OLIVE OIL AND IT HAS AN AROMATIC TOPPING OF RED ONION, FRESH ROSEMARY (DRIED ROSEMARY IS NOT SUITABLE) AND CRUNCHY SEA SALT. IT IS GOOD WITH TOMATO OR PEPPER SALADS OR AS AN ACCOMPANIMENT TO ALL KINDS OF MEDITERRANEAN DISHES.

SERVES FOUR TO FIVE

4 cups all-purpose flour, plus a little extra
1 teaspoon salt
¼ ounce fresh yeast or generous 1 teaspoon active dry yeast
½ teaspoon light brown sugar
1 cup lukewarm water
4 tablespoons extra virgin olive oil
1 teaspoon very finely chopped fresh rosemary, plus 6–8 small sprigs
1 small red onion, halved and thinly sliced
coarse sea salt

1 Sift the flour and salt into a bowl. Cream the fresh yeast with the sugar and slowly stir in half the water. If using dried yeast, stir the sugar into the water and then sprinkle the dried yeast on the surface. Set aside in a warm, not hot, place for 10 minutes, until frothy.

2 Add the yeast, the remaining water, 1 tablespoon of the oil and the chopped rosemary to the flour. Mix to form a dough, then gather it into a ball and knead on a floured work surface for about 5 minutes, until smooth and elastic. You may need a little extra flour if the dough is very sticky.

3 Place the dough in a lightly oiled bowl, slip it into a plastic bag or cover with oiled plastic wrap and let rise. Leave it all day in a cool place, overnight in the refrigerator, or for 1–2 hours in a warm, but not hot, place.

4 Lightly oil a baking sheet. Knead the dough to form a flat loaf about 12 inches round or square. Place on the baking sheet, cover with greased plastic wrap and let rise in a warm place for 40–60 minutes.

5 Preheat the oven to 425°F. Toss the onion in 1 tablespoon of the oil and sprinkle on with the rosemary sprigs.

6 Drizzle the remaining oil onto the loaf, then sprinkle with sea salt. Bake the focaccia for 15 minutes, then reduce the heat to 375°F and cook for another 10–15 minutes. Cool on a wire rack.

VARIATION

To make garlic and thyme focaccia, peel 1–2 heads of garlic, but leave the cloves whole. Fry gently in 1–2 tablespoons olive oil until lightly colored, then cook in the oven at 350°F for about 30 minutes, until soft, browned, but not at all burned. Stir once or twice during cooking, then let cool. When shaping the focaccia, gently knead in the caramelized garlic with about 1 teaspoon chopped fresh thyme. Omit the onion topping, but brush with more olive oil and sprinkle on fresh thyme sprigs and coarse sea salt. Bake as above.

CARAMELIZED ONION AND WALNUT SCONES

THESE SCONES ARE VERY GOOD BUTTERED AND SERVED WITH AGED CHEDDAR OR LANCASHIRE CHEESE. THEY ARE ALSO EXCELLENT WITH SOUP OR A ROBUST VEGETABLE STEW. MAKE SMALL SCONES TO USE AS A BASE FOR COCKTAIL SNACKS, SERVED TOPPED WITH A LITTLE SOFT GOAT CHEESE.

4 Add the cooked onion, walnuts and fresh thyme, then bind to make a soft, but not sticky, dough with the buttermilk.

5 Roll or pat out the mixture to just over ½ inch thick. Stamp out scones using a 2–2½-inch round cutter.

6 Place the scones on a floured baking sheet, glaze with milk and sprinkle on a little salt and a few extra cumin seeds. Bake for 12–15 minutes, until well-risen and golden brown. Cool for a few minutes on a wire rack and serve warm.

MAKES TEN TO TWELVE

7 tablespoons butter
1 tablespoon olive oil
1 Spanish onion, chopped
½ teaspoon cumin seeds, lightly crushed, plus a few extra
1¾ cups self-rising flour
1 teaspoon baking powder
¼ cup oatmeal
1 teaspoon light brown sugar
scant 1 cup chopped walnuts
1 teaspoon chopped fresh thyme
½–⅔ cup buttermilk
a little milk
salt and ground black pepper
coarse sea salt

1 Melt 1 tablespoon of the butter with the oil in a small saucepan and cook the onion gently, covered, for 10–12 minutes, until soft but not browned. Uncover, then continue to cook gently until it begins to brown.

2 Add the crushed cumin seeds and increase the temperature slightly. Cook, stirring occasionally, until the onion browns and begins to caramelize around the edges. Cool. Preheat the oven to 400°F.

3 Sift the flour, baking powder and oatmeal into a large bowl and add ½ teaspoon salt, a generous grinding of black pepper and the brown sugar. Add the remaining butter and rub in with the fingertips until the mixture resembles bread crumbs.

So many sauces, from the classic bases of haute cuisine,

to the lively salsas of modern cooking, rely on the

alliums. Shallots are wonderful in sauces and pickles,

adding strength of flavor without the bulk of an onion.

Strong-flavored onions, shallots and garlic are favorites

for pickling around the globe, from English Pickled Onions

to Hot Thai Pickled Shallots. They are also essential in

many sauces and pastes—Italian Salsa Verde, Indonesian

Peanut Sauce and Indian spice pastes.

Sauces, Pickles and Pastes

OLD ENGLISH BREAD SAUCE

A CLASSIC SAUCE FOR ROAST GAME, CHICKEN OR TURKEY, BREAD SAUCE IS NOW RESERVED ALMOST EXCLUSIVELY TO ACCOMPANY THE CHRISTMAS TURKEY. HOWEVER, IT IS ALSO GOOD WITH SAUSAGES.

SERVES SIX TO EIGHT

INGREDIENTS
   2 cups milk
   1 small onion, stuck with 4 cloves
   1 celery stalk, chopped
   1 fresh bay leaf, torn in half
   6 allspice berries
   1 blade of mace
   1¾ cups day-old bread crumbs, from
     a good-quality white loaf
   freshly grated nutmeg
   2 tablespoons heavy cream
   1 tablespoon butter
   salt and ground black pepper

1 Place the milk, onion, celery, bay leaf, allspice and mace in a saucepan and bring to a boil. Take off the heat, half-cover, and set aside for 30–60 minutes.

2 Strain the milk and place in a blender or food processor. Remove and discard the cloves from the onion and add the onion to the milk with the celery. Process until smooth, then strain the liquid back into the clean saucepan.

3 Bring back to a boil and stir in the bread crumbs. Simmer gently, whisking with a small whisk, until the sauce thickens and becomes smooth. Add a little extra milk if the sauce is too thick.

4 Season to taste with salt, pepper and freshly grated nutmeg. Just before serving, whisk in the cream and butter. Serve warm rather than piping hot.

VARIATION
Muhammara, Middle-Eastern bread sauce with peppers and garlic This sauce is good with grilled fish or chicken or served as a dip with crudités. Crush 2–3 cloves of garlic and place in a food processor or blender with 3 large red bell peppers, grilled, skinned and seeded; 1 hot red chile, grilled, skinned and seeded; scant 1 cup walnuts; and 2 ounces bread, crusts removed. Process to make a paste, then blend in the juice of half a lemon and ½ teaspoon each of salt, pepper and brown sugar. With the motor running, gradually trickle in a generous ⅔ cup extra virgin olive oil. Season with more lemon juice, salt, sugar and a little toasted ground cumin, then stir in 2 tablespoons chopped parsley. If necessary, thin the sauce with more oil or a little warm water or stock.

ONION GRAVY

THIS MAKES A DELICIOUS, DARK ONION SAUCE TO GO WITH SAUSAGES, LIVER, PORK CHOPS OR TOAD-IN-THE-HOLE. IT IS ALSO GOOD WITH A MOUND OF CREAMY MASHED POTATOES.

2 Add the sugar, increase the heat slightly and cook for another 20–30 minutes, until the onions are dark brown.

3 Stir in the flour, cook for a few minutes, stirring constantly, then gradually stir in 1⅔ cups of the hot stock. Simmer, stirring, to make a thickened gravy, adding a little more stock if the gravy is too thick.

4 Add the thyme, season with a little salt and pepper, then cook very slowly, stirring frequently, for 10–15 minutes.

5 Stir in the soy sauce, Worcestershire sauce, if using, and more seasoning, if necessary. Add a little more stock if the gravy is too thick, remove the thyme, and serve immediately.

SERVES FOUR

INGREDIENTS
3 tablespoons butter or
  beef drippings
1 pound onions, halved and
  thinly sliced
½ teaspoon brown sugar
3 tablespoons all-purpose flour
1⅔–2 cups hot beef or vegetable
  stock
1 fresh thyme sprig
2 teaspoons dark soy sauce
1 teaspoon Worcestershire
  sauce (optional)
salt and ground black pepper

1 Melt the butter or drippings over low heat. Add the onions and fry, stirring occasionally, for 15–20 minutes, until soft and beginning to brown.

VARIATIONS
• The onions can be browned in the oven. This is best done in vegetable oil rather than butter or dripping. Place the sliced onions in an ovenproof dish and toss with 3 tablespoons oil. Cook at 375°F for 20 minutes, stirring once or twice. Stir in the sugar, then cook at 425°F for another 15–25 minutes, until the onions are dark brown and caramelized.
• Part of the beef or vegetable stock may be replaced with red wine or dark beer. You may need to add a little extra sugar to balance the acidity of the wine or beer.

SAUCE SOUBISE

THIS IS THE CLASSIC FRENCH WHITE ONION SAUCE. IT IS EXCELLENT WITH VEAL, CHICKEN, PORK OR LAMB. IT IS ALSO GOOD POURED ON SLICED HARD-BOILED EGGS OR POACHED EGGS AND THEN GRATINÉED UNDER A HOT BROILER. IT CAN BE LEFT CHUNKY WITH ONIONS, OR PURÉED.

SERVES FOUR

INGREDIENTS

   3 tablespoons butter
   12 ounces onions, chopped
   ¼ cup all-purpose flour
   generous 2 cups hot milk or stock, or
     a mixture of both
   1 fresh bay leaf
   a few parsley stems
   ½ cup heavy cream
   freshly grated nutmeg
   salt and ground black pepper

1 Melt the butter in a large heavy saucepan. Add the onions and fry gently over low heat, stirring occasionally, for 10–12 minutes, until they are soft and golden yellow but not at all browned.

2 Stir in the flour and cook gently, stirring constantly, for 2–3 minutes.

3 Gradually stir in the hot milk, stock, or milk and stock mixture and bring to a boil. Add the bay leaf and parsley. Part-cover the pan and cook very gently, stirring frequently, for 15–20 minutes.

4 Remove and discard the bay leaf and parsley, then process the sauce in a blender or food processor if you want a smooth sauce.

5 Stir in the cream and reheat the sauce gently, then season to taste with salt and pepper. Add a little more milk or stock if the sauce is very thick. Season with grated nutmeg to taste just before serving.

VARIATIONS

• For leek sauce, substitute leeks for onions, using the white part of the leeks. Cook for just 4–5 minutes in the butter before adding the flour. Omit the nutmeg and stir in 1 tablespoon Dijon mustard just before serving.

• Season the sauce with about 2 tablespoons Dijon mustard at the end of cooking to make *sauce Robert*—a classic French sauce traditionally served with pork chops. It also goes very well with ham or rabbit.

COOK'S TIP

The sauce should be cooked for this length of time to cook out the flour flavor. A heat diffuser mat is very useful to keep the heat as low as possible when cooking delicate foods on the stove.

OLIVE OIL, TOMATO AND HERB SAUCE WITH GARLIC AND SHALLOTS

THIS SAUCE IS BASED ON SAUCE VIERGE, A CLASSIC DRESSING USED IN NOUVELLE CUISINE, AND INVENTED BY FRENCH CHEF MICHEL GUÉRARD. IT IS DELICIOUS SERVED WARM, RATHER THAN HOT, WITH GRILLED OR POACHED FISH. SERVE GOOD BREAD OR BOILED NEW POTATOES TO MOP UP THE OIL.

SERVES FOUR TO SIX

INGREDIENTS

    8 ounces tomatoes
    1 tablespoon finely chopped shallot
    2 garlic cloves, finely sliced
      or chopped
    ½ cup extra virgin
      olive oil
    about 1 tablespoon lemon juice
    sugar
    1 tablespoon chopped fresh chervil
    1 tablespoon snipped fresh chives
    2 tablespoons torn fresh basil leaves
    salt and ground black pepper

VARIATION
Use diced red bell pepper instead of the tomatoes. Broil, peel, seed and finely dice the pepper. Use balsamic vinegar instead of lemon juice and red onion or scallions instead of shallots. Omit the chervil, and use all basil or a mixture of marjoram and basil. A pinch of ground toasted cumin seeds is good in this.

1 Peel and seed the tomatoes, then cut them into fine dice.

2 Place the shallot, garlic and oil in a small saucepan over very low heat and let infuse for a few minutes. The ingredients should warm through but definitely not fry or cook.

COOK'S TIP
It is essential to the flavor of this sauce that you use the best quality extra virgin olive oil.

3 Whisk in 2 tablespoons cold water and 2 teaspoons lemon juice. Remove from heat and stir in the tomatoes. Add a pinch of salt, pepper and sugar, then whisk in the chervil and chives.

4 Let the sauce stand for 10–15 minutes. Adjust the seasoning, adding more lemon juice, salt and black pepper as desired.

5 Reheat gently until just warm, then stir in the basil just before serving.

WALNUT AND GARLIC SAUCE

THIS SAUCE, SEVERAL VERSIONS OF WHICH CAN BE FOUND THROUGHOUT THE MEDITERRANEAN, IS EXCELLENT WITH ROAST OR POACHED CHICKEN AND STEAMED CAULIFLOWER OR POTATOES.

SERVES FOUR

INGREDIENTS

2 ½-inch slices good white bread, crusts removed
4 tablespoons milk
1¼ cups shelled walnuts
4 garlic cloves, chopped
½ cup mild olive oil
1–2 tablespoons walnut oil (optional)
juice of 1 lemon
salt and ground black pepper
walnut or olive oil, for drizzling
paprika, for dusting (optional)

VARIATION

For an Italian *salsa di noci* for pasta, process a scant 1 cup walnuts with 2 garlic cloves and ½ ounce flat-leaf parsley. Blend in 1 slice white bread (crusts removed), soaked in milk, and ½ cup fruity olive oil as above. Season with salt, pepper and lemon juice. Thin with more milk or light cream if very thick.

1 Soak the slices of white bread in the milk for about 5 minutes, then process with the walnuts and chopped garlic in a food processor or blender, to make a rough paste.

2 Gradually add the olive oil to the paste with the motor still running, until the mixture forms a smooth thick sauce. Blend in the walnut oil, if using.

3 Scoop the sauce into a bowl and squeeze in lemon juice to taste, season with salt and pepper and beat well.

4 Transfer to a serving bowl, drizzle on a little more walnut or olive oil, then dust lightly with paprika, if using.

COOK'S TIP
Once opened, walnut oil has a fairly short shelf life. Buy it in small bottles and keep it in a cool, dark place. It is delicious in many salad dressings.

SALSA VERDE

THIS SIMPLE ITALIAN SAUCE IS A PURÉE OF FRESH HERBS WITH OLIVE OIL AND FLAVORINGS. IT IS GOOD WITH POACHED OR ROAST BEEF AND CHICKEN, STEAK OR GRILLED POLENTA.

SERVES FOUR

INGREDIENTS

1–2 garlic cloves, finely chopped
1 ounce flat-leaf parsley leaves
½ ounce fresh basil, mint or cilantro or a mixture of herbs
1 tablespoon snipped chives
1 tablespoon salted capers, rinsed
5 anchovy fillets in olive oil, drained and rinsed
2 teaspoons French mustard (tarragon or *fines herbes* mustard are both good)
½ cup extra virgin olive oil
a little grated lemon zest and juice (optional)
ground black pepper

1 Process the garlic, parsley, basil, mint or cilantro, chives, capers, anchovies, mustard and 1 tablespoon of the oil in a blender or food processor.

2 Gradually add the remaining oil in a thin stream with the motor running.

3 Transfer to a bowl and adjust the seasoning to taste—there should be enough salt from the capers and anchovies. Add a little lemon juice and zest if desired (especially if serving with fish). Serve immediately.

VARIATIONS
• Whisk in 2–3 tablespoons crème fraîche to make a mild sauce that goes well with grilled polenta, cauliflower and potatoes.
• Substitute fresh chervil, tarragon, dill or fennel—or a mixture of aniseed-flavored herbs—for the basil, mint or cilantro to make a sauce that goes particularly well with poached or baked fish, such as hake or sea bass. It is also good with shrimp and langoustines.

YOGURT WITH GARLIC, CUCUMBER AND MINT

VERSIONS OF THIS COOL, MINTY RELISH ARE FOUND IN GREECE (TZATZIKI), TURKEY (CACIK) AND THROUGHOUT THE MIDDLE EAST. IN INDIA, THE EQUIVALENT IS CALLED RAITA.

SERVES FOUR

INGREDIENTS
  6-inch piece cucumber
  1 teaspoon sea salt
  1¼ cups yogurt
  3–4 garlic cloves, crushed
  1 tablespoon dried mint or
   3 tablespoons chopped fresh mint
  ground black pepper
  chopped fresh mint and/or ground
   toasted cumin seeds, to garnish

1 Slice, chop or grate the cucumber, place in a sieve and sprinkle with half the salt. Leave on a deep plate for 30 minutes to drain.

2 Rinse the cucumber in cold water, pat dry and mix with the yogurt, garlic and mint. Season with salt and pepper. Leave for 30 minutes, then stir and sprinkle with fresh mint and/or toasted cumin to garnish.

VARIATION
To make a yogurt and garlic salad dressing, omit the cucumber and use ⅔ cup yogurt instead. Beat in 1 very finely chopped garlic clove, 1 teaspoon French mustard, salt and freshly ground black pepper to taste and a pinch of sugar. Finally, beat in 1–2 tablespoons extra virgin olive oil and 1–2 tablespoons chopped fresh herbs, such as mint, tarragon and chives, to taste.

GARLIC MAYONNAISE

THIS CAN BE AS EASY TO MAKE AS STIRRING CRUSHED GARLIC INTO GOOD QUALITY, READY-MADE MAYONNAISE. BUT HOMEMADE MAYONNAISE, WITH GARLIC STIRRED IN, REVEALS JUST HOW GOOD THIS DELICIOUS DRESSING CAN BE.

SERVES FOUR TO SIX

INGREDIENTS
  2 large egg yolks
  pinch of dried mustard
  up to 1¼ cups mild olive oil or olive
    oil and grapeseed oil, mixed
  1–2 tablespoons lemon juice,
    white wine vinegar or warm water
  2–4 garlic cloves
  salt and ground black pepper

1 Make sure the egg yolks and oil have come to room temperature before you start. Place the yolks in a bowl with the mustard and a pinch of salt, and whisk.

2 Gradually whisk in the oil, one drop at a time. When almost half the oil has been fully incorporated, add it in a steady stream.

3 As the mayonnaise starts to thicken, thin it down with a few drops of lemon juice or vinegar, or a few teaspoons of warm water.

4 When the mayonnaise is as thick as soft butter, stop adding oil. Season the mayonnaise to taste and add more lemon juice or vinegar as required.

WATCHPOINT
The very young, the elderly, pregnant women and those in ill-health or with a compromised immune system are advised against consuming raw eggs or dishes containing raw eggs.

5 Crush the garlic with the blade of a knife and stir it into the mayonnaise. For a slightly milder flavor, blanch the garlic twice in plenty of boiling water, then purée the cloves before beating them into the mayonnaise.

VARIATIONS
• To make Provençal aioli, crush 3–5 garlic cloves with a pinch of salt in a bowl, then whisk in the egg yolks. Omit the mustard but continue as above, using all olive oil.
• For spicy garlic mayonnaise, omit the mustard and stir in ½ teaspoon harissa or red chili paste and 1 teaspoon sun-dried tomato paste with the garlic.
• Use roasted garlic purée or puréed smoked garlic to create a different flavor.
• Beat in about ½ ounce mixed fresh herbs such as tarragon, parsley, chervil and chives. Blanch the herbs in boiling water for 20–30 seconds, then drain and pat them dry on paper towels before finely chopping them.

PEANUT SAUCE

THIS IS BASED ON THE FAMOUS INDONESIAN SAUCE THAT ACCOMPANIES GRILLED PORK, CHICKEN OR SEAFOOD SATÉ. SLIGHTLY THINNED WITH WATER, IT IS ALSO USED TO DRESS GADO-GADO, A WONDERFUL SALAD OF MIXED RAW OR COOKED VEGETABLES AND FRUIT.

SERVES FOUR TO SIX

INGREDIENTS
  2 tablespoons peanut oil
  ¾ cup unsalted peanuts, blanched
  2 shallots, chopped
  2 garlic cloves, chopped
  1 tablespoon chopped fresh ginger root
  1–2 green chiles, seeded and thinly sliced
  1 teaspoon ground coriander
  1 lemongrass stalk, tender bottom only, chopped
  1–2 teaspoons light brown sugar
  1 tablespoon dark soy sauce
  scant ½ cup canned coconut milk
  1–2 tablespoons Thai fish sauce (*nam pla*)
  1–2 tablespoons tamarind purée
  lime juice
  salt and ground black pepper

3 Transfer the spice mixture to a food processor or blender and add the peanuts, lemongrass, 1 teaspoon of the sugar, the soy sauce and 3 fluid ounces of coconut milk and the fish sauce. Blend to form a fairly smooth sauce.

4 Taste and add more fish sauce, tamarind purée, seasoning, lime juice and/or more sugar to taste.

COOK'S TIP
To make tamarind purée, soak 1 ounce tamarind pulp in ½ cup boiling water in a nonmetallic bowl for about 30 minutes, mashing the pulp occasionally with a fork. Then press the pulp through a stainless steel sieve. This purée will keep for several days in a covered container in the refrigerator.

5 Stir in the extra coconut milk and a little water if the sauce seems very thick, but do not let it become runny.

6 Serve cool or reheat the sauce gently, stirring constantly to prevent it from spitting. Garnish with the remaining sliced chile before serving.

1 Heat the oil in a small, heavy frying pan and gently fry the peanuts, stirring frequently, until lightly browned. Use a draining spoon to remove the nuts from the pan and drain thoroughly on paper towels. Set aside to cool.

2 Add the shallots, garlic, ginger, most of the sliced chiles and the ground coriander to the pan and cook over low heat, stirring occasionally, for 4–5 minutes, until the shallots are softened but not at all browned.

ROASTED BELL PEPPER AND GARLIC DRESSING

THIS DRESSING IS DELICIOUS ON CHICKEN SALAD OR TOSSED WITH HOT OR COLD PASTA. IT IS ALSO GOOD WITH SALADS OF GRILLED VEGETABLES, PARTICULARLY EGGPLANT AND ONIONS.

SERVES FOUR

INGREDIENTS

2 large heads of garlic, outer skin removed but left whole

3 fresh thyme sprigs or 2 fresh rosemary sprigs

⅔ cup olive oil

2 red bell peppers, halved and seeded

juice of ½ lemon or 1 tablespoon balsamic vinegar

pinch of sugar (optional)

1 tablespoon snipped fresh chives or basil

salt and ground black pepper

COOK'S TIP

If the dressing starts to separate after standing for any length of time, whisk in 1–2 tablespoons crème fraîche. This is especially good on hot pasta.

1 Preheat the oven to 375°F. Place the garlic on a piece of aluminum foil with the herb sprigs and add 1 tablespoon of the oil. Close the foil around them and bake for 45–60 minutes or until the garlic is soft when squeezed. Place the peppers, cut-sides down, on a baking sheet and bake at the same time as the garlic, until their skin is blistered.

2 Place the peppers in a bowl, cover and set aside to steam for 10 minutes. Then peel off the skins and place the flesh in a blender or food processor.

3 Set the garlic aside until cool enough to handle, then squeeze the soft pulp out of the skins and into the blender or food processor with the peppers. Add any cooking juices from the foil, but discard the herb sprigs and papery garlic skin, then process the mixture until smooth.

4 Gradually blend in the remaining olive oil while the motor is still running. Gradually add lemon juice or balsamic vinegar to taste. Then season with salt and pepper to taste and add a pinch of sugar, if using. Stir in the snipped chives or basil and use immediately.

THAI GREEN CURRY PASTE

A FASHIONABLE, FAVORITE INGREDIENT IN RECENT YEARS, THIS PASTE CAN BE MADE AUTHENTICALLY HOT, OR THE NUMBER OF CHILES CAN BE REDUCED FOR A MILDER TASTE.

MAKES ABOUT ½ CUP

INGREDIENTS

3 Thai shallots, chopped

3–4 garlic cloves, chopped

4 hot green chiles, seeded, if desired, and chopped

2 lemongrass stalks, tender inner parts only, chopped

1-inch piece fresh galangal root or fresh ginger root, chopped

½ ounce cilantro, with root if possible, chopped

2 kaffir lime leaves

1 teaspoon ground toasted coriander seeds

½ teaspoon ground toasted cumin seeds

3–5 teaspoons Thai fish sauce (*nam pla*)

1–2 tablespoons peanut oil

pinch of light brown sugar

salt and ground black pepper

1 Put the shallots, garlic, chiles, lemongrass, galangal or ginger, cilantro, lime leaves, ground coriander and ground cumin in a small food processor or clean coffee grinder. Add fish sauce to taste. Briefly process.

2 Add enough peanut oil to make a paste. Season with salt, pepper and a pinch of sugar. This will keep for 2–3 days in an airtight jar in the refrigerator.

VARIATION

To make red curry paste, process 3 thinly sliced shallots, 3–4 chopped garlic cloves, 6–10 seeded bird's eye chiles, 2 chopped lemon grass stalks, 1 tablespoon chopped galangal or fresh ginger root, 2 tablespoons chopped cilantro root or stem, 2 kaffir lime leaves and 1 teaspoon each toasted coriander seeds, cumin seeds, and paprika, ½ teaspoon black peppercorns and 1 teaspoon dried shrimp paste (*trassi*). Add the peanut oil and sugar as for the green curry paste. Season to taste with salt. For an authentically hot paste, use a small amount of hot chili powder instead of the paprika.

Above right: (clockwise from top left) Roasted Red Bell Pepper and Garlic Dressing, Garlic and Rosemary Vinegar, and Thai Green Curry Paste.

GARLIC AND ROSEMARY VINEGAR

VINEGAR SCENTED WITH GARLIC IS USEFUL FOR FLAVORING SALAD DRESSINGS INSTEAD OF ADDING RAW GARLIC. IT IS ALSO GOOD FOR DEGLAZING THE PAN AFTER FRYING POULTRY OR MEAT.

MAKES 2 CUPS

INGREDIENTS
8–9 large garlic cloves, peeled
2–3 fresh rosemary sprigs
1 long fresh rosemary sprig or long thin wooden skewer (see method)
2 cups good white wine vinegar

1 Blanch the garlic and rosemary in boiling water for 30–60 seconds. Drain and pat dry. Strip the leaves from the long rosemary sprig, if using, leaving a few leaves on top. Blanch the stripped sprig or wooden skewer.

2 Thread the garlic cloves onto the stripped sprig or skewer. (This is easier if you sharpen the end of the branch into a point.)

3 Place the threaded garlic and small rosemary sprigs into a sterilized wide-necked bottle of about 2½ cup capacity. Heat the vinegar to just below the boiling point, then carefully pour it into the bottle and cool before sealing. Let age for 3–4 weeks before use.

VARIATION
You can use other strongly flavored herbs instead of rosemary, threading the garlic cloves on a thin wooden skewer. Try marjoram, basil or tarragon, for example, or a mixture of fresh herbs. You could also use red wine vinegar instead of white for a variation in flavor.

QUICK-PICKLED RED ONIONS WITH DILL, CORIANDER AND JUNIPER

MILD RED ONIONS ARE BEST FOR THIS QUICK PICKLE, WHICH IS BASED ON A TRADITIONAL MEXICAN METHOD OF PICKLING ONIONS THAT WAS POPULARIZED BY AMERICAN COOK DEBORAH MADDISON.

MAKES ONE JAR

INGREDIENTS

    1¼ pounds red onions, thinly sliced
    1 cup rice wine vinegar or
      tarragon vinegar
    1 teaspoon salt
    1 tablespoon sugar
    6 juniper berries, lightly crushed
    2 tablespoons chopped fresh dill
    1 tablespoon coriander seeds, bruised

VARIATION

To make quick Mexican red onions, blanch 1 large sliced red onion, then toss with 1 teaspoon sugar and 7 tablespoons lime juice or rice wine vinegar and a little finely chopped red or green chile. Set aside for 2–3 hours before draining, then season and serve. These onions are very good drained, then tossed with thinly sliced salted cucumber.

1 Place the onions in a large bowl and pour in enough boiling water to cover. Immediately put them into a colander, then set aside and let drain completely. Then return the onions to the dried bowl.

2 In another bowl, mix the vinegar, salt, sugar, juniper berries and chopped dill.

3 Heat the coriander seeds in a dry frying pan until they give off their aroma. Add the the toasted seeds to the vinegar mixture and stir. Pour the spiced vinegar onto the onions, toss to mix, then let stand at room temperature for 1 hour. The onions are now ready for use, and will keep in a covered jar in the refrigerator for up to 1 week. Drain to use.

ENGLISH PICKLED ONIONS

PICKLED ONIONS ARE A TRADITIONAL FEATURE OF PUB FOOD ACROSS THE BRITISH ISLES. THEY ARE SERVED WITH COLD MEATS, PIES AND, MOST FAMOUSLY, BREAD AND CHEESE. THEY SHOULD BE MADE WITH DARK MALT VINEGAR AND STORED FOR AT LEAST 6 WEEKS BEFORE EATING.

MAKES THREE TO FOUR 1-POUND JARS

INGREDIENTS

2¼ pounds pickling onions
½ cup salt
3 cups malt vinegar
1 tablespoon sugar
2–3 dried red chiles
1 teaspoon brown mustard seeds
1 tablespoon coriander seeds
1 teaspoon allspice berries
1 teaspoon black peppercorns
2-inch piece fresh ginger root, sliced
2–3 blades of mace
2–3 fresh bay leaves

1 To peel the onions, trim off the root end, but leave the onion layers attached. Cut a thin slice off the top (neck) end of the onion. Place the onions in a bowl, then cover with boiling water. Let stand for about 4 minutes, then drain. The skin should then be easier to peel with a small, sharp knife.

2 Place the peeled onions in a bowl and cover with cold water, then drain the water off and pour it into a large saucepan. Add the salt and heat slightly to dissolve it, then cool before pouring the brine onto the onions.

3 Cover the bowl with a plate and weigh it down slightly so that it keeps all the onions submerged in the brine. Let the onions stand in the salted water for 24 hours.

4 Place the vinegar in a large pan. Wrap all the remaining ingredients, except the bay leaves, in a piece of muslin or sew them into a coffee filter paper and add to the vinegar with the bay leaves. Bring to a boil, simmer for 5 minutes, then remove from heat. Set aside to cool and infuse overnight.

5 Drain the onions, rinse and pat dry. Pack them into sterilized jars. Add some or all of the spice from the vinegar, but not the ginger slices. The pickle will get hotter if you add the chiles. Pour the vinegar onto the onions to cover and add the bay leaves. Store any leftover vinegar in a bottle for your next batch of pickles. Cover the jars with nonmetallic lids and store in a cool dark place for at least 6 weeks before eating.

COOK'S TIP
For sterilizing, stand clean, rinsed jars upside down on a rack on a baking sheet and place in the oven at 350°F for 20 minutes.

VARIATIONS
• The recipe above produces a crisp pickle. For softer onions, simmer the rinsed, salted onions in the malt vinegar for 2–3 minutes before packing them into sterilized jars, then pour in the hot vinegar. Cool the pickles, then seal with non-metallic lids.
• To make sweet pickled onions, follow the same method, but add 4 tablespoons light brown sugar to the vinegar. A couple of pieces of cinnamon stick and 1 teaspoon cloves are good additions to this version.

HOT THAI PICKLED SHALLOTS

THAI PINK SHALLOTS REQUIRE LENGTHY PREPARATION, BUT THEY LOOK EXQUISITE IN THIS SPICED PICKLE. THE SHALLOTS ARE GOOD, FINELY SLICED, AS A CONDIMENT TO SOUTHEAST ASIAN MEALS.

MAKES TWO TO THREE JARS

INGREDIENTS

5–6 small red or green bird's eye
   chiles, halved and seeded,
   if desired
1¼ pounds Thai pink shallots, peeled
2 large garlic cloves, peeled, halved
   and green shoot removed
For the vinegar
   2½ cups cider vinegar
   3 tablespoons sugar
   2 teaspoons salt
   2-inch piece fresh ginger root, sliced
   1 tablespoon coriander seeds
   2 lemongrass stalks, cut in
     half lengthwise
   4 kaffir lime leaves or strips of
     lime zest
   1 tablespoon chopped cilantro

1 If leaving the chiles whole (they will be hotter if you leave the seeds in), prick them several times with a toothpick. Bring a large pan of water to a boil. Blanch the chiles, shallots and garlic for 1–2 minutes, then drain. Rinse all the vegetables under cold water, then let drain.

2 To prepare the vinegar, put the cider vinegar, sugar, salt, ginger, coriander seeds, lemongrass and lime leaves or lime zest in a saucepan and bring to a boil. Simmer over low heat for 3–4 minutes, then let cool.

3 Discard the ginger, then bring the vinegar back to a boil. Add the cilantro, garlic and chiles, and cook for 1 minute.

4 Pack the shallots into sterilized jars, distributing the lemongrass, lime leaves, chiles and garlic between them. Pour in the hot vinegar. Cool, then seal and set in a dark place for 2 months before eating.

COOK'S TIPS
• Always be careful when making pickles that bowls and saucepans used for vinegar are non-reactive, that is, that they are not chemically affected by the acid of the vinegar. China and glass bowls and stainless steel pans are suitable.
• When packing pickles, ensure that metal lids will not come in contact with the pickle. The acid in the vinegar will corrode the metal. Use plastic-coated or glass lids with rubber rings. Alternatively, cover the top of the jar with a circle of cellophane or waxed paper to prevent direct contact when using metal lids.
• Take care when handling hot jars. Let them cool slightly after sterilizing and before filling to avoid burning yourself. However, do not let them cool completely, as they may then crack when the hot vinegar is poured in.

PICKLED MUSHROOMS WITH GARLIC AND RED ONION

THIS IS A POPULAR METHOD OF PRESERVING MUSHROOMS THROUGHOUT EUROPE. IT IS GOOD MADE WITH ONLY CULTIVATED MUSHROOMS, BUT TRY TO INCLUDE 1–2 SLICED CÈPES FOR THEIR FLAVOR.

3 Add the mushrooms and simmer for 3–4 minutes, then drain through a sieve. Retain all the herbs and spices.

4 Fill 1 large or 2 small sterilized, cooled jars with the mushrooms. Distribute the garlic, onion, herbs and spices evenly between the layers of mushrooms. Then pour in enough olive oil to cover by at least ½ inch. You may need extra oil if you use 2 jars.

5 Let the pickles settle, then tap the jars on the work surface to dispel any air bubbles. Seal with lids, then let stand for at least 2 weeks in a cool, dark place before using.

COOK'S TIP
To keep the mushrooms underneath the oil, wedge 2 wooden toothpicks crosswise in the neck of the jar.

MAKES 2½ CUPS

INGREDIENTS
  1¼ pounds mixed mushrooms such as small cèpes, chestnut mushrooms, shiitake and girolles
  1¼ cups white wine vinegar or cider vinegar
  1 tablespoon sea salt
  1 teaspoon sugar
  1¼ cups water
  4–5 fresh bay leaves
  8 large fresh thyme sprigs
  15 garlic cloves, peeled and halved, any green shoots removed
  1 small red onion, halved and thinly sliced
  2–3 small dried red chiles
  1 teaspoon coriander seeds, lightly crushed
  1 teaspoon black peppercorns
  few strips of lemon zest
  1–1½ cups extra virgin olive oil

1 Trim and wipe all the mushrooms. (It is better not to wash them, as they absorb water easily and can become waterlogged. Simply wipe them with a damp cloth or paper towels.) Cut large mushrooms in half.

2 Put the vinegar, salt, sugar and water in a saucepan and bring to a boil. Add all the remaining ingredients, except for the mushrooms and oil. Simmer for 2 minutes.

COCONUT CHUTNEY WITH ONION AND CHILI

SERVE THIS REFRESHING FRESH CHUTNEY AS AN ACCOMPANIMENT FOR INDIAN-STYLE DISHES OR WITH A RAITA AND OTHER CHUTNEYS AND POPPADUMS AT THE START OF A MEAL.

SERVES FOUR TO SIX

INGREDIENTS

7 ounces fresh coconut, grated
3–4 green chiles, seeded
  and chopped
¾ ounce cilantro, chopped
2 tablespoons chopped fresh mint
2–3 tablespoons lime juice
about ½ teaspoon salt
about ½ teaspoon sugar
1–2 tablespoons coconut
  milk (optional)
2 tablespoons peanut oil
1 teaspoon kalonji
1 small onion, very finely chopped
cilantro sprigs, to garnish

COOK'S TIP
Add more chiles if you prefer a chutney
with a hotter flavor.

1 Place the coconut, chiles, cilantro and mint in a food processor. Add 2 tablespoons of the lime juice, then process until thoroughly chopped.

2 Scrape the mixture into a bowl and add more lime juice to taste. Add salt and sugar to taste. If the mixture is dry, stir in 1–2 tablespoons coconut milk.

3 Heat the oil in a small pan and fry the kalonji until they begin to pop, then reduce the heat and add the onion. Fry, stirring frequently, for 4–5 minutes, until the onion softens but does not brown.

4 Stir the onion mixture into the coconut mixture and let cool. Garnish with cilantro before serving.

ONION, MANGO AND PEANUT CHAAT

CHAATS ARE SPICED RELISHES OF VEGETABLES AND NUTS SERVED WITH INDIAN MEALS. AMCHOOR (MANGO POWDER) ADDS A DELICIOUSLY FRUITY SOURNESS TO THIS MIXTURE OF ONIONS AND MANGO.

SERVES FOUR

INGREDIENTS

scant 1 cup unsalted peanuts
1 tablespoon peanut oil
1 onion, chopped
4-inch piece cucumber, seeded and
  cut into ¼-inch dice
1 mango, peeled, pitted and diced
1 green chile, seeded and chopped
2 tablespoons chopped cilantro
1 tablespoon chopped fresh mint
1 tablespoon lime juice
pinch of light brown sugar
For the chaat masala
2 teaspoons ground toasted
  cumin seeds
½ teaspoon cayenne pepper
1 teaspoon mango powder (amchoor)
½ teaspoon garam masala
pinch ground asafoetida
salt and ground black pepper

1 To make the chaat masala, grind all the spices together, then season with ½ teaspoon each of salt and pepper.

2 Fry the peanuts in the oil until lightly browned, then drain on paper towels until cool.

COOK'S TIP
Any remaining chaat masala will keep in a sealed jar for 4–6 weeks.

3 Mix the onion, cucumber, mango, cilantro and mint. Sprinkle in 1 teaspoon of the chaat masala. Stir in the peanuts and then add lime juice and/or sugar to taste. Set the mixture aside for 20–30 minutes for the flavors to mature.

4 Turn the mixture into a serving bowl, sprinkle on another 1 teaspoon of the chaat masala and serve.

CONFIT OF SLOW-COOKED ONIONS

*THIS JAM OF SLOW-COOKED, CARAMELIZED ONIONS IN SWEET-AND-SOUR BALSAMIC VINEGAR WILL KEEP FOR
SEVERAL DAYS IN A SEALED JAR IN THE REFRIGERATOR. YOU CAN USE RED, WHITE OR YELLOW ONIONS,
BUT YELLOW ONIONS WILL GIVE THE SWEETEST RESULTS. SHALLOTS ALSO MAKE AN EXCELLENT CONFIT.*

SERVES SIX TO EIGHT

INGREDIENTS

2 tablespoons olive oil
1 tablespoon butter
1¼ pounds onions, sliced
3–5 fresh thyme sprigs
1 fresh bay leaf
2 tablespoons light brown sugar, plus
  a little extra
¼ cup prunes, chopped
2 tablespoons balsamic vinegar,
  plus a little extra
½ cup red wine
salt and ground black pepper

1 Reserve 1 teaspoon of the oil, then
heat the rest with the butter. Add the
onions, cover and cook gently for
15 minutes, stirring occasionally.

2 Season well with salt and pepper,
then add the thyme, bay leaf and sugar.
Cook slowly, uncovered, for another
15–20 minutes, until the onions are
very soft and dark.

3 Add the prunes, vinegar and wine
with 4 tablespoons water and cook over
low heat, stirring frequently, for another
20 minutes or until most of the liquid
has evaporated. Add a little water and
reduce the heat if the mixture dries
too quickly.

4 Adjust the seasoning, adding more
sugar and/or vinegar to taste. Let the
confit cool, then stir in the remaining
1 teaspoon oil. The confit is best stored
for 24 hours before eating. Serve either
cold or warm.

VARIATION
Baby onions with tomato & orange Gently
fry 1¼ pounds peeled pickling onions or
small *cipolline* in 4 tablespoons olive oil
until lightly browned, then sprinkle in
3 tablespoons of brown sugar. Let the
onions caramelize a little, then add
1½ teaspoons crushed coriander seeds,
1 cup red wine, 2 bay leaves, a few
thyme sprigs, 3 strips orange zest and
3 tablespoons tomato paste and the juice
of 1 orange. Cook very gently, covered,
for 1 hour, stirring occasionally until the
sauce is thick and reduced. Uncover for
the last 20 minutes of cooking time.
Sharpen with 1–2 tablespoons sherry
vinegar and serve cold, sprinkled with
chopped parsley.

RED ONION, GARLIC AND LEMON RELISH

THIS POWERFUL RELISH IS FLAVORED WITH NORTH-AFRICAN SPICES AND PRESERVED LEMONS, AVAILABLE AT LARGER SUPERMARKETS OR AT MIDDLE-EASTERN FOOD MARKETS.

3 Add a pinch of salt, lots of pepper and the sugar, and cook, uncovered, for 5 minutes. Soak the saffron in about 3 tablespoons warm water for 5 minutes, then add to the onions, with the soaking water. Add the cinnamon stick, dried chiles, if using, and bay leaves. Stir in 2 tablespoons of the sherry vinegar and the orange juice.

4 Cook over low heat, uncovered, until the onions are very soft and most of the liquid has evaporated. Stir in the preserved lemon and cook gently for another 5 minutes. Taste and adjust the seasoning, adding more salt, sugar and/or vinegar to taste.

5 Serve warm or cold, but not hot. The relish tastes best if it is allowed to stand for 24 hours.

SERVES SIX

INGREDIENTS
   3 tablespoons olive oil
   3 large red onions, sliced
   2 heads of garlic, separated into
    cloves and peeled
   2 teaspoons coriander seeds, crushed
    but not finely ground
   2 teaspoons light brown sugar, plus a
    little extra
pinch of saffron threads
   2-inch piece cinnamon stick
   2–3 small whole dried red
    chiles (optional)
   2 fresh bay leaves
   2–3 tablespoons sherry vinegar
juice of ½ small orange
   2 tablespoons chopped
    preserved lemon
salt and ground black pepper

1 Heat the oil in a heavy saucepan. Add the onions and stir, then cover and reduce the heat to the lowest setting. Cook for 10–15 minutes, stirring occasionally, until the onions are soft.

2 Add the garlic cloves and coriander seeds. Cover and cook for 5–8 minutes, until soft.

VARIATION
To make a quick Lebanese onion relish, chop 1¼ pounds ripe tomatoes and combine with 1 bunch of sliced scallions. Crush 2 cloves of garlic with a large pinch of salt and gradually work in 1 tablespoon lemon juice and 3–4 tablespoons extra virgin olive oil. Toss the tomatoes and onions with the dressing and stir in a small bunch of chopped purslane or 2 tablespoons of chopped marjoram or lemon thyme, then adjust the seasoning with salt, pepper, a pinch or two of sugar and maybe more lemon juice. Serve with grilled lamb or chicken or a grain salad made with bulghur wheat or couscous.

INDEX

ACKNOWLEDGMENTS

Photographs are all by William Lingwood except those on the following pages: p6, p7b, p18 The Anthony Blake Photo Library; p7t, p19b Cephas; p8, p13tr, p14t, p17b, p20 The Bridgeman Art Library; p9t, p10t, p10b The Ancient Egypt Picture Library; p9b, p10b, p11t, p11b, p13tl, p14b, p16t, p16b, p21t, p21b, p22b, p23t Mary Evans Picture Library; p12, p14b, p15 e.t. archive; p13b, p22t, p23b AKG Photographic Library; p17t Hulton Getty Picture Library; p19t Food Features; p24,

p28b John Freeman; p28r, p36l, A–Z Botanical Collection Ltd; p37tl Michelle Garrett.

The author would like to acknowledge the following for their inspiration and information: John Ayto, *A Gourmet's Guide* (Oxford, 1994); Lindsey Bareham, *Onions Without Tears* (London, 1995); Barbara Ciletti, *The Onion Harvest Cookbook* (Newtown, CT, 1998); Bruce Cost, *Foods from the Far East* (London, 1990); William J. Darby and Paul Ghalioungui, *Food: The Gift of Osiris*, 2 volumes (London, 1977); Alan Davidson, *The

Oxford Companion to Food* (Oxford, 1999); John Edwards, *The Roman Cookery of Apicius* (London, 1984); John Evelyn, *Acetaria: A Discourse of Sallets* (1699), edited by Christopher Driver and Tom Jaine (Totnes, 1996); *Four Seasons of the House of Cerruti*, edited and translated by Judith Spencer (New York, NY, 1983); M. Grieve, *A Modern Herbal*, edited by C. F. Leyel (London, 1931, 1998); Dorothy Hartley, *Food in England* (1954, 1996); Katy Holder and Gail Duff, *A Clove of Garlic* (London, 1996);

C. F. Leyel and Hartley, Olga *The Gentle Art of Cookery* (London, 1925, 1974); Harold McGee, *On Food and Cooking: The Science and Lore of the Kitchen* (London, 1991); Charmaine Solomon, *The Encyclopedia of Asian Food* (London, 1998); Colin Spencer, *Vegetable Book* (London, 1995); Tom Stobart, *The Cook's Encyclopaedia* (London, 1998); Waverley Root, *Food* (New York, NY, 1980); J. G. Vaughan and C. A. Geissler, *The New Oxford Book of Food Plants* (Oxford, 1997).